Knowledge Production

Knowledge Production is a collection from an impressive international group of educational researchers that explores issues in the production of knowledge about educational phenomena in contemporary society. What emerged from their collaboration is an exploration of the epistemological, methodological, and ethical-political issues arising from the process of knowledge production.

The authors are drawn from three continents – North America, Australia and Europe – and bring diverse perspectives to issues of international concern. Each chapter in the book presents individual responses to the need to challenge assumptions that underpin the conduct of educational research, on the part of both policy makers who sponsor it directly or indirectly, and the educational researchers who carry it out.

The authors address disturbances in educational research practice. For example, they discuss:

- how globalisation is increasing educational opportunities for students and education providers while, at the same time, teachers and teacher educators are heavily constrained by a risk-averse audit culture;
- how human capital theory dominates the rationale for educational endeavours from a policy perspective while, at the same time, others pursue agendas of education as a means of social transformation and personal growth;
- how the idea of usable knowledge seems so obviously apparent while just what it is 'used for' is not all that settled;
- how on the one hand being accountable for our words and deeds is something we all think virtuous, while on the other hand we reject the idea that accountability is solely to be determined by performance, and so on.

These disturbances, taken collectively, constitute interesting times in which to be doing educational research. This collection invites readers to consider what these times mean for their own practice of educational research. The book both breaks new ground and sets the tone for discussions about the future path of educational research in the coming years.

Bridget Somekh is Professor of Educational Research at Manchester Metropolitan University, UK.

Thomas A. Schwandt is Professor of Education at the University of Illinois at Urbana-Champaign, USA.

Knowledge Production

Research work in interesting times

Edited by
Bridget Somekh and
Thomas A. Schwandt

Routledge
Taylor & Francis Group

LONDON AND NEW YORK

First published 2007
by Routledge
2 Park Square, Milton Park, Abingdon, Oxon OX14 4RN

Simultaneously published in the USA and Canada
by Routledge
270 Madison Ave, New York, NY 10016

Routledge is an imprint of the Taylor & Francis Group, an informa business

Typeset in Times by
HWA Text and Data Management, Tunbridge Wells
Printed and bound in Great Britain by
Antony Rowe Ltd, Chippenham, Wiltshire

British Library Cataloguing in Publication Data
A catalogue record for this book is available from the British Library

Library of Congress Cataloging-in-Publication Data
Knowledge production : research work in interesting times / [edited by] Bridget Somekh and Thomas A. Schwandt.
        p. cm.
    1.   Education–Research–Social aspects.   I. Somekh, Bridget.
II. Schwandt, Thomas A.
    LB1028 . K548 2007
    370 . 72–dc22
                                                                2007020935

ISBN10: 0–415–44229–x (hbk)
ISBN10: 0–415–44228–1 (pbk)

ISBN13: 978–0–415–44229–9 (hbk)
ISBN13: 978–0–415–44228–2 (pbk)

Contents

Contributors

Jill Blackmore is a Professor of Education at Deakin University. Her research interests include feminist approaches to globalisation and education policy, administrative and organisational theory, educational leadership and reform, organisational change and innovation, teachers' and academics' work, and all their policy implications. Publications are *Troubling Women: feminism, leadership and educational change* (1999, Open University Press) and *Performing and Re-forming Leaders: gender, educational restructuring and organisational change* (2007, SUNY Press) with Judyth Sachs.

John Elliott is Emeritus Professor of Education in the Centre for Applied Research in Education at the University of East Anglia. He is internationally known for his role in developing the theory and practice of action research in the contexts of curriculum and teacher development. He was Advisory Professor to the Hong Kong Institute of Education (2001–6) and a consultant to the Hong Kong Government on curriculum reform. His publications include *Reflecting Where the Action Is: the selected works of John Elliott* in the Routledge World Library of Educationalists (2007).

Walter Feinberg is the Charles Dun Hardie Professor and a Professor of the Philosophy of Education in the Educational Policy Studies Department at the University of Illinois, Urbana-Champaign. Professor Feinberg's interests centre around issues related to education for democratic citizenship.

Jo Frankham is Senior Lecturer in Educational Research in the School of Education at the University of Manchester. She teaches qualitative methods to postgraduate students. Her research interests include sexualities education and HIV prevention education and methodological issues associated with researching across difference. She recently completed an ESRC funded project with adults with learning disabilities and research for the Joseph Rowntree Foundation with children and young people who have been permanently excluded from school.

Noel Gough is Foundation Professor of Outdoor and Environmental Education at La Trobe University, Australia. His current research focuses on the implications of internationalisation and globalisation for education, and on refining poststructuralist methodologies for curriculum inquiry, with particular reference to environmental education and science education. He is the founding editor of *Transnational Curriculum Inquiry*.

Jennifer C. Greene is a scholar-practitioner in programme evaluation and currently a Professor of Educational Psychology at the University of Illinois at Urbana-Champaign. Greene's scholarship focuses on making evaluation useful and socially responsible, primarily through the development of alternative approaches to evaluation, notably qualitative, democratic and mixed-method approaches.

Barbara Kamler is Professor of Education at Deakin University, Australia. She researches writing across the lifespan as a mode of social action, as a means of producing knowledge and identities, and as a means of speaking against established discourses. Her recent book publications include *Relocating the Personal: a critical writing pedagogy* (2001, SUNY Press) and with Pat Thomson *Helping Doctoral Students Write: pedagogies for supervision* (2006, Routledge).

Maggie MacLure is Professor of Education in the Education and Social Research Institute at Manchester Metropolitan University. Her research interests include qualitative methodology, especially discourse analysis, deconstruction and poststructuralist approaches. She is the author of *Discourse in Educational and Social Research* (2003, Open University Press). See http://www.ioe.mmu.ac.uk/research/res-ppl/m-maclure.shtml.

Luis Miron is a Professor of Educational Policy Studies at the University of Illinois, Urbana-Champaign. His work, recently centred in post-Katrina New Orleans, uses lenses of cultural studies, aesthetics, and the humanities to engage equity issues and the possibilities of establishing deep democracy in inner-city schools serving large numbers of students of colour.

Leonie Rowan is a Senior Lecturer in the Faculty of Education at Deakin University. Her research interests range from early childhood environments through to university settings and relate to the broad fields of equity and social justice. She is particularly interested in the use of transformative pedagogies for disrupting traditional patterns of exclusion in diverse educational and cultural sites. Within this framework she has focused on areas such as early childhood literacy development, boys in schools, girls and ICT, and the role of knowledge producing schools in disrupting traditional patterns of educational success and failure.

Jill Schostak a Visiting Fellow at the University of East Anglia, is interested in contemporary philosophical debates and qualitative methodologies. She has carried out ethnographic research into decision-making in clinical contexts and is currently researching professional development in Emergency Medicine. She co-wrote *Radical Research* (2007, Routledge) with John Schostak.

John Schostak is a Professor in the Education and Social Research Institute, Manchester Metropolitan University. He is interested in qualitative research methods generally and in particular emancipatory research as described in the book written with Jill Schostak, *Radical Research* (2007, Routledge). He also maintains the Enquiry Learning Unit website: http://www.enquirylearning.net/ELU/SubFrame.html.

Thomas A. Schwandt is Professor of Education at the University of Illinois at Urbana-Champaign (UIUC) where he holds appointments in the Department of Educational Psychology, the Department of Educational Policy Studies, and the Unit for Criticism and Interpretive Theory. His books include Evaluation Practice Reconsidered (2004);

Evaluating Holistic Rehabilitation Practice (2004); *Dictionary of Qualitative Inquiry*, 3rd edn (2007), *Exploring Evaluator Role and Identity*, co-edited with Katherine Ryan (2002).

Bridget Somekh is Professor of Educational Research in the Education and Social Research Institute at Manchester Metropolitan University. Her recent research has focused on the theory and practice of transforming pedagogy and learning. Books include *Action Research: a methodology for change and development* (2006, Open University Press) and *Pedagogy and Learning with ICT: researching the art of innovation* (2007, Routledge).

Sheila Stark is a part-time Reader in the Education and Social Research Institute, Manchester Metropolitan University. Sheila's research interests include action research/learning; educational evaluations; professionalism and multi-professional team working. She is also interested in the translation 'space' between theory, policy and practice in a range of contexts.

Sarah Stitzlein is Assistant Professor of Philosophy of Education at the University of New Hampshire. Her primary areas of scholarship are philosophy of education, pragmatism, feminist theory, and poststructuralism. Her most recent work investigates how gender and race might be transformed through the teaching of flexible habits.

Marilyn Strathern is Professor of Social Anthropology at the University of Cambridge. Her ethnographic interests are divided between Melanesia and Britain, and latterly between new medical technologies, intellectual and cultural property, and interdisciplinarity. The edited collection, *Audit Cultures*, subtitled 'Anthropological studies in accountability, ethics and the academy', contributes towards a critique of good practice.

Ian Stronach is Research Professor of Education in the Education and Social Research Institute at Manchester Metropolitan University. His current research interests are in early professional learning, the nature of professional work, qualitative studies, and cultural theory.

Pat Thomson is Professor of Education and Director of Research at the University of Nottingham. Her current research includes an investigation of whole-school change and ongoing work around the active participation of young people in their education. Publications include *Schooling the Rustbelt Kids: making the difference in changing times* (2002, Allen and Unwin) and with Barbara Kamler, *Helping Doctoral Students Write: pedagogies for supervision* (2006, Routledge).

Acknowledgements

Chapter 4 by Maggie MacLure was first published as '"Clarity bordering on stupidity": Where's the quality in systematic review?', *Journal of Education Policy* 20(4) (2005): 393–416. Chapter 5 by Ian Stronach, Jo Frankham and Sheila Stark was first published as 'Sex, science and educational research: the unholy trinity', *Journal of Education Policy* 22(2) (2007): 215–35. Both are reprinted by permission of the publisher, Taylor & Francis Ltd. http://www.informaworld. com.

Chapter 1

First words

Thomas A. Schwandt

"May you live in interesting times" – the expression conveying a wish of sorts – has long been meant to be ironic and something of a curse. Interesting times should be high quality times, good times – exciting, appealing, attention grabbing, stimulating – a kind of cornucopia of possibilities, all, at least, potentially something one would wish for. The irony is that such a richness of possibilities contains within itself its opposite – options that are repellent, boring, tiresome, mind numbing, and confusing – and a longing for simpler, less turbulent times. I was recently told that with the right software I am able to access 2500 television channels through my PC. In 1987, one of the leading publishers of qualitative methods textbooks listed 10 titles in its catalogue; in 2007 they listed 142. When I walk across the street from my office to the coffee shop, the menu board displays at least 30 possibilities for what a cup of coffee means. We now need specialized dictionaries to navigate multiple research languages – dictionaries of qualitative inquiry, social research methods, cultural studies, feminism, postmodernism, poststructuralism, and social theory. We live in a time when the long taken-for-granted conceptual (e.g., family, society, identity, knowledge) and analytical (e.g., objectivity, facticity, validity) vocabulary of social research is no longer the reliable guide to making sense of social reality that we thought it was. The very idea of knowledge is differentially defined, authored by many, widely accessible, distributed, vetted and unvetted. We find it difficult to avoid being bombarded with information – when I recently Googled the phrase "knowledge production", I found 161 million hits and 206 million for "educational research". We live in a time when sweeping processes of political-economic globalization both substantiate performativity as the defining characteristic of knowledge and enable resistance to it, foster convergence on uniform models of the polity and political rationality and simultaneously create the very conditions of opposition to such homogenization. We are vexed with interesting times. The list of what makes this so is endless.

What being troubled in this sense means for ideas of knowledge production and educational research is not all that clear. For some, the troubling is a genuine affliction – disconcerting, disturbing, distressing and foreboding. For others, the troubling heightens their sense of the irony of navigating life and claiming that one "really" knows what is good, true, right, valuable, and so on. For still others, the uneasiness that comes from making problematic long-held understandings is viewed as potentially productive of new and different ways of knowing and being. Interesting times are by definition protean as are the ways in which we live in and make sense of those times as members of society (citizen, consumer, client?), researchers (discoverer, narrator, interpreter, critic, bricoleur, wanderer, reformer?), teachers (sage guide, information broker, cultivator of human capital, skill and drill instructor, nurturer of *Bildung*?), and so on. As a testament to living and working as educational researchers in interesting times, this book is about two things – what is written here and what is shown but not written.

What is written

What is written about educational research here is kaleidoscopic in its coverage of the objects of analysis that are in the viewfinders of the authors. In Part I of this book, authors tackle the intersection of the meaning of knowledge, its production, its justification, and its use(s) in a swirl of contemporary ideas and practices characterized by notions of accountability, quality, and scientific evidence. All of the chapters in this section, in a very broad way, are addressing the questions "How are ideas of (educational) knowledge and knowledge production being shaped in contemporary discursive practices that draw heavily on notions from business models of auditability, process re-engineering (streamlining, cost effectiveness, clearly defined outputs), performance management, and quality assurance? What are the consequences of such framing for institutional practices of educational governance and educational research? What happens to our ideas of knowledge as open-ended, speculative, reflective, and reflexive when this framing occurs?" Marilyn Strathern, thinking anthropologically, takes as her object of analysis the seemingly commonsensical idea that good and relevant knowledge must be useful. She argues for the view that we ought to demand of knowledge more than that it be capable of being accumulated, managed, and put to instrumental use. In her chapter one hears echoes of Clifford Geertz's observation that progress in an interpretive science of society is marked less by the perfection of a knowledge consensus than by a refinement of debate and by an increased capacity to vex each other with our self-understandings. Jill Blackmore's chapter is also concerned with what counts as legitimate knowledge. She offers a more direct critique of the ways in which the notion of educational research quality is being framed both socio-politically and epistemologically at present, particularly in what she identifies as the Australian policyscape. However, she speaks to the concerns of a broader community of educational researchers faced with systems of educational governance favoring evidence-based research as most relevant for decisions of policy and practice. Also writing against the backdrop of an "educational policy machinery" fueled by ideas of quality, utility, auditability, and accountability, Maggie MacLure fixes our attention on one of the knowledge production tools thought to be most generative of useable knowledge for education, namely, the systematic review. She unpacks how systematic reviews made by the EPPI-Centre at the University of London are planned, conducted, and reported. MacLure contends that such reviews are not simply of limited utility in informing educational policy and practice but also emblematic of a dangerously oversimplified, knowledge-product oriented view of what research and scholarship mean. An example of the effects of research framed in accountability discourses is illustrated in the chapter by Ian Stronach, Jo Frankham and Sheila Stark. They explore the framing of the problem of and solution to teenage pregnancy rates in the UK in an allegedly scientific discourse, and conclude that what often is promoted as scientific educational research is more like scientific kitsch. Noel Gough illustrates how what amounts to an agentless flow of quality assurance discourse in higher education works differentially to produce certain consequences and prevent others from occurring as it interacts with local practices. His chapter advises that we would be well served if we worried less about what a notion like "quality" (or evidence, accountability, or performance, for that matter) means and more concerned with how it actually works and what is accomplished in its name.

Part II of the book takes up the conversation about the work of educational research from another set of perspectives. Collectively, the chapters are less concerned with diagnosing the intellectual and moral-political landscape of the meaning of knowledge, and more focused on how the analytic tools employed in educational research must be redefined and used differently in research practices. By analytic tools here I have in mind both the ideas that fashion our ways of understanding what research and methodology mean as well as those concepts (such as innovation, teaching practices, writing, curriculum theory, and the like) that give shape to objects of study. Thus, Leonie Rowan discusses how the study of educational innovations ought to be retheorized to mean genuinely "transformative" responses to educational arrangements that lead to fundamentally new ways of conceptualizing notions of gender, technology, culture, and difference. The notion of an externally imposed educational accountability on teaching practice is criticized in the chapter prepared by Jennifer C. Greene, Walter Feinberg, Sarah Stitzlein and Luis Miron – a familiar tale. The import of their chapter lies in their reconsideration of the lived reality of accountability in the daily lives of teachers as well as in their suggestion that it is valuable to empirically explore a notion of democratic accountability wedded to the mutual, collective responsibilities of those with a stake in an educational practice. John Elliott's chapter invites readers to reconsider human capital theory as the driver of educational curricula. Elliott explores an interpretation of Amartya Sen's capability theory for human development and its potential for curriculum planning. Elliott argues that thinking of curriculum through the lens of capability theory requires a more deliberative, practical, and democratic approach to curriculum planning and design than that suggested by human capital theory. The penultimate two chapters in Part II take up the question of "being" a researcher, but in different ways. Barbara Kamler and Pat Thomson are concerned with research as a practice of writing, and they explore what that means specifically for students engaged in writing their dissertations. John and Jill Schostak invite readers to radically reconceptualize the traditional image (and identity) of the researcher as rational, methodological, cognizing agent firmly in control of the discovery and production of knowledge.

What is shown

A common theme – written about but not directly explored in these chapters – is that traditional ways of conceiving of objects of analysis in educational (and social) research as entities (problems, events, processes, products, tasks, etc.) with definitive structures constituted by a set of components accessible to well-defined procedures of knowing is no longer a viable guide to doing research. Instead, the objects of research analysis – as well as the material, intellectual, and moral-political circumstances in which such analyses are legitimated, authorized, supported, and given value – are complex, complicated, indeterminate, contested, discursive spaces. Generating knowledge in and about such spaces challenges long-held ideas about the disciplinary model of knowledge production wherein the researcher follows a fairly agreed-upon set of ideas, values, methods, and norms defining the research enterprise; where researchers share common training in the skills and means of established research practices; and where mechanisms of peer review serve as quality control (Gibbons, 2000). It is to this theme and the relationship between knowledge and political action that Bridget Somekh turns her attention in the final chapter, "Last words: speculative knowledge".

This book reveals other things about knowledge production as well. At one level, it is an entirely ironic production. Most chapters explicitly or implicitly criticize the business model of knowledge production that animates educational management and research practices concerned with quality, performance, accountability, and the added value of knowledge. In such a scenario, knowledge is a marketable commodity and knowledge outputs are considered justifiable only in terms of the needs they satisfy in a particular market segment. This book, however, depends for its success on precisely the fact that the publishers are able to promote it as a knowledge commodity to a particular segment of the academic market. Although, as contributors to this volume, we may see ourselves as simply reflecting on and adding to the evolution of our collective thinking by pursuing good work and ensuring its effective dissemination to our particular scholarly community, we are complicit in a process of supplying knowledge products to an industry which serves consumers (van der Linde, 2001).

Finally, this book reveals a struggle with being writerly or readerly, to borrow an idea formulated by Roland Barthes (1970). Some of the contributions strive to present their knowledge obliquely or implicitly, thereby inviting the reader to establish her or his own connections and participate in the construction of meaning. Others are clearly more "readerly" contributions in which the knowledge content is more neatly defined, clearly packaged in a linear argument and thereby place the reader in a more reactive and consumptive position. In other words, the contributions show a tension between producing knowledge that is interesting and unexpected, speculative and fragmentary, aimed more at raising questions than solving problems, and with only incidental utility, on the one hand, and producing a kind of authoritative knowledge that diagnoses and treats, on the other hand.

In the circumstance of producing educational research knowledge in interesting times, the book could not be otherwise.

References

Barthes, R. (1970) *S/Z*, London: Cape.

Gibbons, M. (2000) What kind of university? Changing research practices, *Mousaion* 18(1): 28–40.

van der Linde, G. (2001) Alternative models of knowledge production, *Mousaion* 19(1): 53–61.

Part I

Analysis and critique of contemporary audit cultures and performativity in educational research

Chapter 2

Measures of usefulness
A diatribe

Marilyn Strathern

Contemporary social anthropology engages with agendas it regards as 'other people's', whether from within the academy or from among their subjects of study, at the same time as it also responds to demands from national and international agencies. This chapter, first delivered as a keynote lecture at the conference from which this book sprang, takes up some recent developments in anthropological thinking to raise some questions about what is implied in the accompanying idea that good knowledge is 'useful' knowledge.

She would be a fool who tried to demonstrate the uselessness of everything she knew. And for an occasion to which I have been invited as a keynote speaker I fervently trust I shall not make a fool of myself. I do however want to put in a plea for plain speaking. There is much to be gained from acknowledging uselessness – and today's world of knowledge producers and knowledge managers might benefit from knowing why. I also thought the issue might resonate with some of your own interests in applied research.

We run at once into the oxymoron. She would be a fool who tried to demonstrate the uselessness of what she knew, for there is nothing that cannot be useful if by that we mean putting knowledge to human ends. But I do not propose to revel in the revelation that apparently useless knowledge is useful after all, or conversely, how useless our little schemes turn out to be when we try to be relevant to everything. Rather, the question that these categories prompt is how we make or judge things to be one or the other. As values, they are unequally weighted. I wish to borrow from the positive inflection[1] that accompanies the concept of usefulness to give something of a positive cast to 'uselessness'. Hence the subtitle: 'a diatribe'.

At the same time, I also wish to say something about what could have been a second subtitle: 'an anthropological view'. I would be a fool indeed to argue that social anthropology is a useless subject. In fact, many of my colleagues would count that as betrayal. They would regard it as very stupid indeed – not only research funding within the academy but reputation and jobs outside depend on the perception that it is ultimately worthwhile, and its worth includes its usefulness. They would also think I was under-selling it, and (worse) reinforcing the ignorant stereotypes that many hold.

For I think it would be true to say that when people (non-anthropologists) hear about the scope and ambitions of the discipline (its aims and objectives!) they think it must be relevant to everything – but then, when they look at what anthropologists do, are often confused and disappointed. Anthropology comes out neither with grand statements about the human condition nor with findings about behaviour as recognisable rules of thumb. Instead it just seems to make complicated things more complicated. Its preoccupations are thus read as arcane, somehow not of this world, and so forth.

In fact a complaint of social science as a whole, that it makes problems rather than solves them, is especially true of social anthropology. (To my ears, of course, this shows consonance with its subject matter: 'societies' themselves are problem-creating mechanisms, or, rather, every problem solved in social life generates new ones. Anthropology might present this as fundamental to the human condition, but it is hardly the kind of insight ordinarily welcomed under that rubric.) Yet I am afraid that – perhaps in the spirit of Ian Stronach who asked me to come here – I am also being a bit mischievous, since I am taking a liberty with yourselves. I am afraid *you* might think it a bit irrelevant to your concerns if I talk about anthropology, or can't quite see the point of it in relation to your own agendas! So I am acting out the very issue I want to share with you.

The charge of uselessness is my starting point: not to deny it but to run with it. Let us agree there is much that is useless and irrelevant about anthropology and begin from there. Since it is an academic discipline, this means I am in effect talking about the useful/useless-ness of (a type of) knowledge.

Some problems

One would not be prompted to raise the question about the useful/useless-ness of knowledge, in the first place, if there were not some small indications that all is not well in the knowledge economy, at least in the UK.

Here, from many, are three expressions of anxiety. In an evidence-based era, first policy makers and now research councils tell themselves that knowledge that cannot be communicated is useless knowledge, implying that there is the constant danger of a productivity deficit. Remedy: to be productive knowledge must be transferable, have its 'users', that is, be consumed by others than those who produced it (or by producers in a different capacity). Then from BBC Radio 4 comes a lament about the decreasing numbers of students taking A-level physics. Remedy: natural science must be made more relevant to their lives.[2] The *Times Higher* has concerns for university education, as it watches the alarming rise of student plagiarism.[3] Remedy: putting controls on internet access, monitoring take-home course work, and so forth. A moment's thought and one sees the connections. If people learn they should only do what they understand, uselessness is instantly created, and all kinds of knowledge practices will be consigned to the ivory tower. No surprise then that students find other subjects, such as media or environmental studies, more relevant to their lives than science, since they have been taught that they must do things that make sense in terms of their own experience. And plagiarism is not just a matter of getting a degree at any price; it is a symptom of a knowledge regime that values immediately attainable goals, is about acquisition not learning, and looks to acquire information as so many items or pieces of data.

So each of the remedies simply instantiates the problem in the first place (shows how sensitive it is to its initial conditions). Let me spell this out. Productivity is measured by effects outside the sphere of knowledge creation itself – 'users' have to be 'others' – yet use will not (pace Nowotny) automatically increase the processes of generating knowledge in the first place. Relevance is a concept that backfires – if it paraded as a good, people will make up their own minds what is 'relevant' for them. With plagiarism, finally, the more secure you try to make the system of knowledge access, the more you reproduce the idea of knowledge as so many 'things' to get your hands on in the short term.

You do not have to be an anthropologist to have worked out the connection between these anxieties. But it is pertinent to ask what precisely an anthropologist's perspective might be.

Now in showing you what anthropology can do, I shall run very close to the wind of showing you how useful it is. Let us leave that to one side as a premature judgement. Instead I turn to some of the processes by which anthropology arrives at its knowledge, and do so simply in the interest of expanding the mind. Now if the end (aim/objective) of the exercise is some enlarged capacity – and I mean conceptual rather than mental capacity[4] – then so may be the means. That is, one expands the mind by expanding the mind, a means educationalists once called learning for its own sake. However, learning for its own sake is a presumption to which there is no return. Or, at least, no obvious or simple return for the UK academic to the way the sentiment was once nourished under an institutional and funding regime that placed learning and research at arm's length from other interests.[5] So I need to find some aspect of contemporary social practice we take for granted as a means of expansion, and offer one of my current research interests, interdisciplinarity.

Social anthropology likes to think of itself as responsive. It is unusual among the social sciences in the degree to which it engages with the agendas and knowledge practices of its subjects of study quite as much as it engages with the demands of the academy or of national or international agencies. In the recent past there has been much debate about how relativist its knowledge purports to be – today the emphasis would be more on its relational character. This was always evident in its fieldwork mode, learning about social relations by acting out relationships with people. But it has also become applicable to its position vis-à-vis other disciplines (Lederman 2005).

One reason for engaging with interdisciplinarity is because of the way it latches on to that relational facility or capacity, evident in anthropology though hardly unique to it. What I have in mind here is the overdetermination of any relational capacity by the notion of communication. This is particularly so in interdisciplinary contexts, where it is often presumed that the point of demonstrating a connection is to put one discipline's knowledge at the disposal of another. Communication is the aim, and if it can be communicated knowledge is transformed into information that can be passed on. And hereby we slide into the instrumentalism noted at the outset: 'knowledge is useless *if* it cannot be communicated'. I don't know about you, but my instant response would be to feel vaguely guilty and vaguely in agreement, and capitulate without thinking to the assumption that usefulness is a good thing. At the same time, we might pause to note the relational nature of this chastisement (as it is intended), namely that it apparently requires a user from outside, however outside is defined, to convert the useless into the useful. That is to say, a relationship between producer and consumer, an interesting presumption in itself.

Perhaps there is something in those three scenarios of anxiety to work at. I propose to respond to each in turn and in such a way as to give an important role to 'uselessness'. I do so through talking about an anthropology that exists in a world where interdisciplinarity is promoted on all sides. This affords an interesting – as in challenging'– as in 'interdisciplinarily challenged' – context.

I An evidence-based era: applications and negotiations

Others – and from other disciplines – have expatiated at length on one of the drivers of the knowledge economy, the value placed on evidence-based decision-making (e.g. Clarke 2005). It is impossible to object, and I do not rehearse the arguments here. If a precondition of its usefulness is that knowledge can be communicated, an expected outcome is that it will lead to action. This lies behind much applied anthropology, for instance in its continuing and vigorous engagement with development. Practitioners in this sub-discipline offer information that will be applicable, meet perceived goals, respond to the demands of the present, all with a view to informing decisions about the kind of action needed.

Of course, the quality of the evidence being offered matters. Now anthropologists have argued over and again that to best meet immediate goals, it may be wise to rely on information gained independently of the goals now in sight. If so, it will have been gained for other ends altogether. Indeed, anthropologists engaged in development work these days may find themselves drawing on a corpus of data put together with quite other objectives in mind. Those other objectives, such as apparently 'useless' internal debate with colleagues, may have had no practical application in view. This is well appreciated; the point is that such objectives belong to the impetus for data collection and need not affect how the data itself is used.

In many interdisciplinary encounters the situation is otherwise: the objectives are significant and the manner of data collection (the 'methodology') *is* part of the data. Here one might think, for example, of recent experiments in law and anthropology, or its neighbour ethics. This yields a second, and quite different, kind of scenario.

Very roughly, the contrast could be summed up thus. Where what is of value is the data regardless of the process of collecting, anthropology behaves a little like a science or technology, pressing its findings into the service of problem-solving. Information is 'applied' (Schön 2002). Where, however, the mode of assemblage is part and parcel of the data, it begins to resemble the arts and its sister social sciences. As far as interdisciplinary encounters are concerned, successful communication in the first works itself out in terms of the contribution that its data makes to solving a problem overall. In the second case, encounters turn on interpretation and translation, on how far any particular idea or model can cross the disciplinary boundary.

Now if in either of these cases the orientation is to others ('users', 'collaborators') the chances are of course that individual viewpoints become representative of the discipline – and that the outward-looking relation of communication precludes or obscures relations internal to the development of the discipline itself. In the first scenario, one might wish to draw on a model of household relations, say, without going into elaborate definitions of kinship structures. Or, in the second, one might wish to draw on ideas of authorship without also trailing a cosmology of creativity and reproduction. In other words *communication entails a necessary reductionism*, based perhaps on the idea that what has to be shown is how something has 'travelled' between disciplines. So the chances are that it will be a 'thing' (a piece of data) shorn of its original relational coordinates.

No surprise, then, that pre-existing relations (from within a discipline) are erased in the way new relations (across disciplines) are sought out.[6] One consequence is that facts, concepts and so forth, are imagined as though they were entities with their own character and form, and all that has to be got right is their definition, and as though they existed in isolation from one another, so the quest is to bring them into relationship.[7] However, the erasure of internal relations in the embracing of new external ones creates a problem. If one is constructing 'evidence', then the precision with which facts are specified and concepts delineated matter. As with scientific models of chemical formulae, or economic models that deal with prices, or semantic models concerned with the way images work off other images, it is the fixing of concepts by their coordinates that gives them precision.

One can define entities until the cows come home, often an exercise in infinite regress, for each definition will shift the terrain or context (Schlecker and Hirsch 2001). But to treat concepts as nodes at the heart of various coordinates is to give them specificity. That may require bringing in factors that appear to have no immediate connection. Thus the properties of chemical compounds require we know something about the relations between the elements that make them up; the wealth a person has might be best expressed as a function of house prices; the idea of 'nature' has to be pinned down as the antonym of culture, of society, or artifice, of invention or whatever, each of these 'fixing' it in a different way. A virtue of this relationism is that one can specify the conditions under which these different 'meanings' appear. For example, we specify 'knowledge' in distinguishing it from wisdom/information/data – not in order to isolate knowledge as a thing with its own inherent properties but to realise that we have to keep in mind the relationship we wish our concept to have with all these others. But it might look as though we are bringing in a lot of extraneous information.

Let us return to the axiom that knowledge must be communicated for it to be useful. It is clear that, for anything offered as evidence to be credited with any sort of precision, considerable internal relational work is needed first, and possibly even some of that should be conveyed.

Now communication implies finding people willing to be communicated with, possibly even tolerant of extraneous information.

And who cares, for example, that in New Guinea Highlands horticulture gardens are fenced and pigs (the principal domestic animal) roam freely? No-one, until, that is, agricultural officers think it would be more practical to fence the pigs and let the gardens spread. (The principal root crop, sweet potato, is eaten by pigs and people alike, and pigs are always trying to get into the gardens where they grow.) Well, fenced-in pigs do not just get diseased and miss out on the nutritional value of free foraging, and women are not just given more work in harvesting more sweet potatoes to feed them, but the arrangement goes against the very logic of enclosure. Land is enclosed, as clan territories and their associated ancestral spirits are enclosed, so that wealth and produce, including pigs, and including women in marriage, move between local areas. 'To enclose' or 'to fence-in' is fixed by coordinates of meanings the agricultural officers never dreamed of.

Of course, for the present interdisciplinary context, this is a highly reduced account. At the same time reduction is only apparent to those who might have entertained a more detailed version. To them, reduction and thus loss of information is inevitable in purveying information; to those who receive, it is essential. So expansion in one direction also entails loss in others

II Making knowledge relevant to our lives: comparisons and analogies

Obviously, social anthropology has no particular option on these kinds of relational exercises. However, it does deploy a rather distinctive, and *non-reductive*, form of relation to special effect. I refer to the making of analogies.

You will recall the lament about the decreasing numbers of students taking A level physics – in the UK plunging its university future into a crisis. And that the remedy is to make physics seem more relevant to the students' lives. After decades of government propaganda stressing the relevance of teaching and learning, it is not surprising that people are indeed encouraged to think about what knowledge can do for them – and then make up their own mind about what is relevant. In the remedy (make physics more relevant) lies an example of a disastrous attempt at analogy. In fact there are probably several analogies at work. One is an analogy between the critical scrutiny of information to determine what evidence might be relevant to solve a problem (as we have just been considering), and what it is appropriate to teach children in school in order to prepare them for life ahead.[8]

It does not follow that the reductionism in the first case is a good model for advocating reductionism in the second. Another seems to be the analogy between life now and life later. That life ahead is supposed to be already reflected in what children like to do now is a correlation that leaves me gasping. And so on.

So analogies can be treacherous. Here, though, it is I who have pointed to them, and the indigenous holders of such views would probably just think they were drawing obvious conclusions from what they already knew. I am sure analogies are no less treacherous in the hands of anthropologists, but many anthropological analogies are explicitly and intentionally deployed. Anthropologists are always exploring new coordinates, new ways of plotting the meaning of what is to be described; in their hands analogy is a method. A long and continuing investment in comparison has turned away from constructing principles of differentiation and similarity and towards elucidating the character of one thing by reference to another. We can think of it as a latter-day form of cross-cultural comparison.

Let me describe such a moment earlier this year. Listening to a paper being given at the ASA meetings on 'Creativity and cultural improvisation', I turned to the rubric for the panel and my eye fell on the terms 'transplant' and 'context'. The convenors were concerned with creativity as a social capacity. Rather than imagine that innovations, resting on perceptions of discontinuity ('here is something new'), are without precedent because of the unique genius that inspired them, they invited the panel to consider

> appropriations in the sense of practices, information or belief systems being 'transplanted' (through processes including but not limited to colonization, violence, missionization, education, media and trade) and then recontextualized by those who appropriate them.
>
> (Wastell and Demian 2005)

The reference to context suggested that one might consider such appropriations as part of a broader capacity to (re)contextualise that exists in the capacity to switch points of view. The very apprehension of old things in new places as a matter of their travelling between 'contexts' is an epistemological gloss: the imputation is that in being re-located something is now 'known' differently. It is an interpretation that rests of course on a prior understanding that the (same) item has travelled between different, and thus already distinct, places. In any event I saw an analogy between the way that persons create points of view by virtue of their existing difference from one another and the way that existing differences among contexts mean that context casts knowledge in a particular light.

However, the term 'transplant', familiar enough in medicine for example, plunged me as an anthropologist into another world altogether, and into another source of analogy. Transplant is a term by which ethnographers of the Papua New Guinea Highlands (e.g. Muke 1997) refer to the way the men of a patrilineal clan, in bestowing their sister or daughter on another, regard themselves as having a transplant ('sister's/daughter's child') in that second clan. The child is borne by the mother on the father's clan land, but it is as though through the body of the mother the child has travelled from another clan. And here is an apparent local analogy. For the term itself is taken from another domain, horticulture, and from the gardener's technique of introducing sweet potato vines from one plot to another. This may be from old to new gardens, or the vines may come from faraway gardens through all kinds of contacts. Thinking of children as 'planted' implies that some essential part of them has come from elsewhere (from the mother's clan ancestors who bestow nourishment on the father's child). In any event, the imagery of planting a garden is not far from their minds.

Here two quite different 'contexts' (the appropriation of items to create innovations, epistemological and otherwise, and the literal transferring of plants or children from one clan land to another) are joined by a common term ('transplant'). Whether such a series of images typifies relations more familiarly described as the workings of metaphor (planting a sweet potato for talking about bestowing a child onto another clan); or as analogies, drawn out metaphors where deliberate parallels are made evident, such as the parallel between appropriating old things in new ways and taking a point of view; or even as the presentation of comparisons, these operations all depend on keeping the original domains of reference distinct.[9] This suggests parallels with interdisciplinary endeavours. Thus it is presumed both that domains have to be kept discrete and that it is possible to produce new objects of discussion through incorporating elements from elsewhere, in short, that one can learn from other contexts.

The anthropologists' method of cross-cultural comparison means that they are constantly juxtaposing materials from domains they construct as distinct. Explicit comparison aside, they always carry around in their heads examples from some 'elsewhere' or other, and frequently may use the images and languages of one society or culture to talk about another. Here comparison has often remained implicit. So, for example, if models are drawn from Euro-American institutions such as economy or law in order to create a language through which to describe economic or legal practices in non-Euro-American situations, that a comparison between distinct systems or social traditions is implied may remain just that, implicit, unspoken. In effect such *thinking through* happens all the time. These days the relation between such languages is made increasingly explicit, and has become visible in recent works. What is gained from making analogies explicit? We may think of (i) self-consciousness about language of analysis/description; (ii) insights into either domain; (iii) the capacity to write at multiple levels through different genres, tenors; and (iv) monitoring the object of analysis/description through experimenting with what seems a good 'fit'.

So for example, when Maurer (2005) was attempting to describe Islamic financial enterprises, he tried out various analogies with western forms of credit cooperatives and mechanisms for producing profit without interest. Among the analogies are time-bartering and service-exchange associations in urban USA. Nothing is a complete fit, but the parallels are simultaneously illuminating on both sides; they are also likely to introduce more information than one thinks one 'needs'. In other words, far from reducing complexity, such analogies extend it.

Indeed, analogies both conserve and extend. What is non-reductive about this relation is the fact that the two elements to an analogy or comparison are never finally merged: the power of thinking one thing through another lies in keeping them apart. Distinctiveness is conserved, while the understanding of each is extended by introducing the other into its description. What is also non-reductive is that the procedure makes it evident that the grounds of comparison do not lie within but between entities, and are created by, are a function of, the relationship. They do not pre-exist the analysis. One cannot predict, it therefore follows, what might be illuminating as an axis of comparison. (Nor does it follow that all comparisons or analogies are illuminating.) There can, in this sense, be no pre-determination of 'relevance', no 'usefulness' before the extension has been tried.

We come back to a situation surely familiar to educationalists, that there is no way that one can make science or pure maths (say) 'relevant' to the child's world until the relationship has been tried out. If, further, analogic relations are allowed, an exploration of parallel universes with no intrinsic connection between them, each can yield unexpected knowledge about the other. Incidentally, such a method (analogy) could break the impasse of 'proof' – the logic that insists that the only relevant relation between things is that of cause and effect. That is the logic that leads to the extreme position that if there is no connection between items, the one can be of no interest to the other.

III Plagiarism: borrowing and trading

The *THES* article about increasing plagiarism, mentioned at the beginning, itself linked the practice to the erosion of valuing knowledge for its own sake. It makes no sense to cheat when you want to improve your knowledge; things are very different when the goal is an immediate one, the grade at the end. In this view, plagiarism is an outcome of emphasis on grades, rankings, demonstrating what you have achieved, and where knowledge appears a matter of items to accumulate rather than of development or unfolding. In other words, as in making assessments of relevance, knowledge is material to be 'managed'. That is the other message that is coming from the research councils and elsewhere. The irony of research councils participating in this is that one might otherwise have wanted to pitch a research model of knowledge practice against a managerial one (Strathern 2006). In any event, the students have got there as fast as their teachers.

There are some lessons here for how we approach interdisciplinary endeavours. I shall talk about relational extension, but not this time as an intellectual exercise in extending the description of one entity by incorporating elements of other descriptions. In the present case, relational extension is a property of the entity itself.

Now it is well known that interdisciplinary collaboration is invariably difficult, is as often accompanied by anxiety as by exhilaration, and that there are endless attempts to pin down the key negotiations. It strikes me that sometimes we have been looking in the wrong place for the difficulties. We look at the disciplines and at the barriers they create for one another as though the inherent problem rested on their incommensurability. In fact, the fundamental cleavage might instead be between management and research. For it is obvious that the academic practitioner has two kinds of relationship to disciplines. First are those disciplines in which he or she has the kind of investment that leads to primary research and/or training. Second are those disciplines in which he or she has no immediate research interest – and here it follows that the practitioner can *only* have a management interest (the question is how to use it). That affects the perception of means–ends relationships. (If you are not learning for the sake of training, then it is logical to be interested in the grades.)

This applies across the board. Across the board? Perhaps the reason we have sometimes been looking in the wrong place is that we have been so focused on incommensurability, on the difficulties disciplines have as discrete entities in talking to one another, that we do not see what we all know. Namely, that they are *all alike in thinking they have this problem*. That is, the same 'problem' seems to arise in each case. The issue, the endlessly encountered problem, is the impossibility of real communication.[10]

And the way I would phrase it is to say that each discipline comes with, so to speak, the potential for communication and thus for relations beyond itself as intrinsically part of itself. It is that relationality that is now, these days, being made publicly visible and the subject of open debate, and a discipline's success at *performing* its relational capacities is at the heart of assessment, accountability to the public, value for money, and so forth. It is passable, in contemporary policy terms, to perform that relationality in respect of other disciplines as well as to outsiders (Strathern 2004).

Academic disciplines are intrinsically research focused, but they have the spin-off possibility of being useful, of being communicable, of being managed. So when practitioners of different disciplines are in dialogue with one another they are not only, as it might seem, bringing different kinds of expertise to the table, they are also all facing the same challenge of having to operationalise their external antennae, their potential for extension, on pain of appearing weak. That is, present at the interdisciplinary table is both the discipline *and* the problem it has with communicating to others, and that same problem will take as many forms as the disciplines themselves. This makes for another anxiety! For this is a moment when a discipline has to 'manage' its relations to others, and thus has to turn on itself in a managerial capacity. Management, inevitably, is the mode of interaction between any disciplines recognised as 'other' to one another. How useful is the one to the other, what can be got from it, what can be traded, what can we learn, how can we enhance what we already have? These questions all come from a management ethos.

So perhaps in the heat generated over interdisciplinarity, rather than taking differences between disciplines as our starting point we might look to a critical distinction between research and management practices (and the accompanying ethos of each). For going between those two modes requires a switch in the kind of relationship a person has 'with'/'towards' a body of knowledge. I can only guess the perspective from management, but the perspective from disciplines and their research model of knowledge generation is that research has its own internal impetus, such that the demands for it to be commercially useful or useful to society appear 'external' to it. Indeed, they are external to the extent that these are precisely the sites of its extension, its relation with other bodies. We might find versions of this model from diverse areas of social science, e.g., sociology (Luhmann's 1990 system and environment), economics (externalities, from Callon 1998), but I can also offer an anthropological one.

I take from anthropology a model for interdisciplinarity encounters and the anxieties they generate. It comes not from cultural but from social life, a contrast to which I return. This is the figure of the (fractal) person. The person is envisaged as an entity with relations implied (Wagner 1991).[11] You can think of the enclosed New Guinea gardens growing the food that will be fed to people, including women and children, and to pigs, that travel between clan lands. The sweet potato indicates the ground's extensional capacity; planted land is an entity with relations implied. The same is true of persons. A person grows up on their father's clan land, a member of their father's patrilineal clan, but attached to or implied in the person's identity are relations with the mother's patrilineal kin as well.

By analogy, instead of thinking of disciplines as so many individual 'cultures', the parallel so often made, one can think of them socially, with external relations integral to them. This is because that external impetus is not simply a matter of imposed, outside, foreign demands – the impetus to extend outwards may be built into the research as its rationale, or be regarded as its essential outreach to 'society'.

Why did I emphasise a model drawn from social life rather than from culture? The *cultural model* of interdisciplinary encounters is the current orthodoxy, and may seem self-evident to practitioners. It gets us into matters of translation, a sense of boundaries, of interpreters, trading zones, transactions, and so forth. To borrow from economics, basically this is the neo-classical cosmos of discrete entities: a neo-classical model presupposes entities such disciplines as so many distinct cultures, with already established values [production], and you have to find currencies of interchange between them [distribution] in order for them to be communicable [consumption]. Management, in other words, lies outside or between the entities, after the fact of their constitution. Management is all about being productive by bringing pre-existing knowledge together.

A *social model* would look more like a political-economy one, where consumption is entailed in production, and vice versa. That is, a discipline's relational extension is an integral part of itself [productive consumption/ consumptive production].[12] Its place in a research institute or HEI, its drawing in the interests of students, its commercial applications, the handling of its resources and personnel: management is built in, integrally implied. But it is the discipline's fractal remainder – its extension– that gets a discipline elsewhere, to another place. I would add this time, though again I am not on sure ground, that if one thinks of disciplines as having their problems about communication attached, we might also imagine research with management attached. For management, conversely, we might expect to find management practices with expertise attached.

Here I borrow twice over from social anthropology. First is the distinction between cultural and social life, for thinking about two approaches to the relationship between research and management models of knowledge production. Second is recent theorising on personhood and the nature of sociality that began in the Highlands of Papua New Guinea nearly fifteen years ago but has been taken up elsewhere (e.g. Mosko and Damon 2005). Together all this helps us formulate an observation about interdisciplinary work: that we are dealing not with disciplines as single entities, but with disciplines and their fractal remainders. For there will also be disciplinary specificities in what they count as good communication. So rather than, as in the prevalent cultural model, taking practices of communication as neutral enablements, we would focus on what we already know, that how disciplines 'do' their relational extensions – how they communicate – differs too.

Let me return momentarily to the original educational impasse. The plagiarist may be a skilful knowledge manager in the making. But she or he is hopelessly stuck in a cultural or neo-classical world of discrete entities, for in refusing to learn he or she also refuses to admit knowledge as an extension of him or herself.

Diatribe

I said that one reason for engaging with interdisciplinarity is because of the way it latches on to a certain relational capacity evident in anthropology but hardly unique to it. I briefly conclude by hinting at the perversion of the general (human!) relational faculties on which such a capacity draws.

In being responsive to those snippets of information about education in Britain today I wanted both to show anthropology's responsive nature, and suggest that making responsiveness useful has a fatal limitation. The limitation is to assume that responsiveness only gives evidence of itself when its use can be shown by those on whom it has impact. The anxiety *I* have is about the perversion entailed in using such capacities without replenishing them (Brennan 2000). That very human capacity for response to others – a relational capacity – is obviously pressed into the service of communication all the time. It is not a finite good, and willingly replicates itself over and again. But the underlying faculty does have to be nourished. Quite literally, we have to keep the faculty alive.

We demand the same of knowledge as we demand of responsiveness, and they are connected. If a precondition of *its* usefulness is that knowledge can be communicated, an expected outcome is that it will lead to action. However, as I see it, knowledge is more than information to be accumulated (or managed, as our plagiarist does) for the sake of informing others. Knowledge enlarges understanding and keeps the brain alert. Without an enlarged view one cannot make judgements (if only our narrowly 'relevance'-seeking sixth formers knew). And the impetus has to be curiosity, that is, responsiveness to the world at large, not in order to encompass information about everything but to exercise the capacity to know something. Knowledge to satisfy curiosity in the knower (who cares if it is communicable!) never shows a productivity deficit. Along with eye and hand coordination, the great asset of the human species is curiosity, the ability to be interested in many things all at once, indeed, in as many as come into view. We are in peril if we do not cultivate curiosity in what is around us.

And she would be a fool who tried to demonstrate the usefulness of everything she knew.

Acknowledgements

A longer version forms the Isaiah Berlin lecture, British Academy, December 2005, under the title 'Useful Knowledge'. I appreciate the stimulus of an ongoing project, 'Interdisciplinarity and Society', undertaken jointly with Andrew Barry and Georgina Born (ESRC grant RES-151-25-00042) as part of the ESRC Science in Society Programme, where Elena Khlinovskaya Rockhill has been an inspiration. Thanks also to Almut Schneider.

Notes

1 There is a sense in which one cannot not 'want' to be useful, any more than one cannot not allow oneself to be held accountable for one's actions.
2 19 August 2004, BBC Radio 4
3 *THES* opinion piece, summer 2004; Brecher 2005.
4 I do not mean cognitively but in the organisation of ideas.
5 In a very broad brush way I refer here to the post-war 'independence' of the university system from government interests (e.g. McSherry 2001), with antecedents in the idea of education as cultivation (of the mind).
6 One of the issues in apprehending interdisciplinarity is scale – for it repeats at the 'level' of disciplines (areas of knowledge, sub-disciplines, schools of thought) what is intrinsic to language use and to enlightenment knowledge practices alike.
7 This is of course the hegemonic Euro-American model of the way the social world works – the effort to create society by linking people together, persons being pre-existing individual (biological) entities. Moreover, while Euro-Americans love treating entities as things, especially because they think they can consume them/absorb them, reification [figurative mode] is only half of the process of conceptualisation, the other half being the revelation of the relations they contain, their coordinates [literal mode].
8 No judgement here that the life ahead is that of employment (and not, say, the life of the mind).
9 When analogies appear to have explanatory power, that is, offer insights that can be pursued systematically, take many things into account, creating domains that encompass domains, they acquire the status of *models*.
10 Real in the sense of conserving what is meaningful to one discipline in its encounters with others.

11 I give a Euro-American view of the fractal person that emphasises the individual and its extensions … rather than a Melanesian view that has to extract the individual from its relational extensions.

12 The social model would have a comment on the cultural one. From its perspective, the cultural model proposes that the research way of thinking about disciplines, with autonomous lives and independent research trajectories, is consonant with notions of the person exaggerated as 'the individual' in much Euro-American [western] thought, leaving relations as a kind of residue.

References

Brecher, Bob (2005) 'If we insist on playing games …', *Times Higher Educational Supplement* 24 June, 50.

Brennan, T. (2000) *Exhausting Modernity: Grounds for a New Economy*, New York: Routledge.

Callon, M. (1998) *The Laws of the Markets*, Oxford, Blackwell Publishers / The Sociological Review.

Clarke, John (2005) 'Performing for the public: doubt, desire, and the evaluation of public services', in P. Du Gay (ed.), *The Values of Bureaucracy*, Oxford: Oxford University Press.

Lederman, Rena (2005) 'Unchosen grounds: cultivating cross-subfield accents for a public voice', in D. Segal and S. Yanagaisako (eds), *Unwrapping the Sacred Bundle: Reflections on the Disciplining of Anthropology*, Durham, NC: Duke University Press.

Luhmann, N. (1990) 'The autopoiesis of social systems', in N. Luhmannn, *Essays on Self-Reference*, New York: Columbia University Press.

Maurer, Bill (2005) *Mutual Life, Limited: Islamic Banking, Alternative Currencies, Lateral Reason*, Princeton, NJ: University of Princeton Press.

McSherry, Corynne (2001) *Who Owns Academic Work? Battling for Control of Intellectual Property*, Cambridge, MA: Harvard University Press.

Mosko, M. and Damon, F. (eds) (2005) *On the Order of Chaos: Social Anthropology and the Science of Chaos*, Oxford: Berghahn Books.

Muke, J. (1997) Affidavit in 'In the matter of an application under Section 57 of the Constitution: application by Individual and Community Rights Forum Inc. (ICRAF) in re: Miriam Willingal', National Court of Justice, *Papua New Guinea Law Reports*, Port Moresby.

Schlecker, M. and Hirsch, E. (2001) 'Incomplete knowledge: ethnography and the crisis of context in studies of the media, science and technology', *History of the Human Sciences*, 14: 69–87.

Schön, D. (2002) [1st pub. 1983] *The Reflective Practitioner: How Professionals Think in Action*, Aldershot: Ashgate Publishing.

Strathern, Marilyn (2004) 'Accountability across disciplines', in *Commons and Borderlands: Working Papers on Interdisciplinarity, Accountability and the Flow of Knowledge*, Wantage: Sean Kingston Publishing.

Strathern, Marilyn (2006) 'A community of critics', *Journal of the Royal Anthropological Institute*, NS: 112(1): 191–209.

Wagner, Roy (1991) 'The fractal person', in M. Godelier and M. Strathern (eds), *Big Men and Great Men: Personifications of Power in Melanesia*, Cambridge: Cambridge University Press.

Wastell, Sari and Demian, Melissa (2005) Rubric for panel, 'The creativity of social, political and religious life', at ASA conference on *Creativity and cultural improvisation*, Aberdeen.

Chapter 3

How is educational research 'being framed'?

Governmentality, the (ac)counting of, and expertise in, educational research

Jill Blackmore

On 2 July 2005 in *The Age* newspaper (p. 1), a Professor of Education at Melbourne University was cited as arguing that educational research is irrelevant. This type of criticism is not new. The criticism of irrelevance of educational research as a field replicates similar charges made in the UK during the 1990s (e.g. Hargreaves 1996, Hillage *et al.* 1998, Tooley and Darby 1998) and in the USA (Coalition for Evidence-based Policy 2002). But such comments are, in 2005, receiving significant attention. The restructuring (and funding) of higher education is now the focus of significant debate in Australia as elsewhere. The context is that of declining (real) government expenditure in Australian higher education generally. Furthermore, who funds and benefits from research is now at issue, as there is a perceived need to harness knowledge production and transmission to better service the national interest. As stated in the Coalition's policy *Backing Australia's Ability*, universities are now central to knowledge production and dissemination in an 'innovation economy' (Nelson 2003).

In this chapter I argue that the debates over quality are indicative of wider shifts in the nature of educational governance generally (Marginson and Considine 2000), the role of universities within an informational society in particular (Delanty 2001), and the reconfiguring of power/knowledge in terms of the relations between the state, knowledge and expertise within advanced liberalism and global capitalism (Rose 1993). Current debates about quality and research are highly political, driven by neo-liberal ideologies about the role of education as a tool of the market; but also epistemological, as various policy moves are made on particular assumptions about the nature of knowledge production, its dissemination and legitimation in terms of what counts as valued knowledge, who decides what counts, and with what effects. This last point is most obvious when unpacking the 'coincidences' between two rapidly 'travelling' discourses – the discourse of evidence-based policy and practice, and the discourse of quality research assessment – and how they are being articulated in the Australian policy context.

My argument is structured around Yates' (2005a, p. 3) delineations between three approaches to discussions about quality and impact in examining the development of the Research Quality Framework in Australia during 2005–7. In the first section, I will 'ask what agendas and experiences are being brought to a particular development; what are the situation, context, constraints that particular field of discussion is occupied with; what are the tacit as well as explicit terms of the agenda' (p. 3). This requires analysing the changing national and international policyscapes of higher education in relation to the nation state and globalised economies and how universities are being remade to promote innovation and informational economies for global capitalism. Second, I will consider 'quality', and 'impact' as 'events, texts and empirical objects of study' (Yates 2005a, p. 3). I will do this by considering a particular 'case' of the research, policy and practice nexus –gender equity research – from the point of view of a *systematic review*, the preferred approach suggested by 'evidence-based policy and practice' (EPP) advocates. I then move into normative discussions about worthwhileness, the assessment process and criteria of quality. This means 'elaborating and defending and assessing our own aspirations for the work we do; elaborating criteria of methodological quality…defending conceptions of appropriate relationships between research and a field of professional practice…[and] arguing about who or what should be appropriate to judge whether work has in fact been of quality or has an impact" (Yates 2005a, p. 3).

The Australian policyscape

The Australian Department of Education Science and Technology (DEST) established a consultative process during 2004–6 in order to produce a Research Quality Framework (RQF) by 2007. Informed by the Expert Advisory Group chaired by Sir Gareth Roberts, the reviewer of the UK Research Assessment Exercise (RAE) in 2003, the policy debate echoes preceding and ongoing debates about the New Zealand Performance Based Research Fund (PBRF) (introduced in 2004) and the RAE in the UK (introduced in 1985). The RQF will determine in Australia over the next decade what counts as quality research in terms of particular measures of impact on the field and on policy and practice, who gets funded for research in terms of who measures up against particular criteria of quality, and finally which universities count in terms of the measures mobilised to re-distribute both research funds and research training to the 38 Australian universities. This policy has significant implications for all Australian universities and academics, in terms of status hierarchies between universities and academics, the future research capacities and potential of individual universities, and the careers of academics as researchers and/or teachers.

But the quality debate needs to be located within wider debates about the rapidly changing nature of higher education as a result of the internationalisation of education, the rise of knowledge-based economies, the emergence of an international quality movement, decreased Australian federal government funding of universities, increased federal government intervention in higher education to direct teaching and research towards national priorities, and the desire by all governments to be seen to be efficient, effective and more accountable.

With regard to internationalisation and privatisation, quality assurance is now a key aspect of winning and retaining niche overseas and local student markets. The Australian University Quality Assurance Agency, created in 2002 in line with similar institutions in the UK and NZ, completed its first round of assessments in 2006. Its focus was on auditing the paper trail or processes assuring 'quality' of the Australian higher education system in general. But it is quality *research* that will be *the* key signifier in international ranking tables, differentiating between elite global universities and other universities within Australia. Research reputation will attract the 'high flyer' students and research funds. Embedded in current policies, therefore, is the tension. On the one hand, the government wishes to produce greater differential research funding between universities with the concentration of funding in fewer universities, a differentiation that the RQF will deliver. But on the other hand, due to decreased government funding of higher education, government policies encourage all universities to be more internationally competitive by creating a high quality Australian 'brand' of international education (Nelson 2003, Marginson 2006).

But when it comes to defining quality research, how is quality understood? Quality is defined in the Preferred Option of the Australian Expert Advisory Group in two ways: as impact on the field, where quality is judged by citations, quality of journal, theoretical framework, conceptual clarity, methodological rigour etc.; and impact on policy and/or practice as judged by qualified users (Expert Advisory Group 2005). Whereas impact on a discipline is to be judged by peers through a range of 'measurable' proxies (e.g. citations and impact factor of journals) that tend to favour the sciences, how to measure impact on policy and practice is more difficult – who are the users, how does research translate into practice, and how can effect be measured? The latter is a major issue for professional fields such as education.

Educational researchers are precariously caught between a rock and a hard place by contradictory policy pressures. On the one hand, the research quantum measures utilised during the 1990s to fund research increased expectations of Australian researchers to be internationally recognised as judged by their respective disciplinary field (peer esteem) and *quantity* of inputs (research funds) and outputs (publications). As with the UK RAE, old hierarchies of what counts as quality were recreated as universities focused on the production of knowledge for peers and within specialist fields in international peer refereed journals usually inaccessible and incomprehensible to practitioners or policymakers (Morley 2003, Blackmore 2005). On the other hand, as stated in the opening paragraph, since 1996 considerable pressure has been put on educational researchers in the UK, USA and Australia to better inform policy and practice. Criticisms shared across nation states have been that educational research is supply rather than demand driven, lacks coherence as a body of work, is oriented towards research colleagues rather than policymakers or practitioners, and is generally inaccessible in terms of both language and location. In the USA, the No Child Left Behind legislation prescribes scientific research within a particular narrow frame of large-scale randomised control trial (RCT) methodologies (Lather 2003). Education as a professional field is expected to inform professional practice in an ongoing manner. Impact is here equated to immediate use value. These competing agendas about impact mean that politicians and practitioners can blame educational researchers simultaneously for failing to meet the performance indicators in terms of research funds, publications and citations, *and* failing to inform policy and practice, while researchers seek to do both with less time and funding. Thus educational researchers are 'framed' as being irrelevant and inadequate.

The apparent inaccessibility of research to policymakers and practitioners, paradoxically, justifies a further mechanism in order for research to inform practice and policy. It is no coincidence that a discourse promoting *evidence-based* policy and practice (EPP) is currently also being foregrounded. EPP appears to resolve the tension between impact as measured by citations, and impact on policy and practice as EPP advocates claim that systematic reviews can synthesise the evidence for consumption by different audiences. The EPP approach is premised on a particular empiricist view of research that favours large-scale random controlled studies on the basis that it is on the one hand more valid, credible, generalisable and *measurable*, and on other hand, identifies 'what works' premised upon a particularly linear and instrumental relationship between research, policy and practice (Blackmore 2002). These claims are welcome within a political climate in which politicians and practitioners seek simple and immediate solutions to complex problems.

Various versions of what counts as evidence-based policy and practice have been promoted in education by some academics and governments (Lather 2003). The notion of evidence-based practice and policy (EPP) is a new constant in Australian education policy discourses and texts e.g. evidence-based leadership, evidence-based school reviews (Blackmore 2002). The chair of an Australian federal government report on literacy, while citing his own research extensively to advocate that phonics be required in teacher education, also claims the report is 'evidence based' (Rowe 2005; *The Age* 11 December, pp. 1, 12). The EPP discourse within global and local education policy communities takes on significant credibility in the context of the quality research debate given its claims. The proponents of EPP argue that there is need for a more cumulative, rigorous and focused approach to the production of evidence to inform both educational policy and practice (e.g. Hargreaves 1996, Hillage *et al.* 1998). The assumption inherent in much of the argument is that evidence-based research of a particular type derived from the medical model dominant in the health sciences and large epidemiological studies, is of a higher *quality* than other forms of research (e.g. qualitative research based on case studies).

In defining this nexus between quality and impact based on types of research and their application, not only are instrumentalist assumptions about the nature of 'useful' knowledge made, who produces it and for what purpose (cf. Blackmore 2002), but naive assumptions are also made as to the relationship between the fields of educational research, policy and practice (Kirst 2000, Levin 2006).

Even existing performance-based funding based on 'de facto' measures (e.g. research income and publications) do not incorporate much of what educational researchers do. In contrast, Yates (2005b, p. 15) argues research is 'an activity that is defined by most people as a practice with technical/methodological parameters (it investigates something appropriately and systematically) and also substantive parameters (it makes contributions to knowledge)'. That is, the theory/practice divide is not as evident as is claimed by critics when research is defined more broadly and is inclusive of a range of different types of research and different types of researchers. Policymakers still tend to view a model of linear 'dissemination from experts' to practitioners, whereas many educational researchers see knowledge building within the field as complex, two-way and polyvocal, in which practitioners also have a voice. The dissemination process is itself diffuse, and always mediated through publications but also through consultation and advocacy or what Yeatman (1999) refers to as policy activism. This latter perspective sees a more dialogical process between research, policy and practice. Current debates need to be understood within wider shifts in the nature of knowledge, new governmentalities and universities and the re-framing of educational research.

Universities in a knowledge-based economy

The wider issue here is about the changing role, function and idea of the university as the key site of knowledge production, dissemination and application (Barnett and Griffin 1999). It is about challenges to the foundations of knowledge and traditional notions of expertise (Brint 1994), and the changing policy process within the new governmentalities of the twenty-first century that focus on accountability, innovation and competition (Marginson and Considine 2000). A fundamental aspect of the twentieth century university has been as the primary producer of valued knowledge in the form of research and scholarship, regulated through particular methodological, professional and ethical practices as opposed to opinion or ideology, where legitimacy and expertise are based on claims of objectivity (Delanty 2001). The modern university has been idealised as providing critical intellectualism, professional education that imbues a sense of public service, and basic research that in the short term may be applied to problem solving and in the long term will advance the field of knowledge generally. Universities have been largely independent of government, part of the wider cultural field, in which academic freedom has been a central tenet. Knowledge production and modes of organisation within the university were based on the intrinsic more by its utilitarian value of knowledge within strongly bounded disciplinary fields, what Gibbons et al. (1994) refer to as Mode 1 Knowledge. The dominant pedagogic mode was that of expert knower to uninformed learner.

The claims for both objectivity in knowledge and independent governance of universities have been undermined during the latter decades of the twentieth century (Barnett and Griffin 1999, Delanty 2001). The basis of legitimacy for the epistemological claims of one form of knowing over another have been contested by feminist, post-structuralist and cultural studies theorists. Gibbons *et al.* (1994) argue that there is also an epistemological shift, with the old theory/practice divides of the Enlightenment collapsing with a new focus on problem solving and inter- disciplinarity. At the same time, universities have been restructured by governments in order to capture and realign their core work of research and teaching to do the work of the state, as the state increasingly mediates global markets and the democratic demands of their populations for access to higher education (Marginson and Considine 2000, Marginson 2002). Education has become a business central to the nation states economic capacity to compete i.e. academic capitalism (Slaughter and Leslie 1997). This educational restructuring was produced by, and also produced, a shift from government to governance (Taylor *et al.* 1997). New modes of governmentality based on managerialism and marketisation have created a range of performativities based on outcomes, images, efficiencies and hierarchies. These performative measures and audits (quality assurance, performance-based funding) simultaneously appropriate academic labour while alienating academics from their core academic work of teaching and research (Blackmore and Sachs 2007).

Universities are not only being challenged in their monopoly of valued knowledge by new knowledge communities (professional, community-based, social movements) but also by the privatisation of knowledge production with the rise of private sector research and consultancies increasingly utilised by government. As Gallagher (2001), a key education bureaucrat in Australia stated,

> In the knowledge economy, the Academies and university researchers are losing their monopoly in knowledge production. Increasingly, the Academies and universities are becoming knowledge receivers and transformers of knowledge as well as generators of knowledge. In the world of scholarly information, a range of parties interact and form partnerships to develop, create and disseminate scholarly information via a range of national and international networks and publication vehicles. The parties include universities, industry, research organisations, academics, the Academies, researchers, students, librarians and publishers. All bring special interests and concerns to the issue. And all are part of the solution. Each of the parties I have listed above need to review its assumptions about its practice and change that practice if it is inhibiting a solution to knowledge management for the 21st century.

The quality research agenda is not only about production in universities, but also 'embraces both producer and user communities' (Dyson and Desforges 2002, p. 2).

At the same time, the new governmentalities of the performative state have focused on increased accountability of public institutions (and therefore control of the professions that have provided public sector expertise) by government through the audit. The audit has come to replace former reciprocal social understandings that were based on rationalities of trust (Power 1999).

> The constant demands for audit both witness to and contribute to the erosion of trust, and seek to establish new distantiated relations of control between political centres of decision and 'non-political' procedures, devices and apparatuses...
>
> (Rose 1993, p. 295)

Universities are therefore accountable to both government (and the public) for efficient use of research funds, and also to the market (users of research – industry, students, community). But these new accountabilities to government, institutional managers, as well as the market (students, practitioners, and the professions) are often not in alignment, as each stakeholder has different expectations and makes different judgements as to use value.

Meanwhile in Australia, government funding of public universities has drastically decreased, while the user pays and federal intervention on what is taught and researched has increased. Higher education has been vocationalised to meet the needs of the nation state and international capital. These trends have collectively shifted relations between academics (as professional experts and producers of professional labour), the nation state (their employer), and their clients (students, professions and industries), in ways that has devalued academic expertise. There are strong pressures for graduate attributes driven by professional organisations and international standards movements, while reputation (measured by student satisfaction scores) drives local and international markets. Current university reforms are reconstructing professionals as technicians judged by externally determined professional standards and moderated increasingly internationally rather than as advocates who have a commitment to public service and citizens within specific cultural contexts (Brint 1994). Academic expertise is under challenge.

Under the welfare economy, universities were implicated in public policies that involved some state intervention against the market and for social justice and the common good. Now universities are central to knowledge-based capitalism, and the strong accountability upwards to the state and outwards to the market works against public expectations of universities as independent, and catering for public needs and interests. Academics are also accountable to their professional and international communities in terms of knowledge production. And these are based on different rules of the game in terms of advancing the field of study in fundamental as well as applied research. University dependence on the market changes this relationship, can compromise a university's autonomy, and therefore that of its researchers. This is not to argue that professional autonomy be maintained at any cost, but to suggest that professional autonomy is an important aspect that protects the integrity of university-based research and also the capacity of the academic researcher to work independently in public policy. The issue of independent research has now been highlighted by the abolition in 2005 of the 'independent' board overseeing the distribution of funds by the Australian Research Council, making the ARC panels directly responsible to a Minister of Education. He has in turn exercised a previously little-used authority to refuse to fund numerous (largely humanities and social science) applications judged as successful by an extensive national and international peer review process to which all ARC applications are subject. What does this say about independent peer review?

Barnett (1997) argues that what is missing in this process of technologising professional work and commodifying professional knowledge is another dimension of what it is to be a good professional practitioner, that of criticality. This value dimension informs professionals as to the wider debates about ethics, social justice and civic responsibility, about professing for and about their field of expertise (Clegg 2005). Current debates portray criticality and theory as if in opposition to professional practitioner knowledge and problem solving. Yet within education there is an emerging tradition of practitioner research that suggests educational research exemplifies Gibbon's Mode 2 knowledge contrary to Mode 1 knowledge encouraged by the RQF (e.g. Groundwater-Smith and Mockler 2006). Researchers often partner with practitioners, and teachers undertake action research (Groundwater-Smith and Mokcler 2006). What does quality mean for practitioner research (Furlong and Oancea 2006)? Policy is similarly produced in many instances through an ongoing dialogue between researchers, practitioners and policymakers around theorising practice and practising theory (Blackmore 1992). Universities, but particularly professional faculties such as education, are therefore caught in this dilemma between developing critical professionals and being advocates or 'professing'; and servicing the government, the economy and the labour market (Barnett 1997).

> ...the influx of students and the move to student centred learning has placed in juxtaposition the values of those academics who see university education as being about critical thinking and disciplinary study and the values of students, many of whom see university education as being about professional training and the acquisition of a credential which will assist in their chances of career advancement.
>
> (Coaldrake and Stedman 1999, p. 3)

Finally, with the performative state, the nature of policy production, dissemination, and reception has itself altered, and therefore the capacity of research to inform policy in particular ways. Education is a field that is highly politicised and increasingly subjugated to other fields (economics). Politicians are susceptible to rapidly changing public opinion, and also create public opinion through careful media management e.g. market polling (Blackmore and Thorpe 2003). De facto policies are often made by politicians through the media (Lingard 2003). Governments are forced to make decisions within a volatile context, and researchers do not have the same imperatives to draw definitive conclusions or tight policy recommendations, unless required under contractual arrangements. Research cannot provide the certainty in terms of the types of solutions that policymakers seek as research is contested within its own disciplinary boundaries (Levin 2006).

Education policy is often as much about maintaining legitimacy, about being seen to do something, providing a quick solution, rather than being informed by research. That is, policy has performative and symbolic dimensions. Research is often utilised to inform policies post hoc, to confirm decisions already made. And of course research in any field is contested within the discipline, as indicated in the literacy debates between phonics and whole language approaches (e.g. *The Age*, 11 December 2005, pp. 1, 12). Levin (2006) argues that the complexities that governments face in terms of resources, meeting electorates' contradictory demands, dealing with crises, time constraints, electoral promises and priorities, opposition parties and the media, personal experience of politicians etc, support a view that research can only at best expect to be one factor influencing policy decisions. In Bourdieu's (1990) terms, academics and researchers work within different fields, with different vocabularies, boundaries, rules, and practices, that sometimes overlap.

Policy (and how it is read, perceived and received) has become a performative technology of the new governmentality of advance liberalism (Rose 1993). The current research quality policy captures both the market and managerial aspects of performativity: being seen to offer a solution to a problem (the failure of research to inform policy and practice); being accountable in terms of promising greater efficiency and effectiveness through differentiated funding; through its normative capacity to change behaviours to direct research towards national priorities; and its allocative capacity to redistribute resources differentially to quality researchers and universities.

In turn, educational researchers, as teachers, have significant experience of how funding and policy shapes a field of practice, and in turn how institutional practices mediate shifting relationships between individual academics and teachers, their work and their employment conditions. Education professionals were marginalised from policy production during the 1990s with the rise of neo-liberal reforms of marketisation and new managerialism and increased executive power (Blackmore and Sachs 2007). The relationship between government, public bureaucracies, unions and the professions has altered significantly, ending 'licensed autonomy and public service professionalism' (Seddon 1997, p. 230). Whereas public professionals saw advocacy as an aspect of their collective aspirations and responsibility, the technologisation and commodification of technical expertise in the late 1990s, has undermined this aspect of professional practice, at least in theory. Furthermore, the boundaries have blurred between producer/user with increased partnerships, doing and commercialising research, as markets infuse the daily practice of research.

Thus the relationship between government and educational researchers is a difficult, contested and troubled one, in which any prescriptive policy is treated with caution by researchers and where advocacy by researchers (e.g. for social justice) is increasingly less acceptable to policymakers. Levin (2006) goes on to suggest that popular commonsense views of science tend to prevail; therefore education needs to have a veneer of science to gain public credibility. Moves within government and within the research community towards evidence-based policy and practice (EPP) are therefore well received. As Levin (2006, p. 153) argues,

> Some governments or agencies have given a prominent role to research units; while others have dramatically reduced their importance. Where functions of research and use of evidence to support policy are institutionalised there is more potential for research to be available when needed and in an appropriate form. In so far as research has public credibility it will also tend to have more cachet with politicians...

Thus EPPI with its focus on systematic reviews is funded by the UK government, and a Best Evidence Synthesis Unit sits within the NZ educational bureaucracy. The relationship between research, policy and practice, always fraught, is discursively re-articulating earlier depoliticised paradigms of the research–policy relationship. And with the restructuring of education as a field incorporated into economics, policymakers shape what research is done (through funding), how it is done (criteria for funding) and whether or not it is utilised (in policy) (Lingard 2003). Quality research policies can therefore be seen as a mechanism by which the state manages academic capitalism by changing behaviours towards particular types of research that is of immediate value to government (Slaughter and Leslie 1997). So while the discourse is about 'useful knowledge production', 'performativity is both an epistemological condition and, when it comes to the relations between higher education and the state, a political project' (Cowen 1996, p. 252).

(Ac)counting of educational research

Education as a field therefore sits uncomfortably, in the epistemological uncertainties and risk management, economically driven politics of post-industrial societies in global economies. Most academics and Vice Chancellors see the bottom line of the RQF as creating a more differentiated hierarchy between universities that will allow for more efficient distribution of limited research funds and students through research concentration (see DEST 2000 for responses to RQF from AVCC, Australian Councils for Deans of Education, Australian Association for Research in Education). Any hierarchy between research-intensive, teaching and research, and teaching-intensive universities, and any reassertion of old knowledge hierarchies will impact detrimentally on education, a multidisciplinary field rather than a discipline with its institutional base located primarily in the non-research-intensive universities (Lingard and Blackmore 1997). The quality research agenda therefore serves a particular function in a political context where there is an emphasis, as in the UK and Australia, on 'what works' and a desire to change behaviours of educational researchers more towards policy service rather than policy critique or advocacy (Atkinson 2000, Blackmore 2002).

Evidence of past successes no longer protects educational research as a field. For example, the Federal Department of Education, Training and Youth Affairs *Impact of Educational Research on Policy and Practice Report* (DETYA 2000), highlighted the distinctiveness of the field in terms of the nature of educational research and its diffused model of knowledge production and dissemination, but also its quality in terms of its significant impact on the disciplinary field as well as policy and practice, as did earlier reviews (McGaw 1992, 1997). Through five separate, rigorous and methodologically distinctive studies, the *Impact Report* considered both measures of impact: impact on the field of research (a bibliometric analysis and statistical and content analysis of publications); and impact on policy and practice (through backward concept mapping analyses on research impact on policy and another on teacher use of research to inform their practice).

The *Impact Report* indicated that Australian educational research was over-represented in international journals, but that citation rates were low (in part because many educational journals, particularly Australian ones, books and book chapters are not included in citation indexes); that Australian research had significant impact on policy in particular areas (e.g. gender equity reform, critical literacy); and that teachers (exemplary teachers in particular) utilised recent research in their daily practice. Overall, the report was more favourable across a range of criteria than expected. The teacher 'knowledge in action' study (McMeninam *et al.* 2001) indicated that teachers utilised a wide range of resources informed by research directly and indirectly, although exemplary teachers used new concepts more explicitly; and new concepts were disseminated through multiple modes e.g. professional development, policy, colleagues.

The current discourse around quality is therefore as much about new modes of governance seeking to change the nature of the field of educational research rather than recognising the current characteristics of the field. First, the federal educational policymakers felt that educational research did not fit their preferred model of research concentration (modelled on the sciences). Instead, the *Impact Report* indicated that it was diffuse, identifying an unevenness of educational research in Australia (in part due to its geography), and the lack of research concentration due to a more widely distributed nature of educational research locations. There was still a large number of research-inactive educational academics utilising a limited range of methodologies.

Second, the research that was done did not readily answer the questions being asked by politicians and therefore was deemed irrelevant. There was no coherent body of educational research knowledge that provided readymade and consistent answers for policymakers with any certainty. PhD students were seen to be given too much leeway in choosing topics, and not to be working in research teams (as in the science model of research). As with reports in the UK (e.g. Hillage *et al.* 1998, Gorard 2001, BERA 2001, Furlong and White 2001, and McIntyre and McIntyre 2000 as synthesised in Dyson and Desforges 2002), the system was seen to produce numerous small-scale qualitative research reports that lacked some coherence and few large-scale quantitative reports which were replicable and could inform policy.

Third, there was much enthusiasm for practitioner research with some concern about quality. There was concern by government about the lack of cumulative research effort and the absence of attempts to replicate, test and build systematically on previous research (Hillage *et al.* 1998). What the *Impact Report* identifies, as Davies (2003, p. 111) argues in the English case, is that the perceived gap between research and practice is not because teachers do not undertake or utilise contemporary research but that the culture of teaching in general does not encourage utilising research i.e. it is a systemic issue not a research/policy/practice issue (see also Blackmore 2002, Atkinson 2000). To encourage professional learning based on research, and especially teacher practitioner research, would require significant government investment in teacher professional development.

Fourth, what it also indicated was that most teachers were unaware that they were utilising contemporary research in their daily work. This is because of the nature of professional learning in schools. The *Impact Report* showed how impact is diffuse and implicitly embedded in a range of professional and school practices. Yet notions of multiple intelligences and multi-literacies were commonplace in classrooms, ideas disseminated through conferences, texts, workshops, professional development, and by collegial interaction with those teachers who were undertaking post-graduate research. The report also recognised that teachers in reading research without a sound theoretical and conceptual framework were more likely to interpret research differently than is intended.

An updated study (the *Impact Report* considered 1992–8) based on the same mixed methodologies would perhaps reveal the ongoing impact of Australian research; for example, on the Middle Years Research and Development Project (MYRAD), science education (e.g. Science in Schools) in Victoria, and learner-centred pedagogy (e.g. Queensland School Reform Longitudinal Research Study, QSRLS) (Hayes *et al.* 2006). Each of these research projects developed out of different conceptualisations, theoretical frameworks, methodologies ranging from school effectiveness and improvement, to constructivism, and critical sociology. In each instance, the curriculum reforms arising from this research were framed within wider theoretical debates amongst the different communities of researchers, policymakers and practitioners about the nature of curriculum and pedagogy in post-industrial knowledge-based economies. The capacity of educational research to inform policy and practice in these examples also cannot be disentangled from other reforms, both bottom up and top down, that are concerned about developing new ways of organising schools and new forms of teacher leadership in schools (Thomson and Blackmore 2005, Lingard *et al.* 2003). In each instance where there was significant impact on practices in schools, there was a temporary convergence between the political agendas of government and the research agendas of some academics. Other research projects have since developed from these (e.g. Middle Years Research and Development Project and Science in Schools projects in Victoria that now inform an extended project; and in Singapore the QSRLS study is being re-contextualised and enhanced). This research is ongoing with long-term effects on teacher practice.

Paradoxically, the measures of impact within the field of these particular innovations will be limited to publications in international refereed journals. Key books that are most accessible to teachers and principals do not count in research audits or citation indexes (e.g. books from the QSLRS such as Lingard *et al.* 2003, Hayes *et al.* 2006). In the Australian RQF, the current preferred option put forward by the Expert Advisory Committee is that the evidence presented (e.g. four articles) *will not actually be read*, but judged according to proxy indicators (e.g. citations). Yet it is widely acknowledged that education, as humanities generally, have few of their prestigious journals included in citation indexes. And books and book chapters are not in citation indexes. Furthermore, recent 'mock audits' undertaken within some Australian universities indicate that education gains higher ratings when articles are actually read.

Impact, as is relevance, is therefore a complex issue to define, identify and track, and least of all measure. As Davies (2003, pp. 110–11) comments

> relevance depends on questions asked, and in what context and to what practical ends… research that is apparently more generalisable, cumulative, and based on highly representative samples for some purposes may be of little value to those with different practice needs and in quite different contexts from those in which the research took place. There is no such thing as context free evidence.

As the Education sub-panel (2005) of the English RAE argued in a position paper, research can be of high quality, address an important and significant issue within the field, but still have little immediate impact on policy and practice. Indeed, that has been the case for much innovation. And for those who research in and on policy, relevance and wide dissemination alone do not ensure utilisation or impact as intended, as take-up is dependent on the particular context – upon issues of context and capacity, as in the case of teachers, and inclination and political will, as in the case of politicians.

What counts as evidence?

It is therefore understandable that there is significant concern within the educational research community internationally about the trend towards privileging certain types of research as more credible by dominant discourses about evidence-based policy and practice at a time when what counts as quality is also under scrutiny (e.g. Atkinson 2000, MacLure 2005, Torrance 2004). Privileging of particular models of research as a gold standard e.g. No Child Left Behind's prescription of RCT reproduces hierarchies negating the epistemological pluralism of the 1980s and 1990s (Lather 2003). Blair's policy focus on 'research that works' has been institutionalised with the establishment of the National Educational Research Forum (NERF) to develop a national research and development strategy for education, as well as the Evidence for Policy and Practice Information and Co-ordinating Centre (EPPI-Centre) which undertakes systematic reviews. The NERF argued there is a need for research capacity building because there is a lack of sufficient scale and quality in terms of priority issues and what can be used to inform policy and practice (Dyson and Desforges 2002). This is about developing a research *system*, based on particular technologies. In the Australian context, educational researchers feel particularly vulnerable, with the focus on science and technological solutions to the neglect of the social sciences and humanities in the national research priorities (Bullen *et al.* 2004).

Many argue that EPP, and the systematic review in particular, is premised upon large epidemiological studies in health, utilising meta analysis and other statistical methods. While these can inform clinical practice they have less applicability to education because education is unlike health care and medicine – 'its activities, processes, and outcomes are complex and culturally, or contextually, specific' (Dyson and Deforges 2002, p.1) i.e. causation and measurement problems are different. MacDonald states that systematic reviews (2000, p. 131)

> entail a series of techniques for minimising bias and error, primarily though the use of *protocols* which state, prior to the review being undertaken, what the criteria will be to guide the review, search strategies, inclusion and exclusion criteria, standards of methodological adequacy, the precise definition of the intervention in question, unbiased estimation of aggregate effects and so on.

Quality, in the terms of systematic reviewers who undertake a secondary review process of available research, is defined by EPPI, for example, in terms of the clarity of methodology in both the primary research and also the secondary review process; transparency in terms of inclusions and exclusions in that review process; and certainty of outcomes in terms of findings (MacLure 2005, reprinted as Chapter 4 of this book). Key features of systematic reviews according to Evans and Benefield (2001, p. 529) are as synthesised here:

> an explicit research question to be addressed; transparency of methods used for searching for studies; exhaustive searches for published and unpublished studies; clear criteria for assessing the quality of the studies (both qualitative and quantitative); clear criteria for including or excluding studies based on the scope of the review and quality assessment; joint reviewing to reduce bias; a clear statement of the findings of the review.

This ignores, according to MacLure (2005) other measures of quality: inter-textual connectivity, critique, expertise, independence, tacit knowledge, chance ideas with new ideas, and dialogic interactions between the research 'literature' and 'data'. Complex issues such as ethics, values, and professional practitioner knowledge are ignored. Such reviews, she argues, draw from narrow electronic databases which can be searched using keywords in titles and abstracts, again a mode of publication more typical of some fields than others where titles are more 'playful' (Zeller and Farmer 1999). Due to lack of time and cost, the most likely sources gleaned through a desk search (e.g. scholarly networks, reports, discussion papers, books) are not included. Even after this relatively standard approach to a literature review, the research question in systematic reviews is constantly re-focused to reduce the scope. None of the literature tends to be read and reviewed until after the database is subjected to a second phase of meeting inclusion/exclusion criteria of quality. The EPPI protocol for example, considers criteria such as reporting research findings directly, description of intervention, how developed and evaluated; study design and methodology; pre- and post-intervention data; equivalent control group; reports against all outcome measures; and identifying key causal relations. This is the 'experimental model' more typical of psychological research based on particular definitions of reliability, rigour, validity and replicability (MacLure 2005, p. 3). There is little recognition that these are criteria or issues that are not valid for other forms of research that are equally valuable in terms of their explanatory power e.g. case study research. As a consequence of this protocol, as MacLure (2005) points out, the number of studies that are ultimately *read* and reviewed is usually small (e.g. between 10 and 20). Such approaches are applicable to only certain types of research questions (Evans and Benefield 2001, p. 540).

In turn, the lack of studies emerging from such a process is then used to argue that the quality of educational research generally is questionable, rather than the criteria as to what counts as quality evidence or the research question is too narrow or the techniques (software analysis of abstracts only) are limited. Torrance (2004) points out that systematic reviews focus in particular upon the notion of reducing bias or researcher subjectivity, and reducing the role of professional expertise. MacLure argues these approaches are 'backward looking' in a way that

> construes research knowledge as static, transparent and compliant within disciplinary boundaries. It assumes that evidence can be extracted intact from the texts in which it is embedded, and synthesised in a form that is impervious to ambiguities of context, reads interpretations of writers' arguments (i.e. bias). Most of all, systematic review degrades the central acts of reviewing; namely, reading and writing, and the unreliable intellectual acts that these support, such as interpretation, argument and analysis (2005, p. 2).

The question to be asked therefore is whether, given all this, systematic reviews do less rather than more than a 'narrative' literature review which engages with debates in the field, identifies and explores conceptual and methodological issues, addresses context, points to uncertainty and ambiguity in findings, while making useful but qualified suggestions about what works (Hammersley 2001).

Consider the following example. One of the research sub-fields named by the *Impact Report* in Australia as successfully informing policy and practice was that of gender equity research. Yet a systematic review of this subfield would exclude most studies as they did not fit the experimental paradigm. Ironically, while feminists tend to state their values upfront as advocates for gender equity, this form of 'transparency' is viewed as bias and transparency is sought where values are not considered within the methodology. Furthermore, there is an assumption about how knowledge is produced and disseminated out of existing research. Gender equity research arose out of a social movement of the 1970s seeking to promote social change and equity for women and girls through education. The policy process was driven by feminist networks working with/against government amongst policymakers (located in equity units in the bureaucracies), practitioners and researchers. The policy process was bottom-up and top-down (Blackmore 1999, 1992). It was highly contested within government and schools, and amongst feminists, as to appropriate strategies. But gender equity practices derived from this research have now become part of the daily practice of schools and educational organisations and embedded in most curriculum documents. Gender equity for girls was also good for boys, being pedagogically sound and inclusive, and indeed has been adopted but not recognised as feminist informed research (Kenway *et al.* 1998).

Research did make a difference to how gender was theorised, and its influences can be tracked over time through various policy shifts in focus from women and girls and rights (liberal feminism) in the 1970s; to the celebration of difference (cultural feminism) in the 1980s; to gender identity (post-structuralism) and the social relations of gender (and therefore masculinity) in the 1990s. The current policy focus on masculinities and under-achievement is by contrast driven by a narrow conceptualisation of gender that ignores class, racial and linguistic difference and indeed most gender equity research undertaken over the preceding twenty years. But it fits nicely with trends in accountability and outcomes-based education and feminist backlash politics of neo-conservative governments (Lingard 2003).

Finally, 'evidence' or policy did not in themselves change teacher and school practices. There was significant resistance; and legal and normative organisational frames had to be brought to bear. The capacity to institutionalise gender equity reform required multiple approaches: legalistic (equal opportunity legislation), managerialist (e.g. women's budgets and gender audits); accountability for outcomes (e.g. numbers of women in various levels of organisations); but also policy advocacy and activism by researchers and practitioners. Much of the knowledge was not only the result of an accumulated body of evidence, but also arose out of contestation between different ontological and epistemological perspectives as well as from the lived experience of women as teachers and researchers. So would the research field of gender equity for girls have emerged through a systematic review of existing research in 1975? Probably not. But the evidence of impact of gender equity research in 2001 did emerge in the *Impact Report.*

The notion of evidence-based policy is premised upon particular assumptions about the nature of production of knowledge and of research and also of a particular relationship between research and policy – that is, that research is a cumulative process; that research is not contested on political (ideological) grounds; and that research is not about the nature of society, the role of education, or issues of equity and social justice. Furthermore, there is the assumption that policy (and its processes of production, dissemination and reception) is somehow value free, and not value driven and normative, without critique or dissent (Davies 2003).

How policy 'frames' research

Thus the discourse of failure and irrelevance of educational research is not itself based upon 'evidence'. The current push for evidence-based research has an inadequate understanding of the nature of educational research or policy production and also a naïve view of the relationship between research and policy. What the educational research community fears is that the privileging of particular models of research will obliterate important research agendas, agendas arising from more marginalised groups, from stakeholders as well as practitioners. How educational research is counted and 'accounted for' needs to take into account a wider set of responsibilities to the public, to practitioners and to policymakers that are neglected or rejected by this new orthodoxy. What concerns educational researchers is first, whether 'critiques' of educational policy will be funded by government as have critiques of educational research (e.g. Tooley and Darby 1998); second, whether governments will utilise a range of different forms of 'evidence' in their policy making, or, as in the case of Australia and the USA, refuse to move beyond a particular ideological position. Third, will governments be prepared to invest in educational research in the same way as they have in medical research and in a diversity of research? Finally, will the field as understood through the lens of evidence-based policy and practice allow for contestation over the purpose, value and substance of educational research – as more than policy service, but also a matter of critique and also advocacy?

Finally, as MacLure (2005) points out, the language of the systematic review, just as the RQF, are technologies disciplining academics through structures, levels, and taxonomies to institute new orders of importance and create new/reassert old hierarchies (Coaldrake and Stedman 1999). Many would argue that the survival of universities as publicly funded institutions is contingent on them remaining critical and independent. It is the professional and public utility value, the intellectual integrity of university-based research, that is perhaps its most credible commodity. What also characterises public policy on universities is government's refusal to 'accept that university education brings other public benefits which are impossible to quantify' (Poole 1999, p. 29; Yates 2004). Universities are sites of 'conflicting ideas and values that can be articulated and explored without threat to social cohesion' (ibid.) and this is a fundamental function of a democracy. It will be the users of educational research who will be the final judge as they feel the impact of the contradictions between instrumental and democratic notions of intellectual work.

References

Atkinson, E. (2000) In defence of ideas, or why 'what works' is not enough, *British Journal of Sociology* 21(3), pp. 318–30.

Barnett, R. (1997) *Higher Education: A Critical Business*, Open University Press, Buckingham.

Barnett, R. and Griffin, A. (eds) (1999) *The End of Knowledge in Higher Education*, Cassell, London

Blackmore, J. (1992) Policy as dialogue, *Gender and Education* 7(3), pp. 293–313.

Blackmore, J. (1999) Globalisation/localisation: strategic dilemmas for state feminism and gender equity policy, special Issue on Globalisation and Education, *Journal of Education Policy* 14(1), pp. 33–54.

Blackmore, J. (2002) Is it only 'what works' that 'counts' in new knowledge economies? The trend towards evidence based practice and its implications for educational research and teacher education in Australia, special issue, *Social Policy and Society* 1(3), pp. 257–66.

Blackmore, J. (2005) Anticipating policy: institutional and disciplinary responses to the research quality agenda in Australia, paper presented to the European Conference of Educational Research, Dublin, 10–13 September.

Blackmore, J. and Lingard, B. (1997) The performative state and the state of educational research, *Australian Educational Researcher* 24(3), pp. 1–30.

Blackmore, J. and Sachs, J. (2007) *Performing and Reforming Leaders: Gender, educational restructuring and organisational change*, SUNY Press, New York.

Blackmore, J. and Thorpe, S. (2003) Media/ting change: the print media's role in mediating education policy in a period of radical reform in Victoria, Australia, *Journal of Education Policy* 18(6), pp. 577–96.

Bourdieu, P. (1990) *The Logic of Practice*, Polity Press, Cambridge.

Brint, S. (1994) *In an Age of Experts: The Changing Role of Professionals in Politics and Public Life*, Princeton, NJ: Princeton University Press.

Bullen, E., Robb, S. and Kenway, J. (2004) 'Creative destruction': knowledge economy policy and the future of the arts and humanities in the academic, *Journal of Education Policy* 19(1), p. 23.

Clegg, S. (2005) Evidence-based practice in educational research: a critical realist critique of systematic reviewing, *British Journal of Sociology of Education* 26(3), pp. 415–28.

Coaldrake, P. and Stedman, L. (1999) *Academic Work in the Twenty-First Century: Changing Roles and Policies*, Occasional Paper, Higher Education, DETYA, Canberra.

Coalition for Evidence-based Policy (2002) *Bringing Evidence-driven Progress to Education*, Report for the US Department of Education, www.excelgov.org.

Cowen, R. (1996) Performativity, postmodernity and the university, *Comparative Education* 32(2), pp. 245–58.

Davies, B. (2003) Death to critique and dissent: the policies and practices of new managerialism and of 'evidence-based practice', *Gender and Education* 15(1), pp. 89–101.

Delanty, G. (2001) *Challenging Knowledge: The University in the Knowledge Society*, SHRE/Open University Press.

DEST (2000) *What Works in Indigenous Education?* Department of Education, Science and Training, Canberra.

Dyson, A. and Desforges, C. (2002) Building research capacity: some possible lines of action, Paper for National Educational Research Forum.

Education SubPanel (2005) Response to RAE review. http://www.rae.ac.uk/panels/main/k/edu/ (accessed 23 February 2006).

Evans, J. and Benefield, P. (2001) Systematic reviews of educational research: does the medical model fit?, *British Educational Research Journal* 27(5), pp. 527–41.

Expert Advisory Group 2005 *Research Quality Framework: Assessing the Quality and Impact of Research in Australia*. Advanced Approaches Paper. Department of Education, Science and Training, Canberra.

Furlong, J. and Oancea, A. (2006) Assessing quality in applied and practice based research in education; a framework for discussion. In Blackmore, J., Wright, J. and Harwood, V. (eds) *Counterpoints on the Quality and Impact of Educational Research: Review of Australian Research in Education No 6*, Special issue, *Australian Educational Researcher*, pp. 89–104.

Gallagher, M. (2001) 'Innovation and the knowledge economy', www.dest.gov.au/archive/highered/eippubs (accessed 23 August 2005).

Gibbons, M., Limoges, C. Nowotny, H., Schwartzman, S., Scott, P. and Trow, M. (1994) *The New Production of Knowledge: The Dynamics of Science and Research in Contemporary Societies*, Sage, London.

Groundwater-Smith, S. and Mockler, N. (2006) Research that counts: practitioner research and the academy. In Blackmore, J., Wright, J. and Harwood, V. (eds) *Counterpoints on the Quality and Impact of Educational Research: Review of Australian Research in Education No 6*, special issue, *Australian Educational Researcher*, pp. 105–17.

Hammersley, M. (2001) On 'systematic' reviews of research literatures: a 'narrative' response to Evans and Benefield, *British Educational Research Journal* 27(5), pp. 543–54.

Hargreaves, D. (1996) *Teaching as a Research Based Profession: Possibilities and Prospects*, Teacher Training Agency, Annual Lecture. TTA, London.

Hayes, D., Mills, M., Christie, P. and Lingard, B. (2006) *Teachers and Schooling Making a Difference: Productive Pedagogies, Assessment and Performance*, Allen & Unwin, Sydney.

Hillage, J., Pearson, R., Anderson, A. and Tamkin, P. (1998) *Excellence in Research in Schools*, DEE, London.

Kenway, J., Wilis, S., with Blackmore, J. and Rennie, L. (1998) *Answering Back: Girls, Boys and Feminism in Schools*, Routledge, London.

Kirst, M. (2000) Bridging educational research and educational policy making, *Oxford Review of Education* 26, pp. 379–96.

Lather, P. (2003) This is your father's paradigm: government intrusion and the case of educational research, *Qualitative Inquiry* 10(1), pp. 15–34.

Levin, B. (2006) What makes a difference when research speaks to policy? In Blackmore, J., Wright, J. and Harwood, V. (eds) *Counterpoints on the Quality and Impact of*

Educational Research, Review of Australian Research in Education No 6, Special issue, *Australian Educational Researcher,* pp. 147–58.

Lingard, B. (2003) Where to in gender policy in education after recuperative masculinity politics?, *International Journal of Inclusive Education* 7(1), pp. 33–56.

Lingard, B., Hayes, D., Mills, M. and Christie, P. (2003) *Leading Learning,* Open University Press, Buckingham.

Macdonald, G. (2000) Social care: rhetoric and reality. In Davies H., Nutley, S. and Smith, P. (eds) *What Works? Evidence Based Policy and Practice in the Public Services,* Policy Press, Bristol.

MacLure, M. (2005) 'Clarity bordering on stupidity': where's the quality in systematic review?, *Journal of Education Policy* 20(4), pp. 393–416.

Marginson, S. (2002) Nation-building universities in a global environment: the case of Austalia, *Higher Education* 43(3), pp. 409–28.

Marginson, S. (2006) National and global competition in higher education. In Lauder, H., Brown, P., Dillabough, J. and Halsey, A.H. (eds) *Education, Globalisation and Social Change,* Oxford University Press, Oxford.

Marginson, S. and Considine, M. (2000) *The Enterprise University: Power, Governance and Reinvention in Australia,* Cambridge University Press, Melbourne.

McGaw, B. (1996) Linking educational research with policy and practice, *ACER Newsletter Supplement* 85, Autumn, pp. 3–5.

McGaw, B. (1992) *Educational Research in Australia. Report of the Review Panel of Research in Education,* Australian Government Publishing Service, Canberra.

McMeninam, M., Cumming, J. and Bourke, P. (2000) Teacher knowledge in action. In *The Impact of Educational Research,* DETYA, Canberra, pp. 275–550.

Morley, L. (2003) *Quality and Power in Higher Education,* Open University Press, Buckingham.

Nelson, B. (2003) *Backing Australia's Ability,* AGPS, Canberra.

Poole, M. (1999) Reforming higher education: mind the market, *Dialogue: Academy of Social Sciences in Australia* 18(1), pp. 27–43.

Power, M. (1999) *The Audit Society: Rituals of Verification,* Oxford University Press, Oxford.

Rose, N. (1993) Government, authority and expertise in advanced liberalism, *Economy and Society* 22(3), pp. 283–99.

Seddon, T. (1997) Education deprofessionalised? Or reregulated, reorganised and reauthorised? *Australian Journal of Education* 41(3), pp. 228–46.

Slaughter, S. and Leslie, L. (1997) *Academic Capitalism: Politics, Policies and the Entrenpreneurial University,* Johns Hopkins University Press, Baltimore, MD.

Taylor, S., Rizvi, F., Lingard, B. and Henry, M. (1997) *Educational Policy and the Politics of Change,* Routledge, London.

Tooley, J. and Darby, D. (1998) *Educational Research: A Critique. A Survey of Educational Research,* Office for Standards in Education, London.

Torrance, H. (2004) Systematic reviewing: the 'call centre' version of research synthesis. Time for a more flexible approach. ESRC/RCBN Seminar on Systematic Reviewing, 24 June, University of Sheffield.

Yates, L. (2004) *What Does Good Education Research Look Like? Situating a Field and its Practices,* Open University Press, Maidenhead.

Yates, L. (2005a) Is impact a measure of quality? Producing quality research and producing quality indicators of research in Australia. Blackmore, J., Wright, J. and Harwood,

V. (eds) *Counterpoints on the Quality and Impact of Educational Research, Review of Australian Research in Education No 6,* Special issue, *Australian Educational Researcher*, pp. 119-32.

Yates, L. (2005b) What does 'significance' look like? Assessing the assessment process in competitive grant schemes. In Blackmore, J., Wright, J. and Harwood, V. (eds) *Counterpoints on the Quality and Impact of Educational Research, Review of Australian Research in Education No 6,* Special issue, *Australian Educational Researcher*, pp. 57–67.

Yeatman, A. (ed.) (1999) *Activism in the Policy Process*, Allen and Unwin, Sydney.

Zeller, N. and Farmer, F. (1999) 'Catchy clever titles are not acceptable': style, APA and qualitative reporting, *International Journal of Qualitative Studies* 12(1), pp. 3–20.

Chapter 4

'Clarity bordering on stupidity'

Where's the quality in systematic review?

Maggie MacLure

Clarity bordering on stupidity, a dog's life.

(André Breton)

... clever people observe more things and more curiously, but they interpret them ... We need a man either very honest, or so simple that he has not the stuff to build up false inventions and give them plausibility; and wedded to no theory.

(Montaigne)[1]

Introduction

This chapter takes a close, and highly critical, look at 'systematic review' in education, in the form developed and promoted by the EPPI-Centre at the University of London Institute of Education.[2] Systematic review is a form of research synthesis designed to support evidence-informed policy and practice. It is endorsed by the Department for Education and Skills and other government departments, and by the Teacher Training Agency. [3] The method requires teams of reviewers to search the literature in ever-decreasing circles until they have isolated all and only those studies that address a pre-defined question, and are also of high enough quality in terms of research design. 'Quality assurance' procedures are applied in the attempt to ensure that all reviewers think, or at least code, alike.

Systematic review is part of the wider evidence-based, or evidence-informed 'movement' (Oakley 2003: 22). It has been associated with the 'audit culture' and international trends towards control and accountability in knowledge production and use.[4] Its advocates have lent their voices to the criticisms of educational research which have permeated policy and media discourses over the last decade. Exasperated by the inability of educational research to deliver the kind of seemingly hard evidence offered by health and medicine, systematic review favours quantitative methods and embodies a scarcely-concealed positivism that places qualitative research far down the 'credibility hierarchy' (Hammersley 2001: 545).

My interest is in the *discourse* of systematic review, and the research realities and identities that it invokes. I propose to take apart the details of the exhortatory and instructional literature of systematic review, and also to look 'inside' 30 education reviews published on the EPPI-Centre website.[5]

Systematic review, I suggest below, is a backward-looking business. It construes research knowledge as static, transparent and compliant with disciplinary boundaries. It assumes that evidence can be extracted intact from the texts in which it is embedded, and 'synthesised' in a form that is impervious to ambiguities of context, readers' interpretations or writers' arguments (i.e. bias). Most significantly of all, systematic review systematically degrades the central acts of reviewing: namely, *reading* and *writing*, and the unreliable intellectual acts that these support, such as interpretation, argument and analysis. By replacing reading and writing with an alternate lexicon of scanning, screening, mapping, data-extraction and synthesis, systematic review tries to transform reading and writing into accountable acts. It tries to force their clandestine operations – the bits that happen inside people's heads, or in the incorporeal gaps between decoding and comprehension, thought and expression – up into plain view, where they can be observed, quality-controlled and stripped of interpretation or rhetoric. The assumption appears to be that evidence, once it has been filtered out of the source texts and checked for quality, should be able to speak for itself.

I argue that systematic review, and the discredited view of reading that it embodies, is one of the many fantasies of 'presence' (Derrida 1988: 236) that animate contemporary education policy in its rage for clarity, transparency and certainty of outcomes. By trying to regulate reading, writing and interpretation, systematic review suppresses aspects of quality in research and scholarship that are at least as important as clarity, countability and accountability – such as intertextual connectivity, critique, interest, expertise, independence, tacit knowledge, chance encounters with new ideas, and dialogic interactions between researcher, 'literature' and 'data'. The tiny dead bodies of knowledge disinterred by systematic review hold little power to generate new understandings, and are more likely, I suggest, to incapacitate researchers than to contribute to research 'capacity'.

The language of systematic review

Let's begin with the general rationale. The language used to describe and justify systematic review is a mix of old-style scientific positivism (systematicity, reliability, rigour, replicability) and the now-familiar rhetoric of the 'audit culture' (transparency, quality assurance, standards).[6] You can see this mix in Oakley's description of the approach as 'explicit, transparent, replicable, accountable and (potentially) updateable' (2003: 23). Here is an expanded version of the 'key features' of systematic review:

an explicit research question to be addressed; transparency of methods used for searching for studies; exhaustive searches which look for unpublished as well as published studies; clear criteria for assessing the quality of studies (both qualitative and quantitative); clear criteria for including or excluding studies based on the scope of the review and quality assessment; joint reviewing to reduce bias; a clear statement of the findings of the review.

(Evans and Benefield 2001: 529)

Some favoured words belong comfortably to both the scientific and the audit-culture discourses, and can invoke these simultaneously. *Clarity* is one example, as in the quote above, which contains three instances of 'clear', plus one of its near relation, 'transparency', and a second-cousin, 'explicit'. The demand for clarity appeals both to scientific objectivity and to accountability, insinuating that other reviewing practices are both unscientific and shady. Calls for clarity, as several critics have noted, are never innocent. They are usually issued by powerful discourse communities acting as if their world view is 'transcendental': that is, existing 'outside history, language [and] context', while everyone else's is partial and limited (Scheurich 2000: 344). There is, according to Giroux (1992), a 'politics of clarity' which attempts to regulate the diversity of practices of less powerful communities, by obliging them to render themselves intelligible according to terms set by the status quo.

Another example of double-faced vocabulary is *trustworthiness,* which is demanded both of the research evidence, and of reviewers' assessments of it. As a criterion applied to the evidence, the calculation of 'trustworthiness' asserts positivism's concern with certainty – i.e. with reliability, validity, rigour and replicability, for which 'trustworthiness' has become an all-purpose synonym. Simultaneously however, the requirement for trustworthiness also does audit work, as a form of discipline of potentially *un*trustworthy academics through 'quality assurance' mechanisms, in the interests of a putatively more democratic knowledge economy. The term carries an unavoidable moral imputation. Even the evidence itself can, it seems, have bad intentions. The 'EPPI-Centre Review Companion' counsels reviewers to check carefully at the 'keywording' stage as 'this can save a considerable amount of time and effort by excluding studies *which have crept through the inclusion/exclusion stage by mistake*' (EPPI-Centre 2003: 13 of 20; my emphasis). Reviewers are a particular risk in terms of trustworthiness and must be watched carefully. Systematic review 'allows readers to decide for themselves whether the reviewers have looked carefully enough to be able to say they have identified as many as possible of the studies that could help answer the review's research question'.[7] I will argue below that this is an empty claim, since systematic reviews cannot deliver on the transparency that they promise; and in any case, are written in a standardised format that renders large sections of them virtually unreadable. However in terms of the EPPI-Centre's rhetoric, reviewers and researchers must make themselves transparent to scrutiny, not just by professionals but by the public at large, since 'it is the ordinary citizen who is potentially most disadvantaged by the lack of an open, systematic base of evidence concerning the many interventions that intrude into every corner of their lives' (Oakley 2003: 22).

Systematic review, and the 'evidence movement' (Oakley 2003: 23) from which it emerged, thus continually recycles a 'discourse of distrust' of education professionals and academics (Torrance 2004: 3). Research, and researchers, are repeatedly reported or implied to be careless, undemocratic, furtive (i.e. prone to 'hide failures'), biased, incompetent, 'chaotic', 'inward-looking and self-seeking', 'methodologically impoverished' and even potentially life-threatening.[8] All of these accusations can be found, for instance, in Oakley's (2003) article. Most of them are recycled from the small corpus of critiques of educational research that were issued by Hargreaves, Tooley, Hillage and their co-authors, in the mid-to-late 1990s.[9] These originary critiques are repeatedly re-invoked as the root rationale for the necessary rigours of systematic review – despite the fact that none of them are based on evidence that would come close to meeting systematic review's own 'trustworthiness' criteria (see Avis 2003; Torrance 2004). Still, the slurs are, in turn, routinely re-circulated by Oakley and other advocates, and not infrequently by the systematic reviewers themselves.

The systematic reviewers are – or at least one would assume them to be – in a difficult position. They are the vanguard army of the rigorous, accountable, democratic, evidence-informed education 'movement'. Many of the review team leaders are acknowledged experts in their field. But from the EPPI perspective they are also members of the abject community of university researchers who need to be kept under scrutiny. To be seen to be trustworthy in the face of such a dense background of calumny, reviewers must submit to extraordinary degrees of monitoring and regulation. The must show all their workings, leaving a 'clear audit trail from primary research to conclusions' (Oakley 2003: 23). They must follow the EPPI guidelines for teaming up with users and writing protocols, employ the EPPI 'tools' for searching databases, 'keywording', 'data extracting' and 'synthesising', and use 'the EPPI-Centre report structure' for writing up. They must check in at every stage of these proceedings with the EPPI-Centre; work to agreed deadlines, and submit their searching, keywording and data-extracting decisions to 'quality assurance' (i.e. moderation) by EPPI-Centre staff.[10]

Systematic reviewers are intensively managed and monitored throughout the process then, to ensure that they follow procedures to the letter (and I use this cliché intentionally, see below). They are required to embrace not only the positivist epistemological assumptions about the nature of knowledge and research that are built into the EPPI-apparatus, but also to embrace their own subjection to the Taylorist schedules and managerial discipline of the EPPI-Centre regime. Generally, review authors seem to do this quite readily. One team thanks the EPPI-Centre workers for their 'vigilant support' (Penn et al. 2004: i), and concludes with this testimonial:

> This review, its level of scrutiny and use of evidence, has been a wake-up call. We have been forced into thinking more carefully about the nature of

research in early years and the uses it has been put to in justifying policy-making. Even if our own results were not as conclusive as we had hoped, clarifying the issues and highlighting the gaps has been an essential step.

(Penn *et al.* 2004: 43)

Without exception, the review authors always have something positive to say about the EPPI experience, though not all are as openly enthusiastic as the authors above. In fact, between the lines of endorsement and apparent compliance one can detect traces in some reviews of a less straightforward accommodation to the strictures of systematic review.[11] Nevertheless, all the reviews devote many, many pages of text to documenting their compliance with the internal and external quality assurance procedures, and making 'transparent' their coding and synthesising decisions.

The corpus of published reviews testifies therefore to the considerable pains that the academic reviewers took to subject themselves to the EPPI-Centre's requirements. And *subjection* is entirely the right word here. What we are seeing in operation is a technology for forming new academic subjects. New academic identities are being created in which values such as academic independence, intellectual curiosity and expert judgement are being replaced by industriousness, rule-following, compliance and self-imposed endorsement of 'the hegemonic position of managers' (Avis 2003: 373). I am not arguing that those older values are necessarily benign, nor indeed that they have ever been pursued all that energetically. For the moment I want simply to point out the conceptual and ontological distance between them and the new academic virtues of hard work and humility. There is nothing novel in this observation. The trend has been widely noted by critics of the audit culture and the evidence movement (cf. Strathern 2000; Avis 2003). What I want to emphasise particularly here is the way in which compliance and the reconstitution of subjectivity are being enforced *through language itself.*

The tyranny of terminology

Like many other national education policies in England – such as the inspection system, the National Literacy Strategy, the National Curriculum, and the associated training programmes for all of these – systematic review is a regimen that disciplines subjects (reviewers, researchers, teachers, teacher educators) through language. Subjects are not just required to show that they have followed the quality assurance or coding instructions, but to do so *in the correct language.* Characteristically, systematic review is a fabrication of neologisms, borrowings and buzz-words – data capture and data extraction, synthesis, key-wording, mapping, weighting, inclusion and exclusion criteria, screening, handsearching. The published reviews are remarkably uniform in their use of this vocabulary.

It's not just a matter of vocabulary. Like any language, systematic review imposes structure, levels and taxonomies on the flux of experience. It institutes orders of importance amongst entities and concepts, and establishes which ones 'belong' together. Like other discourses, it sets limits on the ways that the world can be viewed and construed, and establishes what will count as truth. As we have seen, it defines what kind of (academic) subject it is possible to be, and of what matters such subjects can legitimately speak. Thus as texts, systematic reviews not only use the authenticated words, but also rigorously observe the same sequential structure, using ready-made chapter headings and sub-headings. They take on board (though not always without demur – see below), the EPPI criteria for weighing research quality. They all employ the EPPI machinery for ensuring that they are adopting the same stance towards the as-yet-uncharted field that they are going to review, and for ensuring that they all 'map' that field using the same techniques.

Those who speak the language of systematic review necessarily bend themselves therefore into the new shapes afforded by its disciplinary syntax and its hierarchies of significance. In Kristeva's terms, this is the symbolic order of the Law at work – 'the legal, phallic, linguistic symbolic establishment' (1982: 72). It's a regime of truth, no doubt about it (cf. Avis 2003: 373). Does any of this matter? It might be argued, legitimately, that we are always subjected to one truth regime or another – summoned to speak and compelled to be silent, bent into shape by prevailing institutional and cultural conventions (cf. Foucault 1980). But this still leaves the question of precisely what shapes and realities are afforded by systematic review. Moreover, while discourses generally exceed the grasp and the control of any one person or group, systematic review is, I would argue, part of a more deliberate policy to reconstitute the cultural and cognitive practices of education professionals *at the very point where words issue from their mouths or their finger-tips.*

It's instructive to look at the silences in the discourse – at what systematic review leaves unspoken. This, after all, is one of the big effects that discourses accomplish: they not only legitimate what can be said, but they also render other things unspeakable. What is *not said* alongside the much-repeated lexicon of scanning, keywording, data extracting, synthesising and so on? For a start, some of the words that one might associate with the cognitive or intellectual acts of research or reviewing are almost wholly absent. *Analysis* does not appear in the EPPI-Centre Review Companion, for instance. *Interpretation* occurs there only once, in a context where the concern is for its 'consistency'. Perhaps most curiously of all, in a document that is a guide to reviewing, there are only two instances of *read/reading* (both in the section entitled 'Data Extraction').

As Fairclough (1989) points out, 'wording' – the summoning of realities into words – is never an innocent matter. So what kind of difference does it make when significant cognitive and textual acts such as reading, analysing and interpreting are diminished or disappeared? How is reviewing differently realised by the insistent 'overwording' of those alternative terms? The EPPI-endorsed terminology carries interesting traces of old and new technologies: nineteenth-century industry, exploration and imperialism (all those tools; all that mapping, mining and capturing), mixed up with computing, medical diagnostics and expert systems (scanning, screening, mapping again). Oakley's description of the two main stages of systematic review exhibits this technicist wording:

> a mapping stage, in which relevant literature is captured and systematically keyworded ... and an in-depth review stage, in which a subset of the literature ... is examined and interrogated in more detail and data extracted from primary studies.
>
> (Oakley 2003: 24; original emphases removed)

The wording of systematic review implies a view of the 'literature' as a bounded territory, containing knowledge that is stable and quantifiable. Reading (or what has replaced it) amounts to the application of (rather aggressive) procedures for mastering the territory and extracting its nuggets of knowledge.

Equally importantly, this new lexicon invokes *auditable* acts. Reviewing is reconstructed as a sequence of tasks that will leave visible and countable residues of themselves, in the form of codes, data entries, maps, weightings and quality assurances. This is how that 'clear audit trail from primary research to conclusions' is supposed to be forged. Acts such as keywording, mapping, data-extracting or synthesising stand in marked contrast to those annoyingly clandestine acts of reading, analysing and interpreting, which are less easy to break down into auditable stages, and are prone to contextual or individual variation, complexity, indirection and qualification.

The lexicon of systematic review thus denies the *textuality* of research; or sees textuality as a kind of enemy or obstacle to be overcome. Evidence is conceptualised as packages of stuff that can be extracted from the base material of texts, weighed and aggregated (synthesised). In bypassing reading and interpretation, which carry the indissoluble marks of their engagement with texts, and replacing analysis and writing with the simple arithmetic of synthesis, the EPPI-lexicon is a fantasy of a text-free knowledge economy, where nuggets of evidence can be extracted from the rhetorical contaminations of persuasion, argument, justification, context, and partiality that are inherent in all texts. This is an ancient and persistent delusion.[12]

Reluctant reading

Still, isn't this all 'just' terminological? One might assume that the reviewers must be reading the articles, even if they're now calling it something different. But reading is strangely absent from systematic review in other ways too. For a start, hardly any of the studies identified as potentially relevant at the outset of the review process are read *at all*. In fact, you could describe the EPPI-Centre method as an algorithm for not-reading as much of the research literature as possible. Here's how it works.

First, a 'protocol' is drawn up which formulates the question to be answered by the review, and the inclusion/exclusion criteria to be used to identify relevant research studies. Reviews are expected to stick to the protocol wherever possible, and diversions into unanticipated areas are not encouraged (although the initial question can be tightened or adjusted later in the process). Learning from adjacent areas is not recommended either. So if, for instance, your review question concerns the effects of small-group discussions in science teaching with students aged 11–18, you may decide not to allow yourself to learn from research into group discussions in other school subjects, nor from research involving younger or older learners (cf. Bennett *et al.* 2004: 76). Reviewers are also asked to state in advance how many studies they will be able to 'data extract' within the time and money allocated, so there is little latitude to expand the scope of the review at later stages.[13] Systematic reviewers often set out to map fairly small fields with secure fences, and do not expect to look over the hedge.[14]

Electronic and 'handsearches' are then done to find research studies that are potentially relevant to the review question. The resulting titles and abstracts – *if* the latter are available – are screened to see if they meet the inclusion/exclusion criteria. In most cases, a huge proportion of studies are screened out at this stage for failing to meet the inclusion criteria, which means that most of the potential field is discarded *without the reviewers having read a single study in its entirety.*[15] In many cases, since abstracts are by no means universal, the reviewers will have eliminated a proportion of studies on the basis of their titles alone. Interestingly, despite the concern with transparency, figures seldom seem to be given for this.

Most potential studies are judged ineligible for inclusion, therefore, without being read at all. Like credit card offers in reverse, they are pre-disapproved. The next step in the process is to get hold of the full text of papers in the remaining corpus, for keywording, in order to draw up the 'map' of the field. This stage seems inevitably to allow yet more studies to be excluded, when the full text makes it clear that they do not meet the inclusion criteria.

This is not the end of the 'filtering' process. However let us pause to note another sense in which not-reading is recommended at this stage. Screening and keywording does not, it seems, require actually reading the full papers in any detail. The EPPI-Centre Review Companion tells reviewers that (by contrast with the lengthier business of data extraction) 'keywords might be applied to a study in as little as 10 minutes' (p. 15/20). Not much reading anticipated at this point therefore.

The next stage usually involves rendering down the corpus into a final selection for full 'data extraction' and 'in-depth review'.[16] This is the point at which something closer to reading in its vernacular sense presumably gets done, since the Review Companion warns that 'the data extraction process takes about 3 hours per study per reviewer', or possibly longer (p. 15/20). However on the evidence of the reviews so far published, pitifully few primary studies make it through to in-depth review. Those studies that do make it through are rated 'high', 'medium' or 'low' for various kinds of trustworthiness including research design.

As noted above, although the EPPI-Centre methodology does not in principle exclude qualitative studies, the weightings strongly favour quantitative designs with large samples. Since, as is widely known, much educational research is not of this kind, it is presumably not surprising to the reviewers and sponsors that further big reductions in the corpus of relevant studies are often in order at this last stage.

The evidential base of many of the in-depth reviews is, as noted, unimpressive. Out of 28 reports on the EPPI-Centre website in September 2004, 16 were based on in-depth reviews of fewer than 10 primary studies (including three that were based on only two primary studies).[17] A list of all the published reports, arranged by size of their in-depth reviews, can be found in the Appendix. Here are some examples of the 'filtering' process from start to finish in published reviews.

What is known about successful models of formative assessment for trainee teachers during school experiences and what constitutes effective practice? (Moyles and Yates 2003):

Initial hits	688
After screening abstracts/titles	233
Keyworded	82
Included in keyword map	58
In-depth review	2

A systematic review of effective literacy teaching in the 4 to 14 age range of mainstream schooling (Hall and Harding 2003):[18]

Initial hits	1265
After screening abstract/titles	1187
Keyworded	107
Included in keyword map	80
In-depth review	3

A systematic review of the characteristics of effective foreign language teaching to pupils between the ages 7 and 11 (Driscoll *et al.* 2004):

Initial hits	5120
After screening abstracts/titles	203
Keyworded	54
In-depth review	4

Supporting pupils with emotional and behavioural difficulties (EBD) in mainstream primary schools: a systematic review of recent research on strategy effectiveness (1999 to 2002) (Harden *et al.* 2003):

Initial hits	1312
After screening abstracts/titles	233
Keyworded	192
Included in keyword map	55
In-depth review	5

A systematic review of the effectiveness of school-level actions for promoting participation by all students (Dyson *et al.* 2002):

Initial hits	14,692
After screening abstracts/titles	336
Keyworded	41
In-depth review (of 'key studies)	6

Is this sort of thing an embarrassment to the EPPI-Centre? Not really. Oakley touches on the 'relatively low yield of usable studies' and gives a figure of 0.3 per cent of initial citations making it through to the in-depth stage in early reviews. The main problem of 'having to search needles to find haystacks', as she sees it, is the cost of time and labour (2003: 27). But the tiny yields of primary studies that are judged methodologically weighty enough for in-depth review serve another, very important purpose within the discourse of systematic review. They allow Oakley and other critics proliferating opportunities to air and extend their 'disappointment' with the quality of educational research. And the authors of these low-yield reviews, faced with the task of justifying conclusions based on a handful of primary studies, and the months of hard work that went into not-reading the rest of the literature, seldom fail to voice their own concerns with the parlous state of their field. Oakley in turn quotes the endorsements of these 'distinguished academics and leaders in their field' (2003: 30).

No time to read...

One might assume that these tiny yields of usable evidence are the unavoidable, if regrettable, result of factors such as narrowly-framed questions or very stringent quality criteria; or indeed of a genuine lack of existing research in the area. And none of these assumptions would necessarily be incorrect. However if you look closely at the instructional literature and at individual reviews, another possible reason emerges – *time*. Several reviewers allude to difficulties of 'time constraints' or 'manageability' – problems which the EPPI-Centre anticipates. At the data-extraction stage – i.e. the point at which reviewers would actually begin to read whole texts – the EPPI-Centre Review Companion advises reviewers:

> It is important to bear in mind the time-intensive nature of this stage of the review, since the resources available to a group may determine what it is feasible to undertake in the in-depth review.... If, when you get to this stage of the review you find that you have too many studies to cope with, the EPPI-Centre can help with ways of making the task manageable. (p. 15 of 20)

The Companion does not elaborate on what kind of help the Centre offers. But there are glimpses of how some individual review teams handled the problem of making the task manageable.

Due to the time constraints, electronic databases were used for initial searches and handsearching was not undertaken

(Moyles and Stuart 2003: 13)

Potentially, a full international search was extremely time- and resource-consuming and beyond the capacity of the group to manage. We therefore chose to review literature in English from other countries insofar as it was accessible via standard international databases available in the UK.... It seemed likely that major, funded studies would be recorded in these databases, but that, inevitably, smaller, local studies would not.

(Dyson *et al*. 2002: 13)

Only 203 full documents arrived in time; these were screened. The other 75 papers did not arrive in time to be considered in the review.

(Driscoll *et al*. 2004: 4)

Due to the time and resource constraints, it was decided that the in-depth review should only include a few studies and that the criteria for the in-depth review should be selected with this in mind.

(Driscoll *et al*. 2004: 21)

It was unfortunate that, given the short timescale, we were not able to take account of one group of users, the students themselves.

(Hall and Harding 2003: 50)

The extent of user involvement in the review process was less extensive than desired but the time constraints meant that the fast pace of the review process made it difficult to involve users at all stages.

(Powell and Tod 2004: 75)

Due to time constraints, we restricted our choice of journals to those available in the library of our host institution.

(Harden *et al*. 2003: 17)[19]

We did not contact experts in the field due to time constraints.

(Harden *et al*. 2003: 18)

Since our review identified a large number of studies, it was not possible to review all of them in depth, so a narrower set of inclusion criteria were developed to select a subset of studies for in-depth review.

(Harden *et al*. 2003: 20)[20]

The application of this 'narrower set of inclusion criteria' left the above reviewers with five studies for in-depth review, which meant that they did not need use their 'reserve' criterion:

> This number was manageable within our timeframe and we did not need to use our 'reserve' criterion which would have enabled us further to exclude studies if they did not evaluate strategies based on a systemic or therapeutic model
>
> (Harden *et al.* 2003: 35)

Slightly less transparently presented in some reviews, then, are a set of additional 'exclusion criteria' that allowed reviewers to keep the corpus of primary studies to a manageable (and in some cases, minute) size. These extra exclusion criteria can be listed as follows.

*   If a journal is not in your institution's library, exclude it.
*   If an issue, or even a whole volume is missing, don't try to get it from other sources.
*   Don't consult experts.
*   Reduce the time spent on the involvement of users.
*   Dispense with handsearching.
*   Set a cut-off time for getting hold of full copies of studies.
*   If too many relevant studies make it through the original exclusion criteria, set some studies aside for a later review.
*   Add some additional exclusion criteria.
*   And keep an extra criterion in reserve.

It should be noted that many reviewers did *not* take such shortcuts. Nevertheless, the EPPI-Centre, which exerts strong control over the form and content of reviews, clearly allows such appeals to time constraints to stand. Indeed Oakley, the Director at the time, refers explicitly to the 'less than ideal short-cuts' that may result when the funding for a review runs out (2003: 28). It appears that the Centre does not consider such shortcuts an insurmountable threat to the 'trustworthiness' of the evidence base.

These time-induced strategies for not-reading source material are undoubtedly the product of the Taylorist time-management procedures imposed on reviewers by the systematic review process. Traditional forms of reviewing are subject to time constraints too of course, and these are seldom explicitly acknowledged. But the ruthless prioritising of time and the quantification of effort in the EPPI-framework contributes to a culture that dismisses intellectual work as mere time-wasting if it cannot conform to schedules and budgets. Any notion of reviewing as involving (amongst other things) slow, careful reading, time for thought, or critique in its wider (non-weighable), sociocultural sense, is stigmatised. As is the idea that reading might actually be pleasurable or personally rewarding. Indeed the whole process of reviewing is often represented as an onerous chore. Here is Oakley, describing the exertions of systematic reviewing.

> Not only is searching for literature a lengthy business, but scrutinising titles and abstracts for relevant information is often exhausting and disappointing, retrieval of hard copies of studies for in-depth review is another time-consuming task, and extracting data from individual studies can take 3–5 person hours per study. (2003: 28)

Seldom has scholarship been represented in such dispiriting terms. The overwhelming impression from the publications emanating from the EPPI-Centre is that reading is an unreliable, unappetising business that can only be rendered respectable and auditable through hard work and disappointment.

What about *writing*?

Writing is equally degraded in systematic review. As noted above, reviewers are not expected – indeed they appear to be actively discouraged – from any display of rhetorical skill or individual style. 'Synthesis' is represented as a matter of assembling the coded data already entered into the EPPI database and 'interrogating' it using the EPPI software. Writing up must follow 'the EPPI-Centre report structure'. This imposes a dreary pattern of identical chapter and section headings, overstuffed methods sections, and overflowing appendices detailing search strategies, coding decisions, application of inclusion criteria, quality weightings etc. Readers have to struggle though pages of empty prose and formulaic phrases that lay out the 'audit trail' that is supposed to lead from conception to conclusion. The ennui induced by these chapters (in this reader at least) contrasts with the introductory 'Background' chapter in most of the reviews, where the authors generally allow themselves to exercise their specialist skills of exposition, argument, conceptualisation and critique according to the generic conventions of traditional academic writing.

Like reading, writing is represented by the EPPI-Centre as not only unhelpfully opaque (which is why reports need to be so closely managed and pre-scripted), but as hard work. The Review Companion, in its final section entitled 'Synthesis and writing the report' rallies flagging reviewers:

> You will be glad to hear that once you get this far, all the hard work is done. The data are present in EPPI-Reviewer, you have a conceptual framework for your synthesis and the software will enable you to interrogate your data in powerful ways. (page 17 of 20)

As with reading, the status of writing is diminished to that of an annoying, if minimal chore. The aim, with the aid of the EPPI-Reviewer codes and the software, is to remove the effort and the opacity of writing, and render 'synthesis' as transparent as possible.

Now you see them, now you don't: finding the findings

Perhaps all of this would not matter (though I rather think it still would), if the EPPI-Centre methodology was living up to its own claims for transparency, sound evidence, fitness of purpose and value for money. But close reading of the reviews so far produced shows that many of them are rather less ample, informative or cost-effective than proponents of systematic review proclaim. The flaccid bodies of semi-hard evidence that many reviews produce can scarcely merit the considerable costs of producing them, even if you exclude the social cost of demoralising and anathematising a generation of research and researchers. Apart from contributing to that culture of calumny, which some would count a benefit rather than a cost, the other merits of systematic review are small. Few of the education reviews published so far provide evidence that could seriously claim to be trustworthy, based as they are on such small 'samples' of primary studies or such narrowly-defined questions. Moreover, these samples may include studies that were of doubtful trustworthiness according to the authors' own criteria. For example, Evans *et al.* report an in-depth review of 27 primary studies (placing them near the top of my 'league table'; see Appendix). However, only 10 of these were judged to be 'methodologically "sound"' (2003: 4). Cordingley *et al.* rated only two studies as 'high' on one of their two sub-questions, and *none at all* on the other (2003: 43). Low and Beverton also rated none of their eight studies as 'high' (2004: 39; see further below).

One might expect that these limitations would result in many reviews with little or nothing to report when they arrive at Chapter 5 of the EPPI report structure, 'Findings and Implications'. Some of the conclusions are certainly lukewarm or banal; and many reviews admit the lack of a secure evidential base. However, *in no case does this prevent the reviewers from drawing implications for policy and practice.* For instance, in a review of effective foreign language teaching at ages 7 to 11, the authors state that they are unable to arrive at 'definitive findings'; yet, in the same paragraph, proceed to offer 'the review findings'.

> As there was a dearth of evidence specifically focusing on the characteristics of effective teaching and as the four studies in the in-depth review are concerned with different aspects of teaching, it is not possible to arrive at definitive findings supported by a substantive body of research [...] Studies, which did consider teaching, tended to focus on topics such as the qualifications of the teacher or the teaching programme used; this may be useful as background but does not enable conclusions to be drawn about effective teaching. Nonetheless, the review findings are as follows...
>
> (Driscoll *et al.* 2004: 4)

A numbered list of 10 findings followed.

Another study, of the impact of ICT on the literacy of learners for whom English is not their first language, describes its limitations thus:

> The primary limitation of the review is that it is small. There are only eight included studies and, of these, none were deemed to provide a 'high' weight of evidence to answer the question at hand; indeed, only three were deemed 'medium' […]. The result inevitably remains that it is hard to draw any firm conclusions or draw much in the way of implications for policy.
>
> (Low and Beverton 2004: 39)

Yet the authors *do* proceed, on the same page, to present 'more detailed implications', albeit 'with a high degree of caution' (39). In fact they present four implications for policy, and two for practice.

Even as they lament the size and untrustworthiness of their shrunken bodies of evidence, therefore, many reviewers still seem to feel able (or perhaps obliged) to offer implications for policy and practice. This can lead to uneasy textual manoeuvres and a kind of 'now you see it, now you don't' effect, as the authors try to handle the incommensurable tasks of reporting a lack of evidence while also drawing implications from it. For instance, a review of formative assessment of trainee teachers during school experience contains, on the same page, an acknowledgement of a lack of evidence, and a discussion of what the evidence 'suggests':

> The main limitation of this review is that it cannot confidently recommend, without further research being undertaken, any successful models of formative assessment, nor can it offer any further insight into the debate of what constitutes effective formative assessment practices.
>
> […]
>
> Evidence suggests that what appears to be a general move in the UK towards the incorporation of US-style reflective journals within ITT courses is potentially an advantageous move. They appear to increase professional and personal growth and allow teacher educators further insight into the depth of their trainee teachers' pedagogical knowledge.
>
> (Moyles and Yates 2003: 38)

To take another example, a review of the impact of headteachers on student outcomes, based on an in-depth review of eight studies, concludes:

> Effective leadership was confirmed as probably being an important factor in a school's success.
>
> (Bell *et al.* 2003: 3)

The tepid nature of this conclusion is doubtless due to the small number of studies on which it was based, and the problematic quality of most of those studies – only one of which seems to have provided wholly trustworthy evidence.[21] Despite this, the authors feel able to commend the results of the review, though the amplitude of their commendation continues to fluctuate:

> [T]he findings broadly confirm the conclusion of the review by Hallinger and Heck (1999) that there is some evidence to support the view that leadership does affect student outcomes, albeit indirectly. (p. 25)

> The overall evidence indicates that headteacher leadership and management does make a difference to pupil performance… (p. 25)

> This review shows that in an area in which significant policy decisions have recently been taken there is very little research evidence available to illuminate the precise nature of the relationship between the leadership and management strategies adopted by headteachers and the learning outcomes of their pupils. (p. 26)

The evidence provided by this particular review is hardly 'transparent'. The conclusions seem to derive as much from the expertise and convictions of the reviewers as from the compromised corpus of research on which they are drawing. This does not prevent them, however, from recommending the EPPI-review process as educative:

> Certainly it has shown the need for many to re-assess their ideas about the nature, purposes and scope of literature reviews, the ways in which articles are prepared for publication, and the role of both journal editors and referees. (p. 25)

In common with many of the other reviews published so far, the one 'finding' that the reviewers are able to present unequivocally is the need for the research community to pull up its socks.

It would appear, then, that the embarrassment of ending up with such small yields after so many months of hard labour can result in systematic reviews that jump to conclusions at least as unwarranted as those of so-called 'narrative' reviews. The fact that reviewers are able to reach such conclusions means that the EPPI-Centre process does not eliminate interpretation and judgement from the review process. It just drives them underground. In other words, it renders the review process *less* transparent. One could cite further examples where the 'synthesis' includes rather more than a straightforward adding-up of numerically-weighted evidence. For instance Harlen's discussion of the findings from her in-depth review of 30 primary sources includes reference to 15 publications that were *not* included in the review (2004: 86–94). This is exactly the kind of interpretive work, based on years of accumulated expertise, that one would expect, and accept, from an experienced academic who is a leading figure in her field. However it does not accord with the strict letter of the EPPI-Centre procedure, since those extra 15 references have not been properly vetted and weighted for trustworthiness. Similarly, Cordingley *et al.* justify referring to studies assigned a 'low' weight of evidence on the grounds that these were 'used to add texture or as illustration only' (2003: 43). Again, this rationale may be persuasive for some readers, especially in the context of a thoughtful discussion of the different criteria that user groups may bring to the issue of trustworthiness (2003: 56–7). But persuasiveness, with its recourse to context, writers' intentions and readers' responses, is not officially included in the EPPI-measuring of quality.

'Synthesis' may involve more, then, than the simple addition or aggregation of evidence culled from the source studies. In fact, I suggest that it must *always* involve more than that. How could it be otherwise? The conversion of weights and numbers back into text – i.e. into conclusions, findings and implications – is always going to require interpretive and rhetorical work. Lurking behind the seeming innocence and transparency of data extraction and synthesis are the familiar 'four R's' of scholarly work – reading, writing, reasoning and rhetoric. By denying that these are taking place, systematic review, against its own professed intentions, renders the business of producing evidence less, rather than more, open to scrutiny.

Conclusion

Despite its overriding concern with quality, systematic review actually closes down on important questions concerning quality and accountability in educational research. Though its implacable insistence that there is only one right way – the EPPI-way – to address issues of quality, accountability and utility, systematic review makes it more difficult to ask the really difficult questions that many educational researchers would like to ask. By refusing to contemplate alternatives to the audit-trailing of scholarly work, the EPPI-system devalues serious consideration of how quality could be improved without suppressing methodological diversity and critical edge; how researchers could work more meaningfully with users, and how they could respond better to the needs of practitioners and policy-makers, without becoming mere service-providers to these constituencies. Contrary to the assertions of many proponents of evidence-based practice and systematic review, educational researchers often have their own concerns about quality, and are interested in pursuing questions of how to improve it, without sacrificing the diversity of approach, interests, values and purposes on which a democratic research community should be based.

There are some useful things to be learned from systematic review, even as it stands. Reviewers could indeed be more specific about what they looked for, and where. We could all benefit from knowing how to search databases effectively. It might indeed be a good idea for reviewers to give an idea of how convincing they found the evidence (without feeling the need to weigh it). 'Users' certainly can productively contribute to the framing of review questions and to other stages of the review process, and there are interesting accounts in the reviews of the range of forms that user involvement can take. Like other national policies – for example, the National Literacy Strategy – there is stuff in there that many professionals and researchers would consider good practice. This is one reason why dissent is so easily framed as dishonourable. ('Oh, so you *don't* think all children are entitled to learn to read?' 'So you *don't* think that reviewers should be answerable for their methods?')

But the overarching framework that bends research to the wheel of accountability counteracts the good practice, especially since systematic review is only one component of a much larger piece of policy machinery that is rolling in one direction. Think again of the National Literacy Strategy. Like systematic review, the NLS also involves prescriptive vocabularies ('bookbanking', 'scribing', 'powerful verbs' 'strategy-checks' etc.), broken-down practice (each literacy hour broken down into segments; each task broken down into pre-set objectives), and ruthless regimentation and monitoring (only one right way to write a recipe or read a poem). Comparison could also be made with Ofsted school inspection, where the regulation of reporting similarly imposes conformity to a ponderous structure of categories, section headings and gradings, and a bland house style that permits inspectors, like reviewers, only to report what falls within the category system, in a voice that is evacuated of interest or equivocation. Systematic review is just one part, I suggest, of a pervasive attempt to reconfigure and regulate professional and academic practices and identities by acting on the very words that people speak and write. It seems to be based on the assumption that discipline, in its Foucauldian sense, can be made to work 'backwards': from word to thought, from speech to self.

The intellectual, social and political implications of this are malign. If the project of disabling critique and disciplining academic work succeeds, the outcome is likely to be a diminution in the social usefulness of research knowledge, the continuing oversimplification of educational problems and solutions, and a less well-educated, less critical community of researchers. It might be tempting to dismiss the EPPI-phenomenon as a small, cultish alternative to a mainstream academic culture that can easily shrug off its impertinences, or bring it round to a more informed understanding of what can and cannot be claimed by an evidence-based approach. And 'behind' some of the reports one can indeed detect traces of attempts to mitigate the extremity of systematic review. Some authors do discuss the difficulties and potentially adverse effects of the approach.[22] It is entirely possible that some reviewers successfully fight their corner with EPPI-Centre staff over issues of principle or procedure, or manage to smuggle some nuance or complexity into their reports. Moreover, as I suggested above, behind the cover story of transparent, interpretation-free evidence accumulation, the traditional work of interpretation and argument goes on. But these are all covert operations, carried out under cover of endorsement of the system in principle; and they rely on an existing body of experienced researchers who know that there are other ways to do things.[23] As long as the EPPI-Centre and its supporters continue to promote the official story of reading-lite reviewing and interpretation-free evidence, and to sell it to novice researchers, a dangerously over-simplified version of research and scholarship is disseminated.

Already systematic review is making inroads into new academic territories. It is now on sale as a taught course or a 20-credit module towards a masters degree at the University of London, and is therefore convertible into the currency of academic qualifications from a high-status university.[24] It is increasingly becoming a requirement in government contracts, and a yardstick by which to measure the quality of proposed research designs (cf. Torrance 2004). The Funders Forum of the National Educational Research Forum (NERF) (disbanded in 2006) identified a 'systematic review skills deficit' and advises commissioners to employ only those properly trained in systematic review procedures.[25] Finally, systematic review is snapping at the heels of journal editors. Supporters of the EPPI system are convening meetings at which editors are exhorted to change their abstracting guidelines to facilitate electronic searching and help prevent unnecessary reading (NERF 2004). Peer review is under attack, and referees and editors who reject papers based on systematic review have been challenged on the grounds that, if it's good enough for the DfES and the EPPI-Centre, it's good enough for a research journal (Stronach 2004).

Like all accountability systems, systematic review is hostile to anything that cannot be seen, and therefore controlled, counted and quality assured. Reading and writing are deeply problematic from that angle, because things happen out of sight, and outcomes are never wholly predictable. Different readers will extract differing meanings from texts, according to their background assumptions and their current priorities and beliefs. Understanding and interpretation leave no traces while they are happening. The only possible access one can have to them is through texts, which are, of course, themselves subject to further acts of interpretation. Reading and writing *always* run the risk of opening up, or calling attention to, the calamitous gaps that exist in the foundations of thought, knowledge and principled action. Writing inevitably opens the gap between representation and reality. Reading does the same for facts and interpretation. As Derrida has shown (e.g. 1980, 1981), this is why they have posed a threat to so many disciplines and cultural practices. This is why the rage for transparency – for unclouded access to the fundamentals that are concealed as well as carried by texts – is a very old, as well as a very contemporary phenomenon (see MacLure 2003: Ch 6). Much contemporary education policy seems to be animated by this fear and distrust: not just of the unreliability of professionals, but of *language itself*. Policy seems to be suffering an acute case of that old ontological panic about 'signs' and the unreliable access that they offer to the stuff that is supposed to lie behind them – truth, knowledge, meaning, evidence, standards.

The EPPI-Centre's response to the threat of reading/writing is not so much a rage, though, as a childish tantrum. It amounts to a continuous, foot-stamping whine about the impasse between texts and truths, and the indirection, ambiguity, contestability, unpredictability and uncertainty that are the price we pay for what we know. In waging war on evidence that can never fully be prised out of its textual embodiment, and on academics whose work resists counting and quality-control, the EPPI-Centre approach is brutishly destructive of some of the most important aspects of research and scholarship – i.e. the reading, writing, thinking, interpreting, arguing and justifying – out of which knowledge is precariously produced.

Appendix

Number of primary studies subjected to 'in-depth review' in 28 systematic reviews published on the EPPI-Centre 'REEL' website in September 2004.*

Review	No. of studies reviewed 'in-depth'
Moyles and Stuart (2003)	2
Moyles and Yates (2003)	2
Totterdell *et al.* (2004)	2
Hall and Harding (2003)	3
Driscoll *et al.* (2004)	4
Powell and Tod (2004)	5
Parker-Jenkins *et al.* (2004)	5
Bennett *et al.* (2003)	5
Harden *et al.* (2003)	5
Dyson *et al.* (2002)	6
Locke and Andrews (2004)	7
Low and Beverton (2004)	8
Bell *et al.* (2003)	8
Burn and Leach 2004)	9
Francis *et al.* (2002)	9
Penn *et al.* (2004)	9
Andrews *et al.* (2004)	10
Harlen and Deakin Crick (2003)	12
Torgerson and Zhu (2003)	12
Bennett *et al.* (2004)	14
Deakin Crick *et al.* (2004)	14
Andrews *et al.* (2002)	16
Cordingley *et al.* (2003)	17
Harlen and Deakin Crick (2002)	19
Howes *et al.* (2003)	24
Gough *et al.* (2003)	25
Evans *et al.* (2003)	27
Harlen (2004)	30

*   Figures for two out of the total of 30 education reviews published on the website at this date have been excluded since these did not report an 'in-depth' review stage: EPPI-Centre (2001) and Fletcher and Lockhart (2003).

Notes

1 References for opening quotations: Breton (1969: 6); Montaigne (quoted in Greenblatt, 1991: 146–7).

2 The full title of the EPPI-Centre is the Evidence for Policy and Practice Information and Co-ordinating Centre (Founding Director: Ann Oakley). The Centre's homepage is http://eppi.ioe.ac.uk/.

3 This is a version of a paper of the same title presented to the Annual Conference of the British Educational Research Association, Manchester, September, 2004. The paper was part of a symposium entitled 'Quality Street and other cul-de-sacs: what is 'quality' in education and educational research, and where are its cutting edges'? Since 2004, names of government departments have changed. The Teacher Training Agency has become the Teacher Development Agency. The Department for Education and Skills disappeared in 2007, to be replaced by two entities: the Department for Innovation, Universities and Skills, and the Department for Children, Schools and Families. There is no space here to discuss the erasure of 'education' from the titles of these bodies. Suffice it to say that such terminological interventions are not irrelevant to the arguments in this chapter.

4 See for example Elliott (2001); Avis (2003); Torrance (2004) and chapters in the second half of Thomas and Pring (2003).

5 These 30 reviews comprised the total corpus of education reviews published on the EPPI-Centre website at September 2004.

6 Cf. Strathern (2000); Hammersley (2001); Avis (2003).

7 'What is a Systematic Review?', http://eppi.ioe.ac.uk/EPPIWeb/home.aspx?page=/reel/about_reviews.htm.

8 Cf. Oakley: 'the disadvantages of not doing this [i.e. introducing more 'codification into the knowledge base'] can ... literally be fatal' (2003: 22). Oakley is referring here to 'areas such as HIV/AIDS education' but the remark comes in the middle of a paragraph about the general importance of making it more difficult for health and education professionals to 'hide failures'.

9 The original critiques are: Hargreaves (1996), Hillage *et al.* (1998) and Tooley and Darby (1998).

10 'How will the [review] group ensure that the methodological and conceptual issues are understood and agreed upon across the review team in time for the protocol to be written?' 'Which computer software are you going to use to manage citations?' 'What will happen if this person is unable to fulfil this role?' The 'Quality Assurance' questions in the Companion are written in red typeface and are presumably especially important: 'Please describe the procedures by which the EPPI-Centre worked with the group to provide external quality assurance of application of inclusion/exclusion criteria'. 'Please describe the procedures by which the EPPI-Centre worked with the group to provide external quality assurance of application of mapping keywords'. 'Please describe the procedures by which the EPPI-Centre worked with the group to provide external quality assurance of data extraction'. (EPPI-Centre Review Companion, *passim*: http://eppi.ioe.ac.uk/EPPIWeb/home.aspx?page=/reel/tools.htm.)

11 One review team considered (but decided against) departing from the EPPI-Centre's framework (Moyles and Yates 2003: 39). Another was somewhat equivocal, describing systematic review approvingly as 'a searchlight', but also debating its inflexibility and narrow focus, and its inability to capture the conceptual complexity of their field (Dyson *et al.* 2002: 53–5). There were also instances of reviewers using their specialist knowledge and skills in ways that went beyond the remit of mere 'synthesis', to incorporate old-school, 'narrative' reviewing habits such as interpretation and argument; see further below.

12   See for example Derrida (1981), Zeller and Farmer (1999). MacLure (2003: Ch. 6) provides an overview of the 'threat of writing', or textuality, and the ways in which philosophers, literary theorists and social scientists have attempted to contain that threat. Systematic review is a particularly extreme reaction to the threat of textuality: see 'Conclusion'.

13   'How much time/how many studies can [the named reviewer] spend/do?' (EPPI-Centre Review Companion: 16/20).

14   Not all reviews start out with narrow questions. For instance Dyson et al. (2002) and Cordingley et al. (2003) both began with broad questions, and their initial searches yielded very large numbers of potentially relevant 'hits'. However this initial breadth had narrowed dramatically by the final, 'in-depth review' stage: from 14,692 to 6, and 13,479 to 17 respectively; see below.

15   Reviewers will, of course, have read those research studies with which they were already familiar, unless the review team are novices to the substantive area – a possibility that is not ruled out in systematic review (cf. Torrance 2004).

16   Some reviewers carried out their in-depth review on the total corpus of studies included in the keyword map; e.g. Harlen and Deakin Crick (2003: 12 studies); Howes et al. (2003: 24 studies); Deakin Crick et al. (2004: 14 studies); Harlen (2004: 30 studies).

17   A total of 30 education reviews were published on the EPPI-Centre website at this date. However two of these did not report an 'in-depth' review stage: EPPI-Centre (2001) and Fletcher and Lockhart (2003). The format of these two reviews also diverged in other respects from the usual EPPI review structure.

18   Three primary studies were 'subjected to the full EPPI procedures of in-depth reviewing' (Hall and Harding, 2003: 30). There is some ambiguity: the reviewers identified a total of 12 studies for in-depth review on the grounds of their 'direct relevance to the Teacher Training Agency'; but only three were subjected to the full treatment because only these gained high enough ratings for quality of empirical evidence.

19   The resulting exclusions included one presumably key journal, since it was listed by the authors in their protocol (*Journal of Emotional & Behavioural Disorders*). Moreover if issues, or even whole volumes, were missing from their institution's library, the authors did not try to obtain these from other sources. 14 issues and 17.5 whole volumes were 'missing' (Harden et al. 2003: 72).

20   The 'narrower set' of inclusion criteria applied by Harden et al. (2003) excluded all studies that did not employ a control or comparison group or a reversal design, or which employed a sample size of less than 20 – thus endorsing the bias towards quantitative design as the benchmark of quality in systematic review.

21   Of the eight studies (which are not assigned numerical 'weights' according to the usual EPPI-procedure), one was 'of limited relevance' (Bell et al. 2003: 17); one was a case study of a single school, from which 'one cannot generalise' (p. 22); one showed 'moderate' and 'negligible' correlations between leadership and student outcomes (p. 17); one found no 'significant, positive relationship' (p. 18); one found that principals made 'a disappointing contribution to student engagement' (p. 19); one found 'indirect' effects (p. 19); one had a faulty design and, in any case, found only a 'weak correlation between leadership and achievement' (p. 20); and one found a 'mediated' (i.e. indirect) relationship between 'transformational leadership' and student achievement in Maths (p. 20).

22   For instance Dyson et al. discuss the features of systematic review that tend towards narrowing of focus and reduced flexibility, referring to the '(understandable) emphasis on tight delineation of review topic, requirement for clear a priori criteria for what forms of evidence can be included and current lack of procedures for "analogical" synthesis.' They also note 'the practical issue of managing a very wide ranging review within a limited timescale and budget' (2002: 55).

23 Amanda Coffey, as Discussant to the symposium in which the original version of this chapter was presented, cautioned against manufacturing a 'moral panic' about systematic review. I take her point. It may be that this chapter over-estimates the power of the evidence 'movement' and its ability to influence research and scholarship. I think I would still argue that the time has come for concerted opposition rather than covert operations. But I could be wrong.
24 Details of the course can be found online by following the link on the EPPI-Centre's homepage at http://eppi.ioe.ac.uk/EPPIWeb/home.aspx.
25 http://www.nerf-uk.org/funders/systematic/.

References

Systematic reviews referred to in the text

All reviews are published in: *Research Evidence in Education Library*. London: EPPI-Centre, Social Science Research Unit, Institute of Education, available online at: http://eppi.ioe.ac.uk/EPPIWeb/home.aspx?&page=/reel/reviews.htm.

Andrews, R., Burn, A., Leach, J., Locke, T., Low, G. and Torgerson, C. (2002) A systematic review of the impact of networked ICT on 5–16 year olds' literacy in English (EPPI-Centre Review, version 1.1).
Andrews, R., Torgerson, C., Beverton, S., Locke, T., Low, G., Robinson, A. and Zhu, D. (2004) The effect of grammar teaching (syntax) in English on 5 to 16 year olds' accuracy and quality in written composition.
Bell, L., Bolam, R. and Cubillo, L. (2003) A systematic review of the impact of school leadership and management on student outcomes.
Bennett, J., Hogarth, S. and Lubben, F. (2003) A systematic review of the effects of context-based and Science-Technology-Society (STS) approaches in the teaching of secondary science. Version 1.1.
Bennett, J., Lubben, F., Hogarth, S. and Campbell, B. (2004) A systematic review of the use of small-group discussions in science teaching with students aged 11–18, and their effects on students' understanding in science or attitude to science.
Burn, A. and Leach, J. (2004) A systematic review of the impact of ICT on the learning of literacies associated with moving image texts in English, 5–16.
Cordingley, P., Bell, M., Rundell, B. and Evans, D. (2003) The impact of collaborative CPD on classroom teaching and learning.
Deakin Crick, R., Coates, M., Taylor, M. and Ritchie, S. (2004) A systematic review of the impact of citizenship education on the provision of schooling.
Driscoll, P., Jones, J., Martin, C., Graham-Matheson, L., Dismore, H. and Sykes, R. (2004) A systematic review of the characteristics of effective foreign language teaching to pupils between the ages 7 and 11.
Dyson, A., Howes, A. and Roberts, B. (2002). A systematic review of the effectiveness of school-level actions for promoting participation by all students (EPPI-Centre Review, version 1.1).
EPPI-Centre (2001) (Gough, D., Oliver, S., Brunton, G., Selai, C. and Schaumberg, H., for the Department of the Environment, Transport and the Regions.) The effect of travel modes on children's mental health, cognitive and social development; a systematic review.

Evans, J., Harden, A., Thomas, J. and Benefield, P. (2003) Support for pupils with emotional and behavioural difficulties (EBD) in mainstream primary classrooms: a systematic review of the effectiveness of interventions.

Fletcher, M. and Lockhart, I. (2003) The impact of financial circumstances on engagement with post-16 learning: a systematic map of research (EPPI-Centre Review, version 1).

Francis, B., Skelton, C. and Archer, L. (2002). A systematic review of classroom strategies for reducing stereotypical gender constructions among girls and boys in mixed-sex UK primary schools (EPPI-Centre Review, version 1.1).

Gough, D.A., Kiwan, D., Sutcliffe, K., Simpson, D. and Houghton, N. (2003) A systematic map and synthesis review of the effectiveness of personal development planning for improving student learning.

Hall, K. and Harding, A. (2003) A systematic review of effective literacy teaching in the 4 to 14 age range of mainstream schooling.

Harden, A., Thomas, J., Evans, J., Scanlon, M. and Sinclair, J. (2003) Supporting pupils with emotional and behavioural difficulties (EBD) in mainstream primary schools: a systematic review of recent research on strategy effectiveness (1999 to 2002).

Harlen, W. (2004) A systematic review of the evidence of reliability and validity of assessment by teachers used for summative purposes.

Harlen, W. and Deakin Crick, R. (2002) A systematic review of the impact of summative assessment and tests on students' motivation for learning (EPPI-Centre Review, version 1.1).

Harlen, W. and Deakin Crick, R. (2003) A systematic review of the impact on students and teachers of the use of ICT for assessment of creative and critical thinking skills.

Howes, A., Farrell, P., Kaplan, I. and Moss, S. (2003) The impact of paid adult support on the participation and learning of pupils in mainstream schools.

Locke, T. and Andrews, R. (2004) A systematic review of the impact of ICT on literature-related literacies in English 5–16.

Low, G. and Beverton, S. (2004) A systematic review of the impact of ICT on literacy learning in English of learners between 5 and 16, for whom English is a second or additional language.

Moyles, J. and Stuart, D. (2003) Which school-based elements of partnership in initial teacher training in the UK support trainee teachers' professional development?

Moyles, J. and Yates, R. (2003) What is known about successful models of formative assessment for trainee teachers during school experiences and what constitutes effective practice?

Parker-Jenkins, M., Hewitt. D., Brownhill, S. and Sanders, T. (2004) What strategies can be used by initial teacher training providers, trainees and newly qualified teachers to raise the attainment of pupils from culturally diverse backgrounds?

Penn, H., Barreau, S., Butterworth, L., Lloyd, E., Moyles, J., Potter, S. and Sayeed, R. (2004) What is the impact of out-of-home integrated care and education settings on children aged 0–6 and their parents?

Powell, S. and Tod, J. (2004) A systematic review of how theories explain learning behaviour in school contexts.

Torgerson, C. and Zhu, D. (2003) A systematic review and meta-analysis of the effectiveness of ICT on literacy learning in English, 5–16.

Totterdell, M., Woodroffe, L., Bubb, S. and Hanrahan, K. (2004) The impact of NQT induction programmes on the enhancement of teacher expertise, professional development, job satisfaction or retention rates: a systematic review of research on induction.

Other work

Avis, J. (2003) Work-based knowledge, evidence-informed practice and education, *British Journal of Educational Studies*, 51(4), 369–89.

Breton, A. (1969) *Manifestoes of Surrealism*, trans R. Seaver and H.R. Lane (Ann Arbor, MI: University of Michigan Press).

Derrida, J. (1980) *The Archaeology of the Frivolous: Reading Condillac* (Pittsburgh, PA: Duquesne University Press).

Derrida, J. (1981) *Dissemination*, trans, with an Introduction by B. Johnson (London: Athlone Press).

Derrida, J. (1988) *Limited Inc* (Evanston, Chicago: North Western).

Elliott, J. (2001) Making evidence-based practice educational, *British Educational Research Journal*, 27(5), 555–74.

EPPI-Centre (2003) EPPI-Centre Review Companion. http://eppi.ioe.ac.uk/EPPIWeb/home.aspx?page=/reel/tools.htm.

Evans, J. and Benefield, P. (2001) Systematic reviews of educational research: does the medical model fit? *British Educational Research Journal*, 27(5), 527–41.

Fairclough, N. (1989). *Language and Power* (London: Longman).

Foucault, M. (1980) *Power/Knowledge: Selected Interviews and Other Writings 1972–77 by Michel Foucault*, ed. C. Gordon (London: Harvester Wheatsheaf).

Giroux, H. (1992) Language, difference and curriculum theory: beyond the politics of clarity, *Theory into Practice*, 31, 219–27.

Greenblatt, S. (1991) *Marvellous Possessions: The Wonder of the New World* (Oxford: Clarendon).

Hammersley, M. (2001) On 'systematic' reviews of research literatures: a 'narrative' response to Evans and Benefield, *British Educational Research Journal*, 27(5), 543–54.

Hargreaves, D. (1996) Teaching as a research-based profession: possibilities and prospects, Teacher Training Agency Annual Lecture (London: TTA).

Hillage, J., Pearson, R., Anderson, A. and Tamkin, P. (1998) *Excellence in Research in School*, (London: Department for Education & Employment/Institute of Employment Studies).

Kristeva, J. (1982) *Powers of Horror: An Essay on Abjection* (New York: Columbia University Press).

MacLure, M. (2003) *Discourse in Educational and Social Research* (Buckingham: Open University Press).

NERF (National Educational Research Forum) (2004) Report from the Third Education Journal Editors' Seminar. NERF, http://www.nerf-uk.org/themes/keyuse/intermediaries/publishers/?version=1.

Oakley, A. (2003) Research evidence, knowledge management and educational practice: early lessons from a systematic approach, *London Review of Education*, 1(1), 21–33.

Scheurich, J.J. (2000) A RoUGH, ramBling, strAnGe, muDDy, CONfusing, e1LIPtical Kut: from an archaeology of plain talk, *Qualitative Inquiry*, 6(3) 337–48.

Strathern, M. (2000) The tyranny of transparency, *British Educational Research Journal*, 26(3), 309–91.

Stronach, I. (2004) Deconstructing 'quality' and reconstructing critique. Paper presented to the Annual Conference of the British Educational Research Association, Manchester, September.

Thomas, G. and Pring, R. (eds) (2003) *Evidence-based Practice in Education* (Buckingham: Open University Press).

Tooley, J. and Darby, D. (1998) *Educational Research: A Critique*, (London: Office for Standards in Education).

Torrance, H. (2004) Systematic reviewing – the 'call centre' version of research synthesis. Time for a more flexible approach. Paper presented to the ESRC/RCBN Seminar on Systematic Reviewing, University of Sheffield, 24 June.

Zeller, N. and Farmer, F.M. (1999) 'Catchy, clever titles are not acceptable': style, APA, and qualitative reporting, *International Journal of Qualitative Studies in Education*, 12(1), 3–20.

Chapter 5

Sex, science and educational research

The unholy trinity

Ian Stronach, Jo Frankham and Sheila Stark

Introduction

> We are led to believe that problems are given ready-made, and that they disappear in the responses or the solution. Already, under this double aspect, they can be no more than phantoms (...). According to this infantile prejudice, the master sets the problem, our task is to solve it, and the result is accredited true or false by a powerful authority.
>
> (Deleuze, 1994: 158)

What is the problem? The problem is straightforward: it is 'rates of teenage pregnancy' (Strange *et al.* 2003b: 201). It is 'one of our most pressing health problems' (DfEE: 1997). What is the solution? It is 'developing more effective ways of delivering sex education' (ibid.). There is some recent consensus about these formulations (Forrest *et al.* 2004; Kidger 2004; Kingori *et al.* 2004), and our own evaluation for the English Department of Health certainly confirms that politicians and policy-makers in England and Wales see both 'problem' and 'solution' that way.[1]

The 'problem/solution' axiomatic is legitimated internationally through OECD tables. These prompted the English government to conclude that they have a problem that must be addressed: 'the under-18 conception rate is among the highest in the world' (Department of Health, 1999). New Zealand was similarly exercised by these tables: it came second, while the US had earlier noted that it was in the worst position, having 'more than double the teenage pregnancy rate of any western industrialized nation' (Center for AIDS Prevention 1996). Indeed an earlier US systematic review of the international situation, involving 23 studies, concluded that the more successful countries, in matters of teenage pregnancy rates, were Canada, England, France, the Netherlands and Sweden. They had the advantages of more 'openness about sex, consistent messages throughout society, and access to contraception' (www.caps.ucsf.eds/sexedtext, 5 August 2004).

Such a conclusion from a systematic review prompts the first doubts about the validity and degree of the problem, constituted as such. Where did England's alleged 'openness about sex' and 'consistent messages throughout society' come from? After all, English researchers more often claim that these things are precisely what is lacking – and to be found elsewhere, perhaps in Holland (Department of Health 1999). Nevertheless, the UK media headlines are fortified by league tables that endlessly repeat the lead story that the 'under-18 conception rate is among the highest in the developed world' (Moore *et al.* 2003: 677; Kingori *et al.* 2004). It seems that moral panic about sex has an enduring fascination for both broadsheet as well as tabloid.[2] But the strongest doubts about the validity of this obsession are prompted by Bonell's historical account (2004) of teenage pregnancy rates in both the UK and the US. These rates have been falling since the 1960s. The 'crisis' can equally be represented as a fairly boring stasis.

So if we ask about the same 'problem' in terms of rates of teenage pregnancy rather than international league table positions, we find a different picture. Even in a *Guardian* article (12 November 2004) headed 'Increase in teenage pregnancies', tucked away in the second last paragraph, is a statement that there were 'nearly twice as many teenage mums 30 years ago than there are today'. Thus the logic of the audit culture constructs 'problem' as 'crisis', when from another angle one might conclude in regard to concerns about teenage pregnancy rates that twice as much as a lot less than before is not very much at all.[3]

Problematising the 'problem' as Official Sex

> The notion that 'teenage motherhood' is a social problem is so deeply ingrained in public consciousness that evidence to the contrary is hard for many people to believe.
>
> (Phoenix 1991: 1)

Thus far, we can see how the problem can variously be represented as a moral crisis, or dismissed as a statistical illusion, or a minor social problem – major for the individuals concerned of course,[4] but not something that ought to be represented as devastating to the moral fabric of the nation. The question then arises: what kind of cultural construction is going on in relation to the 'pregnant teenager' within the discourses that we would like to label for the purpose of our argument 'Official Sex'?

Official Sex is expressed by the state in terms of central constructs such as the 'pregnant teenager' tabulated locally, regionally, nationally and internationally by means familiar in various other educational accountability measures, and addressed through the establishment of key indicators, strategies, guidelines and targets for improvement (in the English case, halved by 2010). We have touched on the statistical ambiguity of this key measure in the Official Sex discourse, and will return to the subject shortly, but the term itself – 'pregnant teenager' – is also very interesting as a symbolic evocation.

First, problems prefaced on the construct of 'the pregnant teenager', being by definition female, involve a covert exemption of the male. Impregnation, as male act, is not an auditable commodity. The 'impregnating teenager' is absent in accountability metrics and so we see – or more often fail to see – a silent substitution of the male by the female. In this way, female agency is foregrounded, activated as a focus for concern, while the male is 'passivated' in audit terms. Such an active/passive articulation is quite the opposite in most early sex education lessons, texts and parental accounts (Frankham 1998) where it is the 'active sperm' that fertilises the 'passive' egg. As Moore points out, the story is also told in competitive terms, each sperm racing to its goal – 'Come on Boys!' (Moore 2003: 290). The sperm is a 'homunculus', a little man (ibid.: 291). Laqueur adds that such depictions construct the process as 'a miniaturized version of monogamous marriage' (Laqueur 1990: 172). The boy takes the lead, proposes to the girl. The girl accepts the ring/seed. So sexual acts in sex education are written as male-led and analogous to a certain version of social relations between the sexes. These analogies, interestingly, are found in biological science as well, whereby the active/passive, donor/recipient 'sexing' of biological processes is common (Spanier 1991: 336). Science is not impervious to male sexism. But in the accountability audits of Official Sex there is a peculiar inversion; an 'unhomunculated' discourse is fabricated (Edwards *et al.* 2004):[5] the little man disappears.

On the other hand, pregnancy constituted as a female state is eminently measurable, and so in the audit culture females get pregnant, as it were, on their own. That conception is both immaculate and shaming, performing an underlying Madonna/whore dichotomy within the parameters of audit discourse and its mediatised expression. The very category of the 'pregnant teenager' thus helps constitute a discourse of Official Sex whose problem-construction is apparently based on 'objective' definitions and enumerations (counts, rates, tables etc.) yet which removes male agency, and foregrounds female responsibility. In Official Sex, Official Science (the construction, measurement and narration of the problem as given) is an instrument of blame, bias and reduction, suggesting that 'sex' and 'sex education' begins with pregnancy, and works its way back to the sexual agency of the female. The 'pregnant teenager', then, is no simple statistic, nor any self-evident concept. In a double sense, she is guilty as conceived.

Second, there is something of the 'father's voice' in this (Haraway 1991). Is this not the State as Father in communication with the Errant Daughter via a 'Science' that Irigaray has already identified as a 'masculine imaginary' (Irigaray 1994: 121)? The conversation takes place via the silent ventriloquism of the audit culture – indeed, behind the very smokescreen of 'transparency'. The state takes over the responsibility of the male as Male. The original father/mother couplet (impregnating male/pregnant teenager) is replaced by a Father–Daughter relation. The State-as-Father redoubles the 'problem' by pathologising the daughter as the Pregnant Teenager – actual or potential – around and through whom national discourses of prevention, blame and remedy must flow. For example, the State as

Father remains centrally interested in the paternity costs, as indeed is the media. When three sisters (aged 12, 14 and 16) were impregnated, the *Sun*'s headline read 'Kid sisters: And guess what … You're paying the 31k-a-year benefit'. The girls' mother follows the logic of the State as Father and is reported as saying that she 'blames the schools for letting all this happen'.[6] Taken together, we see that the discourse of Official Sex *substitutes the State as Father, and as Father Substitute to the Missing Father*, whom the state's accounting erased in making room for itself. In a last twist to these embroilments, the *virtual* figure of the Pregnant Teenager is fathered by the State, as product of its official discourses, in the same movement as the State makes itself surrogate for the actual father. It is an act of incest wherein Freud returns as a commanding virtuality, an Oedipus Rex.

Third, this convolution of roles and attributions carries within it a further substitution, because it is 'pregnancy' that stands in for sex, and encapsulates the central motivation for sex education. In so doing it registers both of these as impurities (Douglas 1984) that must be addressed for the sake of future generations. The impetus for sex education is channelled through the pathology of the 'pregnant teenager' as essentially a remedial, inhibitive and heterosexual education. Thus the initial RIPPLE concern for sex education as a 'relationship issue' is medicalised and pathologised by the Medical Research Council's press release: 'Sex education taught by pupils – a new approach to tackling pregnancy and infection'. Sex education becomes a reductive synecdoche for 'health', 'safety', 'disease' and even 'sex trauma' (Harrison 2000; Tabberer *et al.* 2000: 41; Furedi 2004: 79). Current 'sex education' in England and its associated research therefore typically set out to address and measure the following: 'rates of unprotected sexual intercourse, unwanted pregnancy, sexually transmitted infections and [last and least] the quality of young people's sexual relationships' (Strange *et al.* 2003b: 202, our parenthesis).[7]

Finally, we note the recurrent nature of these 'crises' in morality. As indeed Kellogg *et al.* noted as long ago as 1975, the arguments are unchanged: '… the fear that access to contraceptive information will promote promiscuous sex relations …' (Kellogg *et al.* 1975: 52), the recurrent struggle between 'progressives' and 'conservatives' (ibid.: 27), and the opposition of many churches.[8] Frankham (2006) notes a similar ambivalence in parental strategies. Despite intentions to be 'open' about sex, or at least more open than their parents seemed, parents tend to provide highly constrained and constraining versions of sex, lest too much information translates into too much interest. As Hampshire and Lewis note, '… most recent arguments have tended to recycle arguments that were first articulated in the late 1960s and 1970s' (2004: 310; see also Carol 1983). It would be premature, however, to see such repetition simply as part of the 'problem'. In its iterability, in its recurrent failures and panics may lie a certain functionality, a kind of 'solution': '… it is *in order to function* that a social machine must *not* function well' (Deleuze and Guattari 1977: 151, their emphasis). The state, in moral Keynesian mode, seeks to limit the effects of the market-led pornography and sexualisation it elsewhere licenses or condones. The Social Exclusion Unit demurely refers to these contradictions as 'mixed messages' (Department of Health 1999: 7). Thus, at the same time, the morality of 'family values' can be promoted in a society where '... nothing has replaced the identity status of girls as bodies that men can trade for money' (Irigaray 1994: 61; Thomson 2004). Indeed the need for both morality and immorality to combine synergistically may express a definition of a masculine culture where 'possessing virgins [...] found[s] the symbolic order of [the] culture' (Irigaray 1994: 74). Purity and impurity must simultaneously contain and contest each other, resulting in an impasse whereby sex education can just as readily be presented as a scandalous excess and betrayal of children's innocence, as it can as an introduction that is too little and too late at the same time as it is too much, too soon. The result of this impasse is well illustrated by government policy as explicated by the relevant agency:

> Primary schools in England are required by law to have a policy on sex education (though this does not mean that they have to teach it): the policy could be *not to do so*.
>
> (Department of Health 1999: 37, their emphasis)

Thus, woven through the apparent incontrovertibilities of statistics, the Pregnant Teenager is presented as a target for Official Sex, and as a measurable object for Official Science. As a 'tabloidisation' (Kingori *et al.* 2004: 122) the debate has the 'objective' appearance of certainty; clearly defined, neatly tabulated, and objectively displayed. Against such an apparently simple and clear account, we have tried to pose versions of sex, sex education, and especially the 'pregnant teenager', as a knot of contradictory ideological entanglements. The State periodically takes this 'pregnant teenager', as Errant Daughter, from the margin into the centre of political discourse – in order to be displayed as a sacrificial virtual example and object of national shame. The Pregnant Teenager represents danger (as demonised) as well as purity (as a cautionary tale), thus performing an underlying Madonna/whore dichotomy within the parameters of audit discourse and its mediatised expression.[9] Our account posits the 'pregnant teenager' as a highly complex ritual object, part pharmakon, part auditable object. As such, it is important that it should be neither too numerous nor too powerful. Bonell points out that the concern used to be for 'unmarried mums' but there is a 'decreasing political acceptability of explicitly problematizing unmarried mothers' (2004: 256). In other words, you can only marginalise and pathologise the outsider. The contemporary number of 'unmarried mums' (and hence unmarried votes) is far too high for such scapegoating. Hence the state needs the problem to be sufficiently insubstantial in empirical terms for it to be suitable for this sort of ritual inflation: small problems make the best crises.

> In the present case, however, the clear is precisely the confused; it is confused in so far as it is clear.
>
> (Deleuze 1994: 253)

We hope that it is now possible to see that when Butler (1993: 10) writes that a key question is: 'Through what regulatory norms is sex itself materialized?' we will want to add to her question: 'And how is it virtualised?' That virtualisation influences, as we have argued, the 'problematization of sex education itself' (Hampshire and Lewis, 2004: 310).

Wittingly or unwittingly, the English government, through its accountability and improvement practices has identified a 'problem'. We have tried to show that process as being much more than the innocent identification of statistics that objectively indicate a problem, set it in international perspective, and create targets to redress it. Before inquiring into such redress and the role of educational research in its amelioration, it is helpful to address the questions 'why this, why now?' We do so only in passing and refer readers to the instructive history offered by Bonell and others (cf. Hampshire and Lewis 2004; Kellogg *et al.* 1975). It seems that in 1974 the *Spectator* identified 'one of the most savagely damaging lobbies a society has ever had to confront', a danger so great that it might 'destroy the family' (Hampshire and Lewis 2004: 302, 300). The lobby they had in mind was the 'sex education' lobby, whose educative ambitions were such a goad to promiscuity. As a neoconservative journal, it supported Thatcherite family values, as it does today.[10] Such has been the success of this media campaign over the years, that so-called progressive attitudes to sex education and to sexual mores more generally are widely decried in the – often pornographic – media and loudly denounced by most politicians. The result has been an infantilisation of educational discourses about sex, so that government-funded research already has its hands tied (and an orange stuck in its mouth) by government/media definitions of both problem and solution. Official Sex, we might conclude, is by definition perverse. Its 'politicization of sex' (Hampshire and Lewis 2004: 298) is presumably underwritten by deeper cultural concerns about the 'dangers' of sexual knowledge and desire, especially as expressed by the young, and even more so by the female young. This is 'panic sex' (Kroker and Kroker 1988: 10), seeking to 'quell sexual desire' and suppress the 'exploration of desire and pleasure as part of sexuality' (Allen 2004: 154). As Pollitt (2005: 5) argues: '[s]ensible people continually point out that contraception is the best way to prevent abortion; logically anti-choicers ought to be the pill's most fervent champions. That they refuse to join hands with pro-choicers to support birth control and fact-based sex education shows that their real target is not abortion but modern roles for women, sexual freedom, perhaps even sex itself'.

The problem/solution matrix, promoted by government and acquiesced to by complicit researchers (we too have been there), can be expressed and questioned thus: 'are teenage pregnancy rates the problem to which effective sex education is the solution?' Gilles Deleuze discusses the relation of problem to solution in *Difference and Repetition*. He posits the question as 'the genesis of the act of thinking' and concludes that we need to 'participate in the fabrication of problems' (1994: 158) lest we end up in 'stupidity [...] the faculty of false problems' (ibid.: 159).[11] We will later return to the problem–solution matrix as an overall 'constellation' of state concerns and interventions (Youdell 2005: 252).

Fabricating the problem–solution matrix

Our example of 'solution-rendering', as we earlier called it, is taken from research published by the RIPPLE project (Randomised Intervention of Pupil Peer-led Sex Education). It is chosen for two different sorts of reason. First, it addresses solutions to the above problems of sex and sex education: it is Official Science addressing Official Sex. Second, it is an example of a kind of quantitative research that is increasingly being promoted by governments (UK and US in particular) as a 'scientific' approach to educational research (Lather 2004b). We aim to examine aspects of the 'solution' as well as the research quality of its production, relating both back to the relation of 'problem' and methods that are *a priori* channelled towards the rhetorics of 'what works?'

The problem-as-given

Most of the published accounts of the RIPPLE project repeat some version of the government mantra about social exclusion, or the UK concern that teenage pregnancy rates are the highest in Western Europe, that sexually transmitted infections are rising, and the age of first sex falling (e.g. Stephenson *et al.* 2004). The solution is hypothesised to be improving sex education, in RIPPLE's case by devising peer-led sex education strategies and comparing effectiveness with a control group of conventional teacher-led sex education provision. Such effectiveness has a number of indicators but the 'primary outcome' at the end of the research will be the 'cumulative incidence of termination of pregnancy by 19–20 years' (Stephenson *et al.* 2004: 340). Official Science picks up the problem as defined by Official Sex and sets off in search for Best Practice, though it is interesting that the project acronym coyly elides the 'S' for Sex. Thus far, they conclude that peer-led sex education is a 'promising way forward' (Medical Research Council press release, 23 July 2004). There is an obvious universalism in this quest, a one-size-fits-all assumption that is only lightly hedged around in the RIPPLE accounts. The unspoken social theorem is: if all the world did peer-led sex education 'teenage pregnancy' would decrease.

If we look elsewhere in RIPPLE, the conceptual doubts grow. In Bonell *et al.* we are told that the research 'develops hypotheses on the relation between socio-economic and educational dimensions of social exclusion by examining whether dislike of school and socio-economic disadvantage are associated with cognitive/risk measures' (Bonell *et al.* 2003: 871).

Two major concepts are operationalised in this study. Added together, they make a third. The first is the notion of 'alienation from education'. The second is the idea of 'socio-economic disadvantage'. The third is 'social exclusion', to which 'teenage pregnancy' may contribute. But when we look behind the statistics, we find that the indicator of 'disadvantage' is solely 'self-reported housing tenure' (ibid.: 872). Those pupils reporting that they lived in rented accommodation were counted as 'disadvantaged', the rest were not. The 12 per cent of respondents who didn't know were excluded. On what definition of 'science' can such a reduction be justified? As for 'alienation from education', there is a slippage from 'school' to 'education', and the revelation that 'alienation', a powerful but contested notion in sociological literature (they cite but do not discuss Willis's notion of alienation, 1977), is based on a single question – 'do you like school?' To be exact those who disagreed or strongly disagreed with the statement 'I like school' were 'alienated from education', the rest were not. In this one-stop tick-box sociology the notion of 'social exclusion' is treated as the unproblematic adding up of the first two 'concepts', although it is highly polemical and imprecise, as are all political slogans. In effect, the researchers buy the government's rhetoric of the problem and the targeted solution. They aim to connect these two things through a statistical performance teetering on the conceptual pinheads which found their 'science'. Such extreme reductionism and determinism cannot amount to a secure base on which to build comparisons, however sophisticated the statistical superstructure. It is also interesting how the broad, conceptual and contested assumptions about 'alienation', 'disadvantage', and 'exclusion' come to rest on the tiny props of two questions answered in class by pupils, in social contexts that were very different, where not everyone responded, or responded under the same conditions, or even took the task seriously – as the same group of researchers elsewhere acknowledge (Strange *et al.* 2002). Then that reductionism is followed by a remarkable inflationism, with the authors concluding that '... *alienation* from education may be a particularly important dimension of *exclusion* in the determination of *teenage pregnancy*' (Bonell *et al.* 2003: 876, our emphasis). Such a move then makes schools liable for pregnancy (the Missing Father!), and perhaps explains the recent astonishing moves of the Department of Health in proposing that league tables of teen pregnancies per school catchment might be a 'lever for change' (*Telegraph* 2005).

At any rate, we've already seen how complicated the notion of 'teenage pregnancy' is, for all its apparent self-evidence. Now we can see how simplistic and wildly extrapolative is the inflation of like/dislike school, and rent/own in relation to fattening up 'concepts' such as alienation and disadvantage for the turkey of 'social exclusion'. The statistics in the middle are irrelevant: the argument begins and ends in nonsense.

Number-bending

RIPPLE offers a table of results as objective indicators of research outcomes. It reports the results of an extensive survey of secondary school pupils on their preferences in relation to the organisation of sex education in school (Table 5.1)

The researchers concluded that '*[a]nalysis of the data ... showed that the majority of the girls and about 1/3rd of the boys, would like some or all of their*

Table 5.1 Numbers (%) of boys and girls who reported that they would prefer their sex education in single-sex or mixed-sex classes (n = 1595 girls and 1752 boys)

	Girls	(%)	Boys	(%)
Single sex	527	(34)	263	(17)
Mixed sex	634	(41)	1033	(65)
Both	378	(25)	298	(19)

sex education to be delivered in single-sex groups' (Strange *et al*. 2003b: 201, our stress). Their article in *The Lancet* is more specific, in one sense, but then slips to a more partial summary. Here, they report that 54.9 per cent of the girls and 35.5 per cent of the boys 'would have liked some or all of their sex education to be in single sex groups' (Stephenson *et al*. 2004: 343). Later in the piece, the 'some or all' qualifier disappears: 'Sex education failed to meet the needs of some pupils – *many* [our stress] wanted SRE to be delivered in single sex groups ...' (ibid.: 345). 'Many' is not usually deployed as a descriptor of a minority, i.e. 34 per cent of girls and 17 per cent of boys. We speculate that the 'many' may relate to a felt need to explain why sex education currently seems not to be 'working' in either control or intervention groups. The outcomes are acknowledged to be 'generally modest' (ibid.: 345). Based on previous work (Frankham 1998), we suggest this may be explained by the similarities between the 'intervention' and the 'control' approaches to sex education in terms of objectives and content – protection from unwanted pregnancy and STIs predominates (2004: 339). These sessions may have been peer-'delivered', but they were designed by adults, with adult concerns in mind. Perhaps both groups got the 'placebo'.

On the basis of the same figures in the table, the research could also have 'analysed' the data very differently. Playing the 'some or all' game from the other end we can equally argue that: *'2/3rds (66 per cent) of the girls and more than 3/4ths (84 per cent) of the boys would like some or all of their sex education to be delivered in mixed-sex groups'* (our emphasis).

The conclusion is unavoidable. When the researchers went on to claim that '[t]he views of young people (...) clearly endorse the call (...) for more sex education with girls to be delivered in single-sex groups' (2003a: 213), they were clearly wrong. Indeed, if both statements about percentages wanting single-sex or mixed-sex teaching are admissible and yet contradictory then logically neither can be said to be true.

The implications for such research 'findings' in a policy context of 'what works?' are clearly dangerous. This kind of research is designed to produce a decisionistic text. Do this? Or that? It offers 'answers' to 'problems', and careless policy-makers could easily be deceived into thinking that complicated questions had been satisfactorily if expensively resolved.[12] Instead, a prejudicial arithmetic seems to have been combined with illicit extrapolation to reach a conclusion that the authors may already have had in mind.

Rhetorical gerrymandering

Was there evidence that such prejudices were otherwise evident in the research texts? We turn now to a brief deconstruction of some aspects of the *Gender and Education* article, and suggest a kind of rhetorical gerrymandering.

The research team want to base their research on the 'expressed needs' of young people rather than the normative definitions of need produced by researchers and experts (Forrest *et al.* 2004: 338). One of the authors has written elsewhere about the need to 'allow the voices of research participants to be heard above the (generally) louder voice of the researcher's own' (Oakley 2000: 21). Yet they happily 're-interpret' those expressed needs into normative definitions when it suits their argument. The qualitative data from focus group discussions is interpreted to suggest that whatever girls and boys say about single-sex and mixed-sex classes, their reported experiences would really suggest that single-sex provision would better suit the girls. Here are examples of that privileging of researcher interpretation over pupil voice. 'Although both boys and girls described potential advantages of working with the opposite sex in mixed-sex groups, *these tended not to reflect their experiences*' (2003: 206, our emphasis). Although boys 'were more positive than girls about having sex education in mixed-sex classes, *their descriptions of mixed-sex classes were mostly very negative*' (ibid.: 205, our emphasiss). In both cases the 'voices' were mistaken. The researchers knew better. In addition, views regarded by the researchers as 'surprising' (ibid.: 211) were explained away via *post-hoc* rationalisation. For example, a majority of girls had opted for some or all of 'mixed' classes. This was rationalised in the following terms: '... girls are willing to compromise their own needs in order to create classroom conditions that will be of benefit to boys' (ibid.: 211). No evidence for this essentialist claim was given. A moralising tone was also adopted: 'In general, boys did not take responsibility for classroom disruption' (ibid.: 206). This tone was even strengthened a few pages later, by which time 'none' of the boys would take that responsibility (ibid.: 211).

It is also interesting to see how gender differentiation is worked up in the researchers' analysis. The boys are held to perform stereotypically, 'to conform to particular forms of (heterosexual) masculinity'(ibid.: 211). The girls, by contrast, 'talk more openly and focus on informational issues': a gender-neutral assumption. They were naturally inclined to want information, avoid joking, and be sensible. The analysis then develops a dichotomy whereby a gender differentiation is established between boys and girls:

[male/female]
joking/serious
disruptive/attentive
sexist/neutral
hurting/damaged
(etc.)

There are a number of occasions when the account seems to inflate potential
or actual hurt to the girls, as when a girl reports two occasions when boys were
'messing about, like trying to get your bra undone'. She had not minded that much
as long as 'they don't touch you'. 'If they touch I just turn round and hit them.'
This was reported as 'experiences of physical and sexual assault' and, further,
to be 'part of their everyday school experience'. Similarly, there is a neglect of
data that undermines the simple dichotomy, as when boys do reflect critically on
their behaviour, on the difficulties of sex education lessons, and the psychology
behind the problem: '... some people [boys] are too scared so they cover that up
by being noisy and disrupt the class'. The essentialist dichotomy, of course, is
performative: it helps construct the need for separate sex education of the sexes.
An example of this kind of RIPPLE reading of the boys' contributions can be seen
in the following extract:

[the topic is about getting pregnant]
G[irl]: They haven't got so much to worry about, have they?
I[nterviewer]: Do you think that's true, boys?
B[oy]: No.
G: No, but you don't have to get pregnant. If you get caught being pregnant,
then you gonna get ...
G: Yeah, in serious trouble.
B: We're going to get in trouble.
G: Not as much trouble as us, because just think if we hadn't had the baby...
we're not allowed the baby, we've got to have an abortion or something like
that.

(ibid.: 209)

The passage is interesting to us because it encapsulates an aspect of our
interpretation of the Pregnant Teenager. The girls mark the space of the Missing
Father who 'doesn't have to get pregnant'. Equally the boy resists that expulsion
– 'We're going to get into trouble'. The girls evaluate the different degrees of
'trouble' involved. The boy's contribution to this discussion is dismissed by the
RIPPLE researchers as merely 'reactive', its motivation being 'to interject in order
to disagree' (ibid.: 209). Notions of voice were therefore invoked, differentially
listened to, and sometimes muffled.

Overall, a strange set of displacements is evident in relation to 'pupil voice'.
The authors want to hear what young people have to say, via survey and focus
group. When the discussions suggest that the survey results did not 'really' reflect
what they ought to have said, i.e. mixed-sex sex education is quite difficult in
all sorts of ways, they want both to deny the context within which this data was
generated, and then deny the facts of the survey. They don't, then, take the figures
as reflecting what young people 'really think' and they engage in a naïve reporting
of the girls' voices when it suits their arguments as if voices can somehow
communicate an unmediated, context-neutral 'truth'.

The interpretations we have made above suggest that the researchers knew the answers they were looking for. Added to the manipulation of the table, it seemed that an objective, 'scientific' approach was more of a masquerade than the 'reality' it purported to be.[13] Together, these moves constitute a version of what Spanier has called 'scientific sexism' (Spanier 1991: 330). There were, therefore, elements of the 'science' in these accounts that expressed reductionism, determinism, essentialism, and some unduly selective presentation of the figures and their meanings. We do not wish to claim that such impurities are entirely avoidable in any inquiry or any paradigm, but the official discourse on educational research as a 'new science' makes just such claims on the basis of an objectivity and a scientific comparability that, as we've seen, turns out to be problematic in places, prejudicial in others, and absurd in some. All these reductive and simplifying moves are inevitable for research that accepts government definitions and targets as given.

'Sciencing' educational research

> Driven by the performance goals inherent in standards-based reforms, they seek a working consensus on the challenges confronting education, on what works in what contexts and what doesn't, and on why what works does work. Simply put, they seek trustworthy, scientific evidence on which to base decisions about education.
>
> (Shavelson and Towne 2002: 22)

Finally, some more general thoughts about the relation of sex, science and educational research. In *The Disorder of Things*, Dupré has argued against what he takes to be the essentialism, determinism and reductionism with which certain crude versions of 'Science' invest thinking about social meanings. He identifies 'scientism' and 'mathematicism' as 'a mystifying veneer [which] will sometimes serve to conceal the banality of what is offered as scientific wisdom' (1993: 224). He identifies a persistent Cartesianism in attempts to extend 'so-called scientific thinking into the Social', although his targets are different from ours in this paper – he had in mind the 'neuro-Cartesianism' of brain science and socio-biology. Coming from a very different philosophical tradition, Deleuze has made similar criticisms, especially against a normative science based on the philosophical notion of the Same. His basic argument is against forms of question construction as well as the search for universalistic and simplistic solutions that suppress the nature of differences. Offering a 'post-realist' (ir)resolution, Lather combines critical social science with elements of poststructuralist and late realist thinking, and also inveighs against the simplistic scientism that invests the sorts of research we have been criticising (Lather 2004a,b).[14] The research we have examined can be criticised from all those perspectives, in terms of constructing problems, rendering solutions, as well as producing the requisite *eureka* of 'what works?'

The 'problem' and the 'solution' of sex education in relation to social ills such as 'teenage pregnancy rates' are caught in a pseudo-scientific frame. MacLure describes that current movement as characterised by a 'rage for clarity, transparency and certainty of outcomes' (MacLure 2005: 394). The resurrection of such positivistic approaches as 'Best Science', despite all the unanswered criticisms that led to its first demise in the 1960s and 70s, constitute a kind of Zombie Positivism, feeding in this case on the virtual body of the 'Pregnant Teenager'. Far from being a set of robust comparisons of real outcomes, the surface rhetorics, on which media and populist accounts rely, disguise a whole series of substitutions, displacements, condensations and antagonisms – the Errant Daughter, the Missing Father, the State as Father, the odd synergy of pornography and morality in mobilising 'concern', and so on. That last point is so culturally familiar and yet neglected that it bears exemplification. Recently, the *Sunday Mirror* (29 August 2005) portrayed 'sickening scenes' of holiday debauchery by young Brits, complete with 11 exposed nipples, nude photographs of simulated sex and the demure apology that much was 'too explicit to show'. Morality, of course, was not neglected: 'what would their parents say?' Titillation and tutelation combined. That 'tits 'n' tuts' dynamic is necessary to the recurrence of both problem and solution, especially in that it suppresses history in favour of a certain version of narrow (im)morality, in a kind of statistical neo-Victorianism that constructs the Pregnant Teenager as a pharmakon that is both Madonna and whore.[15] In particular, that neo-Victorianism is caught in the tensions between a largely pornographic media and its 'economy of titillation' and a prudish if hypocritical official morality to which media and politicians also subscribe (Irigaray 1994: ix). In that sense, the shenanigans at the *Spectator* that we earlier reported are emblematic rather than trivially amusing. Each immoral/moral moment is necessary to the dynamic of the other. In this way, the definition of the problem, the stipulation of the solution, and the a priori identification of the methodology that will determine 'effectiveness' provide a kind of discursive veneer wherein oversimplification, reduction and determinism can be brought to play both in order to advocate a 'rational' response to the 'crisis' and to ensure that less comfortable options are excluded (e.g. acknowledging the tight and enduring correlation between poverty and teen pregnancy). Such an epistemology seeks both to fix problem and solution in simple linear associations, and to propel that matrix through a series of unacknowledged recurrences as manifestations of 'panic' (Hall 1980), 'hysteria' (Stronach and Morris 1994), 'rage' (MacLure 2005) and 'frenzy' (Lather 2004a). These are all effects of the scapegoating ritual.

In addition, the surface lamination of problem and solution depends on the suppression or erasure of a whole range of discrepant 'facts of life' and motivations. The impregnating teenager largely disappears. So too does any discourse on sex/sex education/pregnancy as positive and desirable. 'Sex' becomes 'pregnancy', with a few gestures in the direction of 'positive relationships' – usually heavily skewed towards 'how to say no'. And Teenage Pregnancy becomes an economic as well as a moral concern, a matter of wasted productivity in an age when 'societies and economies have become ever more dependent on skills and knowledge' (Department of Health 1999: 7). In New Labour rhetorics the ultimate immorality is to *appear* to be unproductive. What is performed in these various mobilisations is a kind of virtual 'bio-power' (Foucault 1990) whereby the state can represent itself (to itself as much as to others) as organising forms of vernance linked to productivity. Thus the discursive veneer makes invisible a series of contesting discourses and explanations. Indeed, such is the simplicity of the schema that, here as elsewhere, it is the emic power of international league tables (Stronach 1999) that determine the moral scale of the 'problem' (twice as much as…) and the urgency of a 'solution' (halved by…). These normative scales constitute a new auditable morality, expressed within the rubrics of 'effective' education, and expressible as league tables – even, as we saw for Teen Pregnancy rates.

Our argument has been that this statistically constructed morality is highly patriarchal in its presentations of problem and solution, and it is a deep irony that the fabricating of 'solutions' within this frame (e.g. by Strange *et al.*) should presume itself to be 'feminist' and emancipatory (see Lather 2004b). In effect, 'sex education' becomes an impossible object, forever rehearsing its own postponement – as the sexual act, the sexual relationship – in a series of paradoxical educational events that exhibit, inhibit and prohibit its subject matter.[16] Little wonder that it 'does not work' since it is far from clear what it is supposed to be doing, educationally speaking. Its essentially recursive nature also ensures that educational debate on this subject – and many others caught in the media-state complicity – is in the UK a 'stuck discourse'.[17]

But we wish to end on a different and more culturally specific note. It seems that the research/policy discourse we have been interrogating, with research an acquiescent female partner (no Errant Daughter, she) to the dominant male of government, offers an instructive series of defining characteristics. As an example of 'scientism' it exhibited:

1 *Gestures imitative of Science*, especially through a statistically validated normativity, invoked in order to provide 'correct' answers based on simplistic questions that were political 'givens' (Hayek 1952; Stenmark 2001).

2 *'Mathematicism' as a validating cover*, a manifestation of Dupré's 'fetishistic reverence' (1993: 167), and therefore the apparition of the 'robust' findings of a 'hard' science. It also related to a 'new kind of medicine [which] made subjectively reportable states, such as pleasure, of relatively little scientific interest'. Pleasure and desire play no part in its therapeutic moves (Laqueur 1990: 188; Furedi 2004).

3 *Educational research posited as a future Science*, a way forward that is part of a future fantasy of the Grand March of Science, alleged to be achieved in Medicine, and increasingly powerful in Nursing, Social Work/Care and Education. This is 'redemptive scientism' at last (Stenmark 2001; Oakley 2000; Lather 2004b).

4   *An imperialistic nature*, dismissive of alternatives and criticisms, what Arendt called 'a dogmatic absolutizing of a special area' (1970: 124); as well as a willingness to let power decide arguments,[18] in addition to determining what will count as 'problems' and how their 'solutions' ought properly to be sought.

5   *An aspect of 'shoddy production*,' as we have seen, in terms of the 'solution' we have examined. Yet at the same time, an assertion of the formulaic, of production over craft, of science over subjectivity

6   *A matter of public sentimentality*, promoted by the 'tabloidisation' of the discourse, and its reduction to scare stories, moral panics and policy hysterias (Kingori *et al.* 2004: 122; Stronach and Morris 1994). And also the romanticism of a 'peer-led' initiative in which the young learn to save themselves.

All of this is a denial of what Kundera called in relation to social and political life in general, 'shit' (1984: 243). He meant by that the untidiness and uncertainty of the social, its indetermination and lack of hygiene, order, and predictability. Its serendipity. But we can offer some conceptual purchase on this disorder. The constellation of these six factors is familiar to a certain sort of aesthetic – 'enchanted by the consonance of [its] own system' (Arendt 1970: 123). 'What works?' is a rendering of complicated questions into oversimplicities and a schooling of answers to decisionistic banalities. At the same time these reductions can be paraded as both 'Science' and the most absolute common sense, even if that is no sense at all. They constitute the 'relation of pseudo-science to science in the modern mass age' (ibid.: 122). As Scruton, Arendt, Greenberg, Kundera and Adorno would all attest, from across a broad political spectrum, these features listed above are defining characteristics of *kitsch* rather than science. What we have been examining, then, is *educational research as 'scientific' kitsch*. This new Education Research of Science (EROS, of course) constructs reality in a problem/ solution matrix wherein sex has to be represented as 'parodic [...] beyond the ethical subject in relation to its sexual conduct to a little sign-slide between *kitsch and decay'* (Kroker and Kroker 1988: 96, their stress). As Lyotard noted a quarter of a century ago (in 1979), such an ambition towards 'realism' 'always stands somewhere between academicism and kitsch' and reflects an absurd demand for 'correct' images, 'correct narratives' – a demand for 'reality' that is always prefaced by an insistence on 'unity, simplicity, communicability etc.' (Lyotard 1986: 75). And, in 2005, here we still are.[19]

Finally, how are we to respond to the emergence of educational research as scientific kitsch? We need to see both the funny and the serious side of this social phenomenon, and it is for this reason that we earlier labelled its odd combination of fascism and farce, 'farcism' (Stronach *et al.* 2002b). Kundera illustrates this kind of totalitarian kitsch in his early writings on communist Czechoslovakia:

Kitsch causes two tears to flow in quick succession. The first tear says 'How nice to see children running on the grass!' The second tear says: 'How nice to be moved, together with all mankind, by children running on the grass!'

(1984: 244)

Let *our* first tear say: 'How nice to teach effectively!' And the second one say: 'How nice to be seen to make a Science of 'peer-led' Sex Education available to all!'[20]

As Kundera concludes: 'It is the second tear that makes kitsch kitsch'. That is, the fantasy of a simple universalism available as Best Practice for Virtual Outcomes which are, in this instance, improvements in 'teen pregnancy' international league table positions. But perhaps the last, and also the best, word on the new kitsch science should be left to Oscar Wilde, and his epitaph for the death of the unfortunate heroine in *The Old Curiosity Shop*.[21]

A man needs a heart of stone not to laugh at the death of Little Nell.

Notes

1   The research consisted of a national evaluation of inter-agency initiatives designed to address (amongst other things) rates of teenage pregnancy by offering improved sex and health education in primary schools. The evaluation reported in 2003 (Stark *et al.* 2003).

2   For example, 'School for Sex', *Sunday Times* 16 April 2004; 'Oral sex lessons to cut rates of teenage pregnancy', *Observer* 9 May 2004; 'School. For sex', *Sunday Times* 16 May 2004; 'Schools fail to hold back surge of sexual diseases', *Observer* 25 July 2004; 'Increase in teenage pregnancies', *Guardian* 12 November 2004; 'Abortions for under-15s top 1000', *Sunday Times* 20 February 2005;'If we leave sex education to parents alone, many teenagers will suffer', *Observer* 29 May 2005; 'Teenage kicks', *Observer* 14 August 2005; 'Hannah White gave birth to a baby in the middle of her GCSEs', *Guardian* 17 September 2005.

3   For the same sorts of moral panic concerns re South Africa, see Macleod (1999). For a similar scepticism about the statistical evidence see also Burghes and Brown (1995).

4   This paper in an earlier form was a keynote address to the British Educational Research Association conference, Manchester 2004. A questioner criticised such representations as ignoring the actual individual tragedies that might lie behind these statistics. But this aspect of the critique is not directed at individuals at all: it looks at and criticises the statistical manipulation that can be skewed towards a declaration of 'moral panic' or a prompt to 'policy hysteria'. It is interested in how government and media 'work up' such a generalised political response. Our concern is not teenage pregnancy as such, but 'teenage pregnancy' as an official construct of government and media.

5   Edwards *et al.* use the notion of 'fabrication' to acknowledge that discourse is always a rhetorical achievement. We suspect that they would regard our use of that term in this article to be more 'ideological' than they would desire, and they would be right.

6   *The Sun* 23 May 2005.

7   The antiquity of these fears, according to Foucault, is impressive. Galen, in his tract 'On the usefulness of the parts of the body' at least asked a positive question about

sex and sex education: 'Why is a very great pleasure coupled with the exercise of the generative parts?' (cited Foucault 1990: 107).

8 They cite St Anthony, as quoted by Pope Pius XI in 1929, not without what seems a disguised relish: 'So great is our misery and our disposition to sin that … a good father, when talking to his son on a matter of such insidiousness, should be mindful not to go into details … so as not to inflame the fire in the innocent and tender heart of the child instead of extinguishing it' (cited p. 35).

9 If that seems too much, consider the *Guardian* report of 17 September 2005. Paula [mother] recalls visiting a chemist with her [pregnant] daughter in school uniform, and seeing how badly she was treated by the assistant, 'That's when I realised just what a bad press teenage mums get.'

10 Non-UK readers might wish to note that the recent past editor of the *Spectator*, Boris Johnson MP, had to resign as editor following publicity about an affair, concerning which he had lied to the then (2004) Conservative leader. Meanwhile one of the owners confessed to an affair with the then Home Secretary, David Blunkett, who eventually had to resign. Unusually, Blunkett claimed paternity of at least one of the owner's children. Perhaps literalising the notion of the State as Father? Meanwhile again, the same owner was discovered to have had a further affair with a married journalist for the paper, the well-known columnist Simon Hoggart. It is clear, then, why the *Spectator* is interested in sex, but less clear where the family values come in.

11 Maggie MacLure has also criticised EPPI-style reviewing as 'clarity bordering on stupidity' (2005).

12 These interpretations were contested by S. Gorard (2004). His principal argument in relation to the above was that the call for more single-sex education was justified, since presumably all teaching was mixed-sex. The article makes it clear that there was single-sex teaching as well. The response (Stronach 2004) agreed that it 'would be possible […] to work out whether students wanted more single-sex education than they currently got, but that was not a line explored by the [Strange *et al.*] article, and therefore neither was it by myself. I sought merely to deny that the table "showed" what the authors claimed.'

13 As was made clear in the BERA plenary presentation on which this account builds, we offer these criticisms of these specific articles, and make no comment on the qualities of the rest of the RIPPLE study. No doubt, a broader investigation of RIPPLE might seem to be necessary, given the weaknesses reported here, but that is not our current purpose.

14 These are not uncommon criticisms. Hannah Arendt made a parallel attack on 'pseudo-science' (1970: 122). De Certeau offers similar criticism, although of course both were criticising 'positivism' first time round: 'The law, which is given in numbers and data (that is, fabricated by technicians), but presented as the manifestation of the ultimate authority, the "real", constitutes our new orthodoxy, an immense discourse of the order of things' (1986: 207).

15 The virgin/whore dilemma is noted by Youdell (2005) in her empirical study of secondary school female students, for whom 'reputation' is a central issue.

16 An example of that 'prohibition': we produced a case study for the Department of Health. It portrayed explicit but sensibly handled sex education for 10-year-olds. An aspect of the worksheet was included in the study: it was a sketch of an ejaculating erect penis. The Department decided it could not have such a drawing on its website. Nor indeed could the words 'erect penis' penetrate the electronic firewalls of the Teenage Pregnancy Unit. We were told: 'What would happen if the media got hold of it?' (fieldnote)

17 We have written elsewhere about the nature of such 'stuck discourses' in educational debate. See Stronach *et al.* 2002a on the nature of contemporary professionalism.

18   For example David Gough of the EPPI-Centre replied to criticisms such as the above, and those made elsewhere and separately by MacLure and Torrance, with the threat of quasi-legal action. The free and open debate that ought to characterise research – and science – is quickly subordinated to more coercive strategies, 'totalitarian' in effect (Kundera 1984: 245).

19   It is worth reminding ourselves of Lyotard's prescience: 'The decision makers, however, attempt to manage these clouds of sociality according to input/output matrices, following a logic which implies that their elements are commensurable and that the whole is determinable. They allocate our lives for the growth of power. In matters of social justice and of scientific truth alike, the legitimation of that power is based on its optimising the system's performance – efficiency. The application of this criterion to all of our games entails a certain level of terror, whether soft or hard: be operational (that is commensurable) or disappear' (Lyotard 1986: xxiv). Whether we should solemnise such totalising farce with the descriptor of 'soft terror' is another matter.

20   The Teacher Training Agency in England has a manager called Head of Effective Practices. In common with most such government agencies in the UK, the TTA is being renamed and rebadged at the moment. It will be called the Teacher Development Agency.

21   Cited by Roger Scruton (2004).

References

Allen, L. (2004) Beyond the birds and the bees: constituting a discourse of erotics in sexuality education, *Gender and Education*, 16(2), 151–67.

Arendt, H. (1970) *Men in dark times* (London: Jonathan Cape).

Bonell, C. (2004) Why is teenage pregnancy conceptualized as a social problem? A review of quantitative research from the USA and UK, *Culture, Health and Sexuality*, 6(3), 255–72.

Bonell, C., Strange, V., Stephenson, J., Oakaley, A., Copas, A., Forrest, S., Johnson, A. and Black, S. (2003) Effect of social exclusion on the risk of teenage pregnancy: development of hypotheses using baseline data from a randomised trial of sex education, *J. Epidemiol. Community Health*, 57, 871–6.

Burghes, L. and Brown, M. (1995) *Single lone mothers: problems, prospects and policies* (London: Policy Studies Institute).

Butler, J. (1993) *Bodies that matter: on the discursive limits of 'sex'* (London: Routledge).

Carol, L. (1983) *The ostrich position: sex, schooling and mystification* (London: Writers' and Researchers' Collective).

Center for AIDS Prevention (1996) Does sex education work? University of California (accessed at www.caps.ucsf/sexedtext.html, 5 August 2004).

De Certeau, M. (1986) *Heterologies: discourse on the Other* (trans B. Massumi) (Manchester: Manchester University Press).

Deleuze, G. (1994 [1968]) *Difference and repetition* (trans P. Patton) (London: Athlone Press).

Deleuze, G. and Guattari, F. (1977) *Anti-Oedipus* (trans R. Hurley, M. Seem and H. Lane) (New York: Viking).

Department of Health (1999) *Teenage pregnancy*. Report by the Social Exclusion Unit (Cm 4342), June.

Douglas, M. (1984) *Purity and danger: an analysis of the concepts of pollution and taboo* (London: Ark/RKP).

Dupré, J. (1993) *The disorder of things: metaphysical foundations of the disunity of science* (Cambridge, MA: Harvard University Press).

Edwards, R., Nicoll, K., Solomon, N. and Usher, R. (2004) *Rhetoric and educational discourse* (London: RoutledgeFalmer).

Forrest, S., Strange, V. and Oakley, A. (2004) What do young people want from sex education? The results of a needs assessment from a peer-led sex education programme, *Culture, Health & Sexuality*, 6(4) 337–54.

Foucault, M. (1990) *The care of the self: history of sexuality, Vol. 3* (trans R. Hurley) (London: Penguin).

Frankham, J. (1998)Peer education: the unauthorised version, *British Educational Research Journal*, 24(2), 179–93.

Frankham, J. (2006) Sexual antimonies and parent/child sex education: learning from foreclosure, *Sexualities*, 9(2) 236–54.

Furedi, F. (2004) *Therapeutic culture: cultivating vulnerability in an uncertain age* (London: Routledge).

Guttmacher Report on Public Policy (2002) Teen pregnancy: trends and lessons learned (New York), February.

Hall, S. (ed.) (1980) *Culture, media and language* (London: CCCS/Hutchinson).

Hampshire, J. and Lewis, J. (2004) 'The ravages of permissiveness': sex education and the permissive society, *Twentieth Century History*, 15(3), 290–312.

Haraway, D. (1991) A cyborg manifesto: science, technology and socialist feminism in the late 20th century, in *Simians, cyborgs and women: the re-invention of nature* (New York: Routledge) (accessed at www.stanford.edu/dept/APS/Haraway/Cyborg Manifesto, December 2002).

Harrison, L. (2000) Gender relations and the production of difference in school-based sexuality and HIV?AIDS education in Australia, *Gender and Education*, 12(1) 5–19.

Hayek, F. (1952) *The sensory order* (Chicago: Chicago University Press).

Irigaray, L. (1994) *Thinking the difference: for a peaceful revolution* (London: Athlone).

Kellogg, E., Kline, D. and Stepan, J. (1975) *The world's laws and practices on population and sexuality education*, Law and Population Monograph Series 25, (Medford, MA: Fletcher School of Law and Diplomacy).

Kidger, J. (2004) Young mothers delivering school sex education, *Sex Education*, 4(2), 185–97.

Kingori, P., Wellings, K., French, R., Kane, R., Gerresso, M. and Stephenson, J. (2004) Sex and relationship education and the media: an analysis of national, regional newspaper coverage in England, *Sex Education*, 4(2), 111–24.

Kroker, A. and Kroker, M. (eds) (1988) *Body invaders: sexuality and the postmodern condition* (London: Macmillan).

Kundera, M. (1984) *The unbearable lightness of being* (trans M. Heim) (London: Faber & Faber).

Laqueur, T. (1990) *Making sex: body and gender from the Greeks to Freud* (Cambridge, MA: Harvard University Press).

Lather, P. (2004a) Scientism and scientificity in the rage for accountability: a feminist deconstruction, Glimcher Inaugural Lecture, Wexner Center, Ohio State University, March.

Lather, P. (2004b) This is your father's paradigm: government intrusion and the case of qualitative research in education, *Qualitative Inquiry*, 10(1) 15–34.

Lyotard, J.-F. (1986) *The postmodern condition: a report on knowledge* (trans B. Massumi) (Manchester: Manchester University Press) (1st published 1979).

MacLure, M. (2005) 'Clarity bordering on stupidity': where's the quality in systematic review? *J. Education Policy*, 20(4) 393–416.

Moore, L. (2003) 'Billy, the sad sperm with no tail': representations of sperm in children's books, *Sexualities*, 6(3/4), 277–300.

Moore, L., Graham, A. and Diamond, I. (2003) On the feasibility of conducting randomised trials in education: case study of a sex education intervention, *British Educational Research Journal*, 25(5), 673–89.

National Statistics Online Sexual Health (2005) (accessed at www.statistics.gov.uk/cci/ nugget, October).

Oakley, A. (2000) *Experiments in knowing: gender and method in the social sciences* (Cambridge: Polity).

Phoenix, A. (1991) *Young mothers* (Cambridge: Polity Press).

Shavelson, R. and Towne, L. (eds) (2002) *Scientific research in education*, Committee on Scientific Principles for Educational Research (Washington DC: National Academic Press).

Spanier, B. (1991) 'Lessons' from 'nature': gender ideology and sexual ambiguity in biology, in Epstein, J. and Straub, K. (eds) *Body guards: the cultural politics of gender ambiguity* (London: Routledge).

Stark, S. Franks, F., Jarvis, J., Jones, E., Stronach, I. and Wibberley, C. (2003) National Evaluation of Primary School/Primary Care Health Links Initiative, MMU for Department of Health, December.

Stenmark, M. (2001) *Scientism: science, ethics and religion* (Sydney: Ashgate).

Stephenson, J., Strange, V., Forrest, S., Oakley, A., Copas, A., Allen, A., Babiker, A., Black, S., Ali, M., Montiero, H. and Johnson, A. (2004) Pupil-led sex education in England (the RIPPLE study): cluster- randomised intervention trial, *Lancet*, 364(9431), 338–46.

Strange, V., Forest, S., Oakley, A., and RIPPLE study team (2003a) Using research questionnaires with young people in schools: the influence of the social context, *Int. J. of Social Research Methodology*, 6(4), 337–46.

Strange, V., Oakley, A. and Forrest, S. (2003b) Mixed-sex and single-sex education: how would young people like their sex education and why? *Gender and Education*, 15(2), 201–14.

Stronach, I. (1999) Shouting theatre in a crowded fire: 'educational effectiveness' as cultural performance, *Evaluation*, 5(2), 173–93.

Stronach, I. (2004) Reply to Stephen Gorard, *Research Intelligence*, (89), 11–12.

Stronach, I. and Morris, B. (1994) Polemical notes on educational evaluation and the age of 'policy hysteria', *Evaluation and Research in Education*, 8 (1/2), 5–19.

Stronach, I., Corbin, B., McNamara, O., Star, S. and Warne, T. (2002a) Towards an uncertain politics of professionalism: teacher and nurse identities in flux, *Journal of Education Policy*, 17(1) 109–38.

Stronach, I., Halsall, R. and Hustler, D. (2002b) Future perfect: evaluation in dystopian times, in K. Ryan and T. Schwandt (eds) *Exploring evaluator role and identity* (Greenwich, CT: Information Age Publishing).

Tabberer, R., Hall, C., Prendergast, S. and Webster A. (2000) *Teenage pregnancy and choice – abortion or motherhood: influences on the decision* (York: YPS Publishing Services Ltd).

Thomson, R. (2004) 'An adult thing?' Young people's perspectives on the heterosexual age of consent, *Sexualities*, 7(2), 133–49.

Youdell, D. (2005) Sex-gender-sexuality: how sex, gender and sexuality constellations are constituted in secondary schools, *Gender & Education*, 17(3), 249–70.

Chapter 6

Internationalisation, globalisation, and quality audits

An empire of the mind?

Noel Gough

The empires of the future are the empires of the mind.
Winston Churchill, Speech at Harvard University, 5 September 1943[1]

The decline in sovereignty of nation-states... does not mean that sovereignty as such has declined. ...sovereignty has taken a new form, composed of a series of national and supranational organisms united under a single logic of rule. This new global form of sovereignty is what we call Empire.
Michael Hardt and Antoni Negri, *Empire* (2000, pp. xi–xii; emphasis in original)

Empire as concept

I suspect that the term 'empire' is an anachronism to many academics – perhaps especially to those of us who reside in the UK's former colonies and are old enough to remember when 'Commonwealth' displaced 'Empire' in everyday speech.[2] But the theme of empire has also been revived recently, partly in the context of European history (see, e.g., Niall Ferguson, 2003), but more obviously in debates about the role(s) of the United States as imperialist oppressor and/or more-or-less benevolent global superpower (see, e.g., Andrew Bacevich, 2002; Max Boot, 2002). Simon Dalby (2004) notes that in many popular discourses 'America is not supposedly an empire, not like the European states from which its political rhetoric works hard to distinguish it', but he also argues that the global presence of the US navy, the ubiquity of its troop garrisons in many 'independent' nation-states, and its pre-emptive use of military force to impose its political and economic will, 'has finally cut through the taboo on calling America an empire' (p. 1). Understanding US power in terms of empire adds weight to R.B.J. Walker's (1993) long-held view that there is much more to global politics than many contemporary 'international relations' models of competing and cooperating autonomous states seem to suggest. In a world dominated by imperial power, territorial assumptions about sovereignty might not be particularly useful.

Churchill's figure of speech, 'empires of the mind', anticipates a conception of imperialism that avoids territorial assumptions. Michael Hardt and Antoni Negri

(2000) provide an extensive and sophisticated exploration of this concept in their aptly titled monograph, *Empire*.[3] They argue that even the most dominant nation-states have ever-diminishing powers to regulate the flows of capital, technologies and people across national boundaries and that sovereignty now is passing to an amorphous series of regulations and shared processes that exceed the mandates of nation-states and determine the rules for incorporating numerous institutions and peoples into what they simply call 'Empire', which they distinguish from imperialism:

> In contrast to imperialism, Empire establishes no territorial center of power and does not rely on fixed boundaries or barriers. It is a *decentered* and *deterritorializing* apparatus of rule that progressively incorporates the entire global realm within its open, expanding frontiers. Empire manages hybrid identities, flexible hierarchies, and plural exchanges through modulating networks of command. The distinct national colors of the imperialist map of the world have merged and blended in the imperial global rainbow.
>
> (pp. xii–xiii; emphasis in original)

Hardt and Negri (2000) emphasise that they use 'Empire' not as a metaphor, 'which would require demonstration of the resemblances between today's world order and the Empires of Rome, China, the Americas, and so forth, but rather as a *concept*' (p. xiv; authors' emphasis) characterised chiefly by a lack of boundaries: 'Empire's rule has no limits. … No territorial boundaries limit its reign' (p. xiv).[4]

Audit cultures or audit Empire?

A number of recent news items from different countries have led me to speculate that quality assurance in higher education might be becoming – to reiterate Hardt and Negri's (2000) words – 'a *decentered* and *deterritorializing* apparatus of rule that progressively incorporates the entire global realm within its open, expanding frontiers' (p. xii), and that this marks a shift from what Marilyn Strathern (2000) termed 'audit cultures' (plural) to a singular *audit Empire*.

For example, the *Sowetan* (South Africa's largest selling daily newspaper) reported recently that 'The Higher Education Quality Committee of the Council on Higher Education (HEQC) has just signed a memoranda [sic] of understanding with quality assurance agencies in the UK and India'.[5] According to this report, signing the memorandum will enable the three national agencies to exchange information and expertise on, for example, 'key policy documents and operational information' and 'collaboration in joint research of mutual benefit'. Similarly, the executive director of the Australian Universities Quality Agency (AUQA), David Woodhouse (2005), recently publicised 'the signing of a memorandum of cooperation with the Hong Kong Council for Academic Accreditation, and the Malaysian Lembaga Akreditasi Negara exploring the possibility of AUQA assisting it in a review of Malaysian providers' (p. 34). Woodhouse claims that

AUQA is 'acting in the best interests of the overseas operations of Australian universities', but adds that 'we are conscious of "quality imperialism" and must acknowledge that many countries have their own quality assurance systems in place'.

I am familiar enough with the higher education quality agendas in three of the above-named countries/regions (Australia, Hong Kong and South Africa) to wonder what such 'free trade' between national quality agencies might produce (and/or prevent). For example, as Maureen Tam (1999) points out, the Hong Kong Council for Academic Accreditation (HKCAA) 'was set up in 1990 ... to advise on the academic quality of degree courses proposed or offered by *the non-university organisations*' (p. 222; my emphasis). I initially found it a little puzzling that the Australian *Universities* Quality Agency would sign a memorandum of cooperation with a council that accredits non-university courses, given that the Hong Kong agency with the equivalent jurisdiction to AUQA is not the HKCAA but the University Grants Committee. Given that both of the Hong Kong agencies already cooperate with each other and with AUQA as full members of the International Network for Quality Assurance Agencies in Higher Education (INQAAHE),[6] I am also curious as to what additional purposes such a memorandum of cooperation between AUQA and HKCAA might serve. Woodhouse (2004b) regards the establishment of INQAAHE during the 1990s as playing a 'major part' in the development of 'quality assurance as a profession' (p. 78) and notes that: 'In 2002, the Board of INQAAHE formally recognised the emergence of a quality assurance profession, and INQAAHE's role as the professional association for EQAs [external quality agencies]' (p. 79). He also predicted that the 2000s would be 'the decade of international quality' (Woodhouse, 2004b, p. 77). Thus, although Woodhouse disavows AUQA's potential to be an instrument of 'quality imperialism', he perhaps overlooks the possibility that quality professionals might be becoming the apparatus for ruling the global realm of quality in higher education. Nations might well have their own quality assurance systems in place but might also, in effect, be ceding their authority and responsibility to determine quality in their own locations to a global cadre of quality professionals. In other words, quality in higher education internationally will be reduced to that which quality professionals can audit.

I was less surprised by the news that South Africa's HEQC has signed a memorandum of understanding with its UK equivalent. As Nico Cloete *et al.* (2002) demonstrate, in recent years South Africa has received a great deal of advice from other countries on how to establish a national quality assurance system. A.H. and J.F. Strydom (2004) add that South Africa's political and historical ties to the UK and other major education-selling nations created some pressure to conform to their quality assurance practices. However, they also argue that the unique circumstances in which quality assurance systems are being developed in South Africa (and in southern Africa more generally) mean that 'conformity with... quality assurance systems in other countries should not idealistically be accepted as the answer for South Africa' (Strydom and Strydom, 2004, p. 111).

In the remainder of this chapter I explore some ways in which concepts drawn from Gilles Deleuze and Félix Guattari's 'geophilosophy' might be used to analyse 'quality' in contemporary contexts of globalisation, multiculturalism and international communication networks, with particular reference to translating, interpreting and/or 'trading' 'quality' across national, linguistic and cultural borders.

Geophilosophy

Deleuze and Guattari (1987) offer a new critical language for analysing thinking as flows or movements across space, creating concepts such as *nomad, rhizome, assemblage, deterritorialisation,* and *lines of flight* that refer to spatial relationships and to ways of conceiving ourselves and other objects moving in space. Thinking rhizomatically and nomadically destabilises arborescent and sedentary conceptions of knowledge as hierarchically articulated branches of a central stem or trunk rooted in fixed and firm foundations. As Umberto Eco (1984) explains, 'the rhizome is so constructed that every path can be connected with every other one. It has no center, no periphery, no exit, because it is potentially infinite. The space of conjecture is a rhizome space' (p. 57).

In a world of increasingly complex information/communication/knowledge technologies, the space of educational research is also becoming a 'rhizome space'. A rhizome is to a tree as the Internet is to a letter – networking that echoes the hyperconnectivity of the Internet. The structural reality of a tree and a letter is relatively simple: a trunk connecting two points through or over a mapped surface. But rhizomes (see Figure 6.1) and the internet (see the Birch/Cheswick map at http://www.cheswick.com/ches/map/gallery/isp-ssgif, accessed 9 May 2007) are infinitely complex and continuously changing. Imagining knowledge production in a rhizomatic space is particularly generative in postcolonialist educational inquiry because, as Patricia O'Riley (2003) explains: 'Rhizomes affirm what is excluded from western thought and reintroduce reality as dynamic, heterogeneous, and nondichotomous; they implicate rather than replicate; they propagate, displace, join, circle back, fold' (p. 27).

In their last book together, Deleuze and Guattari (1994) ask: *What is Philosophy?* They answer by plotting the 'geography of reason' from pre-Socratic times to the present, and characterise philosophy as the *creation* of concepts through which knowledge can be generated. As Michael Peters (2004) points out, this is very different from the approaches taken by many analytic and linguistic philosophers who are more concerned with the *clarification* of concepts:

> Against the conservatism, apoliticism and ahistoricism of analytic philosophy that has denied its own history until very recently, Deleuze and Guattari attempt [a] geography of philosophy – a history of geophilosophy – beginning with the Greeks. Rather than providing a history, they conceptualise philosophy in spatial terms as *geophilosophy*. Such a conception immediately complicates

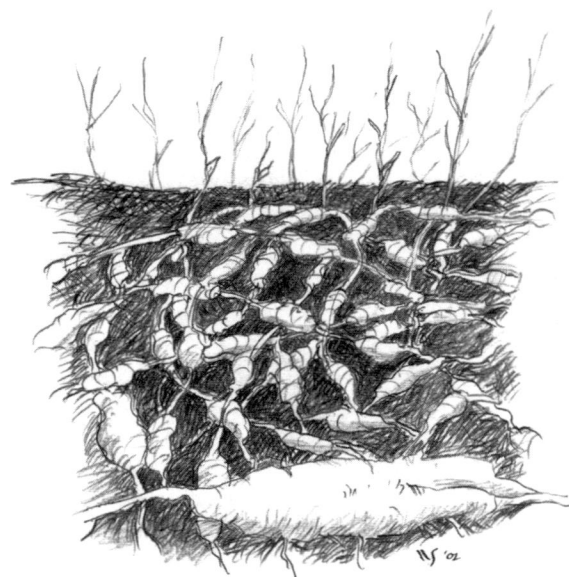

Figure 6.1   A tangle of rhizomes (Image © Warren Sellers, published with permission)

the question of philosophy: by tying it to a geography and a history, a kind of historical and spatial specificity, philosophy cannot escape its relationship to the City and the State. In its modern and postmodern forms it cannot escape its form under industrial and knowledge capitalism. (p. 218)

One of Deleuze and Guattari's (1987) conceptual creations is what they call *mots d'ordre,* usually translated as 'order-words', which are not commands but terms that link implicit presuppositions to social obligations and produce locatable effects:

> We call *order-words*, not a particular category of explicit statements (for example, in the imperative), but the relation of every word or every statement to implicit presuppositions, in other words, to speech acts that are, and can only be, accomplished in the statement. Order-words do not concern commands only, but every act that is linked to statements by a 'social obligation.' Every statement displays this link, directly or indirectly. Questions, promises, are order-words. . . . language is the set of all order-words, implicit presuppositions, or speech acts current in a language at a given time. (p. 79)

Brian Massumi, in his 'Translator's endnote' to Deleuze and Guattari's (1987) *A Thousand Plateaus*, notes that *mot d'ordre* means 'slogan' or '(military) password' in standard French and argues that Deleuze and Guattari use it literally to mean 'word of order', that is, to suggest a command as well as a word that creates a political order (p. 523). Similarly, Robert and Kerry-Ann Porter (2003) suggest that 'order-word' signifies 'the immediate, irreducible and pragmatic relation between *words* and *orders*' (p. 139), which can in turn be viewed in two ways:

1. Words or speech acts are pragmatically implicated in a *social order* or in forms of, what Deleuze and Guattari call, 'social obligation'. These forms of 'social obligation' always presuppose *imperatives* ...
2. Words or speech acts can perform an *ordering function*: that is, they can *imperatively* or immediately change the circumstances in which they are formulated. (p. 139)

To exemplify their first point, Porter and Porter (2003) consider the imperatives presupposed by the 'social obligations' that 'order' the ways in which a PhD student and an examiner perform the *viva*:

Think about the *social-institutional setting* in which the communicative exchange takes place, and the roles the examiner and student are *obligated* to perform in order to make their discourse function in this context. It is *imperative* that the examiner makes judgements relevant to the substantive content of the text under discussion. It is *imperative* that the student exhibits an intimate knowledge of the work she is required to defend. Clearly, all bets would be off if the examiner insisted on asking the doctoral candidate questions concerning her personal life rather than her thesis. Similarly, there would be no pragmatic grounds on which to proceed if the student responded to questions by turning cartwheels around the room. This is just another way of saying that forms of 'social obligation' – that is, the imperatives implied by the social order or social-institutional setting – precede the performative assumption of speech action roles. (pp. 139–40)

Kaustuv Roy (2004) offers a succinct example of the second way in which Porter and Porter (2003) see words relating to orders: 'when the judge pronounces "Guilty", the result is not simple penitence but the *production of the convict* with its own intricate social structure' (p. 304; emphasis in original). Roy (2004) argues that for Deleuze and Guattari language is neither information nor communication but, rather, 'a leaping from order-word to order-word, punctuated by action, as each statement performs an act or an act is performed in the statement ... A word is what a word does or prevents from doing' (pp. 304–5).

If we approach 'quality' as an order-word in educational discourses, then we will not ask what quality *means* but ask how it *works* and what it *does* or *produces* (or prevents) in specific locations.[7] Understanding 'quality' as an order-word might help us understand what national quality agencies are able to 'trade' across national, linguistic and cultural borders – which may be especially significant if such boundaries also designate power differentials.

I explore this speculation further by focusing on examples of the effects of the ordering functions of 'quality' discourses in three different nations, including the auditing processes managed by the Australian Universities Quality Agency (AUQA), the promotion and auditing of 'quality' in both higher education and school education in Hong Kong, and continuing debates about 'balancing quality and equality' in post-apartheid South Africa.

Some effects of auditing quality in Australian universities

The Australian Universities Quality Agency (AUQA) describes itself as 'an independent, not-for-profit national agency that will promote, audit, and report on quality assurance in Australian higher education'.[8] Among other things, AUQA is responsible for 'conducting quality audits of self-accrediting Australian higher education institutions... [and] providing public reports on the outcomes of these audits'. AUQA provides an online glossary which includes stipulative definitions of 'quality' and eight other 'quality' terms, namely, 'quality approval', 'quality assessment', 'quality assurance (QA)', 'quality audit', 'quality control (QC)', 'quality management', 'quality management system (QMS)' and 'quality system'. For example, the AUQA glossary defines 'quality' as:

> Fitness for purpose, where 'purpose' is to be interpreted broadly, to include mission, goals, objectives, specifications, and so on. This is an inclusive definition, as every organisation or activity has a purpose, even if it is not always precisely stated. 'Fitness for purpose' means both that an organisation has procedures in place that are appropriate for the specified purposes, and that there is evidence to show that these procedures are in fact achieving the specified purposes.

AUQA therefore requires each university to prepare a 'performance portfolio', a self-study of the 'fitness' of its procedures for achieving its specified purposes. This portfolio is then scrutinised by an audit panel which may ask further questions of clarification, seek further documentation, and undertake a site visit in which they observe aspects of the university's operations and interview various members of staff. The audit panel eventually prepares a report containing commendations (statements about what the institution is doing well), recommendations (things that need to be done) and, since 2004, affirmations (matters in need of attention that the auditee has already diagnosed).

In the Australian higher education community, 'quality' is thus a word that has created a socio-political order (materialised in AUQA, the activities it 'orders' in universities, and the portfolios and reports these activities produce). Enunciations such as 'quality assurance' and 'quality audit' are pragmatically implicated in forms of social obligation that presuppose imperatives for all of the parties concerned. The roles and actions that AUQA and the universities are obligated to take in order to make their discourse function are implicit presuppositions, but they become more visible when these imperatives and obligations are challenged or ignored, as would also be the case in Porter and Porter's (2003) PhD *viva* scenario, quoted above, if (for example) the examiner *did* ask inappropriate personal questions or the student *did* turn cartwheels around the room in response to the examiner's academic question.

The social order in which communicative exchanges between AUQA and Australian universities take place, and the roles each party is obliged to perform in order to make their discourse function, was challenged by Edith Cowan University (ECU) in 2004. Immediately after AUQA released its report on ECU, the university placed a quarter-page advertisement in the Higher Education Supplement (HES) of *The Australian* newspaper which began with the following claims:

> In the latest audit undertaken by the independent Australian Universities Quality Agency (AUQA), Western Australia's Edith Cowan University (ECU) gained strong endorsement for its strategic focus, reputation and performance across many operational areas.
> **Leading outcome**
> … ECU attained the highest number of commendations of any University audited by AUQA during its three years of operation. And its ratio of commendations to recommendations for improvement is also the best of all Universities so far examined: 23 to 12.[9]

The advertisement included a table that ranked institutions based on the number of commendations each university received from AUQA (see Figure 6.2). The table presents the names of ECU and three other Western Australian universities – the University of Western Australia (UWA), Curtin University and Notre Dame University – in block capitals and bold type, and the numbers of commendations and recommendations received by each of these four universities were also displayed in bold type.

One week later, the HES carried three letters to the editor, grouped in three columns under the common headline, 'Audit comparisons controversy'. Reading from left to right, the first letter was from the Executive Director of AUQA, Dr David Woodhouse (2004a); the second letter was from Dr David Hamilton (2004), Director, Planning and Resource Development, University of Canberra; the third letter was from ECU's Vice-Chancellor, Professor Millicent Poole (2004).

Woodhouse's (2004a) letter refers to ECU's advertisement as 'unfortunate and misleading':

> unfortunate because it purports to use the outcome of the AUQA audit process as a basis for producing comparisons among universities. These audits were not set up for this purpose – in fact quite the converse. Each audit reviews the auditee against its own objectives… Under such circumstances, comparisons become meaningless. The universities themselves expressed repeated concerns

SUMMARY AUQA AUDIT REPORTS		
	Commendations	*Recommendations*
EDITH COWAN	**23**	**12**
Griffith	21	16
Queensland	19	16
UWA	**18**	**21**
James Cook	17	16
Macquarie	17	23
South Australia	16	10
Newcastle	16	19
Southern Queensland	14	22
Australian Maritime College	13	16
Southern Cross	13	18
New England	12	16
Australian Catholic	12	19
Canberra	11	21
CURTIN	**10**	**20**
NOTRE DAME	**10**	**22**
RMIT	10	24
Swinburne	8	18
Adelaide	7	26
Ballarat	6	26

Figure 6.2 Copy of table featured in Edith Cowan University's advertisement in *The Australian*, 3 November 2004, p. 25; capitalised names and bolder numerals are as in original.

that AUQA's audit reports would lead to the media generating league tables, and AUQA promised to attempt to write them in such a way as to discourage this tendency. It is particularly unfortunate therefore that a member of the AVCC [Australian Vice-Chancellors Committee] has chosen to take such an approach. (p. 31)

Woodhouse adds that 'AUQA was conscious that the only area that might lend itself to – admittedly spurious – comparisons would be the numbers of recommendations and commendations' and explains how the ECU advertisement misleads readers by making such comparisons.[10]

Hamilton's (2004) letter begins by supporting Woodhouse's interpretation of the purposes of AUQA's audits:

'Never, never' was the mantra chanted by the inaugural executive director of the Australian Universities Quality Agency, David Woodhouse, as he made his way from university to university a couple of years ago introducing the compulsory audits. Never would the audits be used to rank universities.

That was until last week when Millicent Poole, vice-chancellor of Edith Cowan University, broke ranks with her higher education colleagues and purchased space in the *HES* to publish her rankings of institutions based on the number of commendations each university received in their AUQA report. (p. 31)

I doubt if it was any coincidence that the letters from Woodhouse, Hamilton and Poole were placed alongside a one-and-a-half page feature article, 'Ranking mania reflects distortion of priorities', in which Colin Steele (2004) discusses the scores achieved by Australian universities in *The Times Higher Education Supplement* World University Rankings. Elsewhere in the same issue of *HES*, columnist Dorothy Illing (2004) alludes to these rankings in a very forthright commentary on the ECU advertisement:

Forget the international league ladders: Edith Cowan University has established its own set of quality rankings. And it has already raised the ire of the Australian Universities Quality Agency. Last week the uni took out a big advertisement trumpeting the positive findings of its first audit by AUQA... To demonstrate its success the uni drew up a table ranking the ratio of commendations to recommendations[11] (never mind the new category of affirmations) for all unis audited so far. Of course, ECU was at the top. And by its spurious measures, two competing West Australian unis were highlighted near the bottom. Bit cheeky. The number of recommendations and commendations – the standard reporting format used by AUQA – does not reflect winners and losers. Nor are the reports to be used as rankings. ECU vice-chancellor Millicent Poole should know that. She sits on the AUQA board. (p. 34)

Poole's (2004) letter defends the advertisement by claiming that 'ECU was seriously disadvantaged by the circumstances' of the public release of the AUQA audit report and the subsequent press coverage, 'and felt compelled to defend its reputation'. The circumstances to which she refers include *The Australian* publishing a story (within hours of the AUQA report's public release) 'which focused almost entirely on criticism contained in the report and made no attempt to offset the criticism with a response from ECU'. Poole argues that the advertisement 'was chosen as an effective way of establishing some degree of balance on the public record and responding to public perceptions' and also makes the extraordinary claim that: 'There was no intention to rank other institutions' (p. 31). As Figure 6.2 clearly demonstrates, ranking other institutions is precisely what the ECU advertisement does.

The imperatives implied by the social-institutional setting in which AUQA produces quality audit reports for Australian universities include a social obligation *not* to use the reports to make meaningless comparisons between institutions or to produce spurious rankings. If we use Porter and Porter's (2003) PhD *viva* scenario as an analogy, we could say that Poole has responded to AUQA's report (and media stories based on it) by turning cartwheels around the room – and then vehemently denying that she did so.

The ECU advertisement might itself have performed an ordering function and changed the circumstances in which it was formulated. Hamilton's (2004) response reveals some ambivalence about the 'order' in which AUQA and universities are mutually implicated. For example, he agrees that 'audit commendations and recommendations are meaningful only in the context of the particular institutional quality framework to which they refer' and that 'counting commendations contributes nothing to assessments of institutional quality or quality frameworks' (p. 31). But having asserted that 'counting commendations contributes nothing', Hamilton begins his very next sentence by writing: 'Even if the count of commendations meant something ...'. Is this wishful thinking? Does Hamilton imagine that a 'count of commendations' *could* conceivably mean something? His initial support for AUQA's position shifts ground a little towards the end of his letter:

> An analysis reveals the counts of AUQA commendations have varied over time. There are clear signs of commendation inflation – there has been a steadily increasing trend in the number of commendations ...
>
> Analysing the median number of commendations for each of AUQA's auditor directors shows one auditor has a median number of commendations of nine, compared to another, who has 16 ...
>
> Commendation inflation, auditor impact and the ... oscillations in the number of commendations included in reports all suggest that now is just the right time to audit the auditor – independently. (p. 31)

This 'audit comparisons controversy' provides a snapshot of what 'quality' as an order-word *does* and *produces* and *prevents from doing* in the audit culture of Australian higher education. It has produced a new bureaucracy (AUQA) and produces flurries of intense activity in universities as teams of academics and administrators strive to generate a 'performance portfolio' that demonstrates the 'fitness for purpose' of its plans, policies, procedures, protocols, programmes etc. At the same time it prevents (or at least distracts) these same academics and administrators from other 'quality'-related activities, such as considering the fitness *of* purpose of various university operations. As this example demonstrates, 'quality' in Australian higher education also produces controversy, dissent, and the somewhat bizarre public spectacle of a Vice-Chancellor attempting to deny the undeniable.

Quality effects in Hong Kong

In Hong Kong, 'quality' as an order-word in education produces a number of different effects from those it produces in Australia. As previously noted, two organisations – the Hong Kong Council for Academic Accreditation (HKCAA) and the University Grants Committee (UGC) – identify themselves as quality assurance agencies in higher education, and each performs functions that are different from one another and from AUQA. The HKCAA conducts academic accreditation of degree courses offered by non-university institutions. The UGC is a non-statutory advisory committee responsible for advising the Government of the Special Administrative Region (SAR) of the People's Republic of China on the development and funding needs of higher education institutions in the SAR. For example, the secretary-general of the UGC, Nigel French (1997) describes its roles and functions as follows:

> The UGC in its mission statement pledges to uphold the academic freedom and institutional autonomy of the institutions while at the same time seeking to assure the quality and cost-effectiveness of their education provision, and being publicly accountable for the sums of public money devoted to higher education. (pp. 42–3)

Thus, as Ka Ho Mok (2000) points out, the quality assurance activities driven by the UGC emphasise 'value for money' and attempt to measure the quality of the output (i.e., graduates) and 'value added', that is, 'the value of the output minus that of the input' (p. 158). Control mechanisms introduced by the UGC include Research Assessment Exercises (which, like their UK equivalents, link resource allocation to research performance), Quality-Process Reviews (evaluations of the extent to which universities have institutionalised quality assurance, assessment and improvement systems; see Massy 1997), and Management Reviews (examinations of each university's roles, missions, academic objectives, resource allocation, planning and financial process mechanisms; see Mok 2000).

Quality as value for money also seems to be one of the prime ordering functions of Hong Kong's Quality Education Fund (QEF): 'Formally established on 2 January 1998 with an allocation of HK$5 billion [approx. AUD$800 million], the QEF provides an effective channel for worthwhile projects from the school education sector to be funded'.[12] However, a more significant effect may be that it produces innovation. An exhaustive search of the QEF homepages reveals no stipulative definitions of 'quality'. Rather, it seems to be left largely to applicants for funding to demonstrate that their projects are likely to be 'worthwhile' within a very broad range of parameters. For example, the 2004 Call for Applications/ Guide to Applicants describes the scope of the QEF as follows:

> The Quality Education Fund (QEF) mainly sponsors worthwhile projects that benefit pre-primary, primary, secondary and special education. These projects

should be non-profit-making, pioneering or experimental in nature and aim to further the development of quality education in line with the prevailing education policies in Hong Kong.[13]

The 'prevailing education policies' include a major cultural shift from a highly centralised school education system to one that gives much more autonomy to teachers and school administrators in curriculum matters. Thus, the assessment criteria for QEF proposals foreground school development and teacher/principal professional development as well as cost-effectiveness. These criteria seem to be consistent with interpretations of the QEF's purposes by researchers such as Edmond Law and Maurice Galton (2004), namely, that QEF exists 'to promote and support various forms of teachers' participation in school-based initiatives' (p. 44).

Thus, in the context of Hong Kong's QEF, 'quality' can be seen to be pragmatically implicated in a new socio-political ordering of schooling and new forms of social obligation which presuppose imperatives to 'pioneer', 'experiment', and participate in school-based initiatives.

Quality and equality in South African education discourses

In post-apartheid South Africa, 'quality' can also be seen to be pragmatically implicated in a new socio-political ordering of education and schooling, but here the new forms of social obligation presuppose imperatives toward social *transformation*. Johann Steyn (2004) characterises transformation in South African education as:

- the transformation from a fragmented educational system to a unified system;
- the efforts to remover inequalities and the move towards equal education;
- the shift away from a monocultural educational system;
- the intention to shift from a content based education to Outcomes Based Education;
- the repealing of anti-democratic policies;
- the transformation from a closed society to a more open society;
- the 'catching up' with leaders in the field of education, and
- the intention to create a just system that provides for access to quality education. (pp. 101–2)

A distinctive characteristic of South African discourses of educational transformation is that the enunciation of 'quality' orders conversations around 'equality', and vice versa. For example, Willem Du Plessis (2000) argues that during the apartheid years 'all good quality education was the sole property of schools for Whites, in White residential areas, beyond the reach of non-White students' (p. 65). Similarly, writing in the run-up to the first democratic elections in 1994, Pam Christie (1993) asserts that the pursuit of quality education 'has become a catch cry limiting the influence of Black students on the existing practices of historically privileged schools' (p. 11). Five years after those elections, Ken Hartshorne (1999) insists that little has changed: 'quality education is only a strategy to slam doors in the faces of Black learners' (p. 7). More recently, Steyn (2004) characterises contemporary perceptions of quality and equality in South African education as opposing positions in a 'debate', with some protagonists arguing that 'the quest for quality education is an attempt to maintain standards in White schools and universities and to exclude Black learners', and others arguing that 'the eradication of gross inequalities is not a viable option in the light of the hard [economic] realities' (p. 106).

Thus, in South Africa, the enunciation of 'quality' not only orders conversations around 'equality' but also orders these concepts into an inverse or adversarial relationship. For example, Steyn (2004) describes 'balancing quality and equality' as a 'dilemma' and as 'a kind of juggling act' (p. 97), which implies that increasing one's commitment to quality *necessarily* reduces one's commitment to equality (and vice versa). This is not the case in a number of other nations from which South Africa has made policy borrowings, where equality (or equity) is understood to be a *necessary condition* of quality.

South Africa's discourses of social transformation produce a socio-political ordering of education and schooling that emphasises economic and racial equity, which in turn leads to a positioning of equality as being in tension with quality. This contrasts with 'equality' in nations such as Australia and the UK, which produces 'orders' (such as policy directives) on equity issues that extend beyond race and class to include gender, sexuality, disability, etc. In Australia it is relatively easy to demonstrate that (say) gender equity is an *achievable condition* of quality education, rather than something that is economically or socially 'beyond the reach' of the majority of learners.

Conclusion

'Quality' (as a Deleuzean 'order-word') produces different effects in different locations. For example, the deployment of 'quality' in the audit discourse of Australian higher education clearly produces very different effects from its mobilisation in debates about 'quality versus equality' in South Africa's social transformation. One implication of this analysis is that when we engage in conversations about 'quality' across national, linguistic and cultural borders, we cannot be content with stipulative definitions. It would be nonsense to say that *here* quality 'means' fitness for purpose, or that *there* quality 'means' value for money, or that somewhere else quality 'means' social transformation. Rather, we need to understand how quality works and what it does, what it produces, and what it prevents from being done in specific locations through a more determined scrutiny of its locatable effects. Such scrutiny should perhaps also precede any 'trading' of quality assurance artefacts such as policy documents and operational information and might help us to resist 'quality imperialism'.

Notes

1 The Churchill Centre, http://www.winstonchurchill.org/i4a/pages/index.cfm?pageid =424, accessed 5 September 2005.
2 For example, from 1905 to 1957 Australians celebrated Empire Day on 24 May (Queen Victoria's birthday), although in my own childhood it was better known as 'Cracker Night' and was the main annual event for releasing fireworks. It was renamed British Commonwealth Day from 1958 to 1965, after which it effectively disappeared. In fact, it was renamed Commonwealth Day from 1966 and moved to 11 June (the present Queen's 'official' birthday, which is recognised in most Australian states by a public holiday on the second Monday in June).
3 I want to record my admiration for Hardt and Negri's restraint in resisting any temptation to expand (or add a subtitle) to *Empire*. Their use of this single word intensifies the persuasiveness of a very lengthy (496 pp.) argument.
4 Hardt and Negri explicitly acknowledge Deleuze and Guattari's (1987) *A Thousand Plateaus* as a significant influence on their thinking, which is evident in their references to *deterritorialisation,* and their creation of Empire as a *concept* rather than as a metaphor.
5 *Sowetan*, 14 March 2005, p. 8 (no byline).
6 http://www.inqaahe.org/, accessed 17 November 2004.
7 Several recent studies demonstrate the generativity of this approach to analysing the semiotics of institutions such as schools and universities; see, for example, Roy (2003) and the recent special issue of *Educational Philosophy and Theory* 36 (3) 2004 on Deleuze and Education.
8 Unless stated otherwise, all quotations pertaining to AUQA are taken from its website at www.auqa.edu.au, accessed 16 November 2004.
9 *The Australian*, Higher Education Supplement, 3 November 2004, p. 25.
10 Woodhouse argues that comparing the numbers of recommendations and commendations assumes that they all have equivalent weight, whereas in any given audit some are rather specific and confined, while others are of broader import.
11 Illing is not correct here. The table in the ECU advertisement (see Figure 6.2) ranks the universities by numbers of commendations, although the preceding text claims that ECU's ratio of commendations to recommendations is 'the best of all Universities so far examined'.
12 See http://www.info.gov.hk/qef/object/index.htm, accessed 17 November 2004.
13 See http://www.info.gov.hk/qef/download/qa_tod/8th/appform_8e.doc, accessed 17 November 2004.

References

Bacevich, Andrew (2002) *American Empire: The Realities and Consequences of U.S. Diplomacy*, Cambridge, MA: Harvard University Press.
Boot, Max (2002) *The Savage Wars of Peace: Small Wars and the Rise of American Power*, New York: Basic Books.
Christie, Pam (1993) Equality in curriculum in post-apartheid South Africa, *Journal of Education*, 18(1), 5–18.

Cloete, Nico, Fehnel, Richard, Maassen, Peter, Moja, Teboho, Perold, Helene and Gibbon, Trish (eds) (2002) *Transformation in Higher Education: Global Pressures and Local Realities in South Africa*, Kenwyn: Juta & Co.

Dalby, Simon. (2004) Ecological politics, violence, and the theme of empire, *Global Environmental Politics*, 4(2), 1–11.

Deleuze, Gilles and Guattari, Félix (1987) *A Thousand Plateaus: Capitalism and Schizophrenia* (Brian Massumi, trans.) Minneapolis,MN: University of Minnesota Press.

Deleuze, Gilles and Guattari, Félix (1994) *What is Philosophy?* (G. Burchell and H. Tomlinson, trans.) London: Verso.

Du Plessis, Willem (2000) *Official policy related to quality and equality in education: a documentary study*. Paper presented at the Democratic Transformation of Education in South Africa, Stellenbosch, South Africa, 27–28 September.

Eco, Umberto (1984) *Postscript to The Name of the Rose* (William Weaver, Trans.) New York: Harcourt, Brace and Jovanovich.

Ferguson, Niall (2003) *Empire: The Rise and Demise of the British World Order and the Lessons for Global Power*, New York: Basic Books.

French, Nigel (1997) *Financing Higher Education in Hong Kong: Outline of the UGC Funding Methodology*, Hong Kong: Government of Hong Kong, University Grants Committee.

Hamilton, David (2004) Letter to the Editor. *The Australian*, November 10, p. 31.

Hardt, Michael and Negri, Antoni (2000) *Empire*, Cambridge, MA: Harvard University Press.

Hartshorne, Ken (1999) *The Making of Education Policy in South Africa*, Cape Town: Oxford University Press Southern Africa.

Illing, Dorothy (2004) Snitch, *The Australian*, November 10, p. 34.

Law, Edmond and Galton, Maurice (2004) Impact of a school-based curriculum project on teachers and students: a Hong Kong case study, *Curriculum Perspectives*, 24(3), 43–58.

Massy, W. (1997) Teaching and learning quality-process review: the Hong Kong programme, *Quality in Higher Education*, 3(3), 249–62.

Mok, Ka Ho (2000) Impact of globalization: a study of quality assurance systems of higher education in Hong Kong and Singapore, *Comparative Education Review*, 44(2), 148–74.

O'Riley, Patricia A. (2003) *Technology, Culture, and Socioeconomics: A Rhizoanalysis of Educational Discourses*, New York: Peter Lang.

Peters, Michael (2004) Geophilosophy, education and the pedagogy of the concept, *Educational Philosophy and Theory*, 36(3), 217–31.

Poole, Millicent (2004) Letter to the Editor, *The Australian*, November 10, p. 31.

Porter, Robert and Porter, Kerry-Ann (2003) Habermas and the pragmatics of communication: a Deleuze–Guattarian critique, *Social Semiotics*, 13(2), 129–45.

Roy, Kaustuv (2003) *Teachers in Nomadic Spaces: Deleuze and Curriculum*, New York: Peter Lang.

Roy, Kaustuv (2004) Overcoming nihilism: from communication to Deleuzian expression, *Educational Philosophy and Theory*, 36(3), 297–312.

Steele, Colin (2004) Ranking mania reflects distortion of priorities, *The Australian*, November 10, pp. 30–1.

Steyn, Johann (2004) Balancing the commitment to quality education and equal education in South Africa: perceptions and reflections. In Yusef Waghid and Lesley Le Grange (eds), *Imaginaries on Democratic Education and Change* (pp. 97–110), Pretoria: South African Association for Research and Development in Higher Education.

Strathern, Marilyn (ed.) (2000) *Audit Cultures: Anthropological Studies in Accountability, Ethics and the Academy*, London: Routledge.

Strydom, A.H. and Strydom, J.F. (2004) Establishing quality assurance in the South African context, *Quality in Higher Education*, 10(2), 101–13.

Tam, Maureen (1999) Quality assurance policies in higher education in Hong Kong, *Journal of Higher Education Policy and Management*, 21(2), 215–26.

Walker, R.B.J. (1993) *Inside/Outside: International Relations as Political Theory*, Cambridge: Cambridge University Press.

Woodhouse, David (2004a) Letter to the Editor, *The Australian*, November 10, p. 31.

Woodhouse, David (2004b) The quality of quality assurance agencies, *Quality in Higher Education*, 10(2), 77–87.

Woodhouse, David (2005) Global perspective, *The Australian*, May 18, p. 34.

Part II

Engagement and transformations

Reconstructing research and theory to meet the challenges and opportunities of the contemporary world

Chapter 7

Theorising innovation and knowledge creation in pursuit of educational justice

Leonie Rowan

Summits of innovation

In 2005 I was invited to take part in a conference focused on the benefits of reading aloud to children in the early years. During the course of this two day event – an event that actually had the impressive title of 'Summit' – the audience was presented with data taken from a wide range of research studies all of which demonstrated fairly convincingly the important point that kids who are read aloud to more than three times a week (from 4 months till age 3) were significantly more likely to develop high levels of literacy than those who were not. Not surprisingly, these same studies also demonstrated that the kids who were regularly read aloud to, and those who were not, were differentiated around the usual kinds of lines: kids in poorer, isolated families, indigenous children and folk who have a language background other than English were substantially less likely to prioritise (or even to attempt) reading aloud with their children.

The data presented at this forum illustrated yet again that kids in Australia – kids, indeed, throughout the world – continue to be positioned in different relationships with a whole range of educational experiences depending upon their socio-economic status, their cultural background, their first language, their nationality, their ability, disability and their gender.

The creativity and sophistication of the various innovations showcased at the conference – each one of which sought to respond to the challenge of uneven literacy achievement – was truly astonishing. But sitting alongside discussions of initiatives that seemed to offer so very much to so many kids, was a different kind of presentation. These came from various literacy experts who made powerful claims about such things as: the 'right' or 'best' kinds of books to be reading ('I cannot accept this idea that kids can learn about language reading just anything ... there are books and there are good books'); the 'attitude' necessary to be a 'read-aloud parent' ('if you can't spare 15 minutes a day to read aloud to your child then you should get a goldfish instead'); and the 'correct' and 'most effective' way for parents to actually go about reading aloud.

Now obviously I can understand the intention behind these claims – and I have probably made precisely the same statements myself in various forms.

Nevertheless, I confess to feeling extraordinarily intimidated by the notion that there was some kind of 'read aloud' competency test that I needed to pass before being let loose on my own children. I was also vaguely troubled by the suggestion that letting my children occasionally choose their own books – even if this happened to include overtly commercial texts such as magazines about Winnie the Pooh or books about Bob the Builder – would undermine their understandings about what it 'really' means 'to read' and would also reduce their capacity to appreciate 'language'. And this led to me to wonder, of course, how this kind of high culture right/wrong attitude towards reading would impact on other parents, particularly those who may already feel themselves to be at odds with educational systems, 'culture', books and reading generally.

Underpinning my reflections was a feeling that the idea of the conference itself, and many of the key activities it supported, certainly and absolutely qualified as 'innovative' and transformative. But it seemed to me that at this conference – as at so many other educational forums I have attended in the past five years – it was possible to identify a key moment when the 'truly' (or at least the potentially) innovative was constrained – even chained? – by a decidedly authoritative reassertion of narrow, traditional, and, frankly, elitist perspectives; perspectives, moreover, that seemed to be fundamentally at odds with (but granted more 'status' than) the aims of the most innovative innovations in the first place. Indeed, I believe this Summit illustrated beautifully a distinction I have been concerned with for some time: the distinction between innovations which are transformative for those traditionally at risk, and those which simply re-package, re-mediate or re-badge the kind of existing process that contributes to the production of marginality and risk in the first place. On this point I believe it is possible to distinguish between what Shiv Visvanathn (2001: np) describes as 'innovation chains' – dynamic, rhizomatic, transformative responses to the contemporary world that lead to fundamentally new ways of conceptualising such things as gender, technology, culture and difference – and between chains of innovations that actually work to reassert hegemonic and restrictive understandings.

It seems to me that the ability to make this distinction is one of the key challenges facing educators and educational researchers in these current, turbulent times. In a world where educational researchers are constantly pressed to provide justifications for – and evidence concerning – the validity of their findings, it is not at all surprising that we might find ourselves trending towards authoritarian, absolute claims. But if we wish to contribute to debates about – and richer understandings concerning – the on-going persistence of educational (and social) inequities, then it is imperative that we continue to ask better, sharper, more focused questions about the relationship between our own practices and the education of those most at risk.

There is much to be said about this issue and this is only the early stages of my own attempts to articulate and theorise this distinction. Indeed, this chapter is as much a discussion about the processes through which one creates knowledge about innovation, as it is about understandings of innovation itself. In this regard, the chapter is an attempt to suggest some new ways in which educational researchers might think about literacy practices in the early years: frameworks that open up, instead of closing down, the transformative potential of education.

My starting point for this enquiry is a strong belief that the persistence of educational and social inequities in a time of so very much change warrants urgent and on-going attention. Unfortunately, however, the likelihood that social justice – in whatever guise – will become once again (or even at all) a sustainable educational priority is severely diminished by at least three particular elements of our contemporary context: the pervasiveness of claims to 'innovation' found across almost every field of endeavour, a widespread cultural suspicion of (and some degree of weariness regarding) debates around 'difference' or diversity, and the rise of consumer-oriented innovations that have worked to reproduce difference as popular commodity.

These are the key issues that I aim to explore in this chapter. In doing so I will bring together a number of arguments that I have explored in regards to various educational contexts over the past few years, all of which I believe are relevant to the broad questions associated with innovation, transformation, technology and social justice. In addition I will outline some of the theoretical perspectives I have found useful in thinking not only about what it might mean – right now – for educators to claim the status of 'innovative' but also how educators can participate in the circulation of new forms of 'knowledge' about innovation and its connection to educational justice.

The status of innovation in changed and changing times

> ... I link therefore I am ...

Any discussion about the ways in which 'innovation' is conceptualised needs to acknowledge that the term is now very much a part of day-to-day discourse. It is often used, fairly unreflectively, to refer to pretty well anything that is (or seems) 'new' (such as the CD player or spray-on tans), or to things that are being (re)presented or re-delivered in new and different ways (such as the use of videoconferences to deliver classes 'at a distance'). And in many cases, of course, 'innovation' is seen to occur, as if automatically, whenever there is the addition of some form of technology to a particular task or context. This is particularly the case where computer and communication technologies are involved. So 'going online', 'using the net', 'working virtually', and 'blogging' are all represented – in one context or another – as educational innovations regardless of how badly (or boringly) they are handled. Alan Kay makes a powerful point about how the presence of technology has largely been seen as an indicator of quality within schooling systems:

Perhaps the saddest occasion for me is to be taken to a computerized classroom and be shown children joyfully using computers. They are happy, the teachers and administrators are happy, and their parents are happy. Yet, in most such classrooms, on closer examination, I can see that the children are doing nothing interesting or growth-inducing at all! This is technology as a kind of junk food – people love it but there is no nutrition to speak of. At its worst it is a kind of 'cargo cult' in which it is thought that the mere presence of computers will somehow bring learning back to the classroom.

(cited in Shenk 1998: 74; see also Kay 1996)

The conflation between 'computers' and 'innovation' that Kay identifies here is not unique to education. Nor is the unproblematic assertion that the pursuit of innovation – innovative capacities – is a good thing found only in educational debates. At the same time as 'innovations' are sold to us in our professional, educational and personal lives, the ability to not only buy innovations but also, ourselves, to *be* 'innovative' is increasingly being emphasised. Political and economic leaders across the globe have long proclaimed the importance of producing a 'clever country' (e.g. Bob Hawke, Prime Minister of Australia in 1998), a 'knowledge nation' (Barry Jones for the Australian Labor Party in 2001) 'smart cities' (a label born by towns as diverse as Edmonton, Hamburg, Atlanta, Dubai, Kansas) and learning organisations: all of which improve our capacity to innovate and thus 'compete' in a global economy.

The claim routinely made is that the knowledge and 'innovation' so valued by local, state and federal governments will form the key to economic and social security into the future. As a corollary to this, national educational policies are increasingly filled with references to the need for a contemporary workforce of 'active citizens' able to contribute in innovative ways to the 'knowledge economy' over the course of their lifetime. This link between 'innovation' and economic usefulness is made quite explicit in the Australian Federal Government's policy paper, *Backing Australia's Ability*, where innovation is explicitly defined as: 'the process by which new ideas are transformed, through economic activity, into sustainable, value creating outcomes – into tradeable products, processes and services' (Department of Education, Science and Training 2004: np).

In this kind of context it is hardly surprising to see people claim change as the new constant. Certainly we have no shortage of 'changed' and changing circumstances. As Rushkoff notes:

The degree of change experienced by the past three generations rivals that of a species in mutation. Today's 'screenager' – the child born into a culture mediated by the television and computer – is interacting with his *[sic passim]* world in at least as dramatically altered a fashion from his grandfather as the first sighted creature did from his blind ancestors, or a winged one from his earthbound forebears … what we need to adapt to, more than any particular change, is the fact that we are changing so rapidly. We must learn to accept change as a constant. Novelty is the new status quo.

(Rushkoff 1997: 3)

At one level the ubiquity of claims to innovation is of little consequence. Just another example of the consumerist society within which everything old is, at some point, made new again. At another level it is possible to argue that the mere existence of this climate in which almost anything can be claimed as an innovation can actually serve to obscure the extent to which this very same climate (and many things labelled innovative) masks the persistence of educational and social risk and decidedly un-innovative realities. For not everything in our contemporary landscape is so very new or different. It is to this point that I will now turn.

The more things change ...

Buffy: *Hey Dawn. How was school today?*
Dawn: *The usual: a big square building filled with boredom and despair.*
Buffy: *Just how I remember it ....*

In a world where things that are new are replaced by things that are newer often before the original is out of warranty (Moore's law tells us that computing capacity doubles every 18 months: *Webopedia Computer Dictionary,* 2004) it seems reasonable to argue that 'innovation' itself is an increasingly meaningless term. In many locations, across many contexts, we can map year after year of activity associated with changing *processes* or inventing new cultural artefacts without *any* significant concomitant changes in the *outcomes* that those processes support. This is as much the case in education as in any other context. In the past thirty years we have certainly witnessed wave after wave of educational reforms, many of which are motivated by belief in the significance of computer and communication technologies, or by a desire to respond more effectively to a heterogenous student population. But in the year 2005 – 21 years after the launch of the revolutionary 'learning technology' of the Macintosh computer and a full half century since the 'universal' declaration of human rights with all its ambitions for education – educators throughout the world are still seriously challenged by the persistence of long-standing patterns of educational advantage and disadvantage.

Indicators from various national and international organisations continue to demonstrate the fact that some individuals and groups are consistently more likely to experience 'positive' educational outcomes than others. The specific groups most at risk of educational alienation and failure are those that depart from the 'mythical norms' of western culture generally, or particular discipline areas more specifically, that is to say, those who are not white, male, middle class, physically able, financially secure, Christian, heterosexual (Lorde 1990).

Thus while the world may indeed look, act, and interact quite differently in 2005 as opposed to 1945, I have little doubt that the ways in which poor kids relate to school – and the world around them – is actually fairly similar to the way poor kids viewed themselves and their education back in the 1940s. On literacy and numeracy indicators it is clear to see that rich kids do better than poor kids. Rich girls do better than rich boys, and also better than middle class girls. In English-speaking countries, kids from Language Backgrounds Other than English do less well than kids with English as their first language, and indigenous kids – on all educational measures, across all colonised countries – do less well than all other kids in the country. In such an uneven, unfair context it is hardly surprising that so many kids demonstrate the classic signs of educational alienation: lack of attention, disruption of classes, disinterest in subject matter, absence and withdrawal.

In the past twenty years, many interventions designed to focus on this problem have turned to computer and communication technologies (CCTs) with the belief that these will somehow automatically engage the disinterested, and re-connect the alienated. But many of the resultant 'innovations' have been woefully inadequate in their understandings of both processes of marginalisation, and the capacities of CCTs. In 1998 a group of leading-edge North American commentators on the cultural evolution of new technologies in social practices drafted eight principles of 'technorealism', signed it, and launched it as a charter. They aimed to intervene in a situation where 'despite the complicated and often contradictory implications of technology, the conventional wisdom is woefully simplistic' (Shenk 1998: 217). The fifth principle of technorealism states that 'wiring the schools will not save them'. The authors elaborate as follows:

> The problems with America's public schools … have almost nothing to do with technology. Consequently, no amount of technology will lead to the educational revolution prophesied by President Clinton and others. The art of teaching cannot be replicated by computers, the Net, or by 'distance learning.' These tools can, of course, augment an already high quality educational experience. But to rely on them as any sort of educational panacea would be a costly mistake.
>
> (Shenk 1998: 218)

Costly indeed. While schools have taken on board all manner of educational 'innovations' (i.e. things they can do with computers) it is not in any way possible to argue that the problems faced by schools twenty years ago have changed at all. That means that the consequences of educational alienation which do not, of course, end at the school gate, continue to shape social and life futures. Pathways into and through high school, further education and employment (and all the associated factors such as periods of employment/unemployment, income/benefits, health, mental health, stability of relationships and so on) are all connected to educational success and failure.

The persistence of uneven patterns of educational success and failure is alarming to me as both a parent and an academic and I have been interested for many years in coming to a better understanding of both the possibilities and limitations of equity-based educational reforms. In recent years I have identified three particular obstacles to the re-invigoration of social justice agendas in education – and the innovations that may be linked to this project – and I want to review each of these briefly here.

Not-so-popular attitudes to difference ...

I'm not gay! Not that there's anything wrong with that!

(*Seinfeld*: *The Outing*)

Although there are undoubtedly more technical and academic ways to describe the phenomenon I want to refer to here, it seems to me that many people are well and truly over the whole 'difference', acceptance, and 'social justice' thing. Long-standing attempts to draw attention to the experiences of girls, people of colour, gays and lesbians have certainly 'raised awareness' about their 'historical plight' and increased base-line levels of 'tolerance' but they have also, and simultaneously, lowered public and policy interest. Some folk today argue that so called 'majority' groups are now themselves the victims of 'political correctness' and that education and social systems have gone 'too far' in their efforts to cater for heterogeneity. It strikes me as somewhat ironic that this new conservatism is in many ways fuelled by a particular kind of anti-authority/populist criticality that is today prevalent in popular television and radio. Over the past ten years, just about every comedy and panel show on TV has taken to using extreme versions of sarcasm or ridicule in the pursuit of a laugh: *Seinfeld*, *The Simpsons*, *Becker*, *Buffy*, *Everybody Loves Raymond*, *Good News Week*, *Rove*, *The Panel* and so on. Each show uses characters and character types renowned for their 'plain speaking' and 'wit' and frequently direct their scathing observations at figures of authority such as members of government, high-profile bureaucrats, business people or sports stars.

Allegiance to these kinds of TV shows and to some very high-profile 'critical' comics, seems, in many ways, to fuel the claim that Australians are an aware and insightful bunch of folk, capable of looking critically at every issue. Unfortunately, these high-profile 'performances' of popular criticality are in many ways a new form of 'tokenism' and increasingly seem to be functioning as proxies for what might be thought of as more substantial forms of critique. It cannot be a coincidence that at the same time as popular 'wise-cracking' has reached an all-time high, we've also seen an increasing tolerance by the 'Australian people' of government policies that work to position people in minority or 'at risk' groups – refugees, the unemployed, single parents, people in low-socio-economic backgrounds – in increasing negative ways. This shift, it seems, is acceptable because Australians have ensured that it's not them who have the problems with diversity because, hey, they watch *Rove*....

Educators working towards social justice outcomes, are therefore challenged not only by a context that celebrates 'newness' and therefore has little interest in the persistence of 'old' problems, but also by significant shifts in the way 'difference' is popularly understood. This understanding is, of course, fuelled by dominant political discourses and it is important to acknowledge the role of the rather precipitously mourned 'nation state' in the creation of new levels of resistance to justice agendas.

States of anxiety

> How could this happen?
> We started out like Romeo and Juliet but it ended up in tragedy.
>
> Milhouse, *The Simpsons*

New and emergent resources, practices and relationships associated with information technologies; communication technologies; media activities; finances; and the rapid and dramatic flow of people and ideas have been cited as some of the 'hallmarks' of globalisation. Arjun Appadurai (1990) captures a general sense of the nature of these changes when he refers to developments across five 'scapes': mediascape; technoscape; ethnoscape; finanscape; and the ideoscape. Developments on each of these 'scapes' are seen not only in the rise and rise of technologically (re)mediated practices and performances, but also in significant changes to understandings of the 'nation state' and the way individuals and communities conceptualise themselves/their identities/their subjectivities. One particularly significant issue concerns the ways in which the nation state (in what is allegedly the time of its decline) works to reassert its power and authority over its citizens – and, indeed, all non-citizens – through increasingly conservative claims about what it means to 'belong' to a particular country, nation or 'way of life'.

In an era of global competition and suspicion, both new and old technologies and media processes are manipulated by governance technologies to try and preserve the fiction of a worthy 'us' protecting our country from the problematic of 'them'. As Appadurai notes: 'minorities are the major site for displacing the anxieties of many states abut their own minority or marginality (real or imagined) in a world of a few mega states, of unruly economic flows and compromised sovereignties' (2001: 6). He reminds us that 'minority groups' (and outsiders) 'do not come preformed. They are produced in the specific circumstances of every nation and every nationalism' (2001: 5).

It is this kind of logic that has informed, in Australia, the demonisation of immigrants, refugees, non-Christians and, indeed, any group represented by the government as other to 'mainstream Australia'. The ability of political parties to represent the marginal in this particular way is directly connected to a third characteristic of the contemporary environment: the construction of difference as a commodity.

Cappuccino cultures: popular consumption of 'difference'

> Five people. After lunch coffee:
> *'I'll have a decaf coffee"; 'I'll have a decaf espresso'*
> *'I'll have a double decaf cappuccino'; 'Give me decaffeinated coffee ice cream'*
> *'I'll have a half double decaffeinated half-caf, with a twist of lemon'*
> *'I'll have a twist of lemon'; 'I'll have a twist of lemon'; 'I'll have a twist of lemon';*
> *'I'll have a twist of lemon'*
>
> Steve Martin: LA Story

Additional insights concerning the contemporary challenges associated with re-engaging public and policy concern for the consequences of difference are outlined by feminist philosopher Rosi Braidotti who points to the way that difference is now being reinvented as a product or commodity in contemporary western economies. She writes:

> 'post-industrial' societies have taken 'differences' into a spin, making them proliferate with an aim to ensure maximum profit. Advanced capitalism is a difference engine – a multiplier of de-territorialized differences, which are packaged and marketed under the labels of 'multiple or multicultural identities'. It is important to explore how this logic thereby triggers a consumeristic or vampiric consumption of 'others', and how this logic fuels the new forms of contemporary social and cultural practice. From fusion cooking to 'world music', the consumption of 'differences' is a common practice.
>
> (Braidotti 2003: 1)

Conservative media and political environments regularly proclaim the (long-standing) liberation of women, homosexuals and lesbians, people of colour, people with disabilities and so on. And while there have quite obviously been certain and significant changes to the status of these groups in the past 100 years, the vampiric consumption of otherness referred to by Braidotti – signalled by everything from the rise of 'multi-cultural food', 'world music', and dinner sets that feature 'authentic' ceramic versions of cardboard Japanese noodle boxes (seriously: how bizarre is that??) – masks the ongoing production of some bodies in less powerful relationships to contemporary culture than others. Braidotti makes the powerful point that 'the bodies of the empirical subjects who signify difference (woman/native/earth or natural others) have become the disposable bodies of the global economy' (Braidotti 2003: 10) and goes on to say:

> Looked at from the angle of the disposable bodies of 'others' of the dominant subject, the on-going new scientific revolution is neither very new, nor particularly scientific. What we have, in fact, is the return of the masters'

narratives: science turns into technological applications, gets fuelled by a massive hype and it perpetuates traditional modes and patterns of exclusion. This is the contemporary variation on the theme of the ruthless exploitation of bodily materialism and bodily matters. The age of globalization has shown rawer and more brutal power relations that we had seen since the first industrial revolution. What we are getting is a perversion of the subversive and creative potential of those very technologies which we have invented. It is old (master) narratives in new (scientific) bottles.

(Braidotti 2003: 9–10)

Braidotti highlights here a point that is central to this chapter: invocations of innovation in education may regularly refer to technological 'newness', changes to how things are 'done', the development of innovative capacities (and the creation of a socially useful (compliant?) workforce) but none of this necessarily addresses long-standing, underlying issues concerned with the way different *bodies* are positioned in *different relationships* with the practices that result. There are innovations which open up possibilities to transgress hegemonic understandings of gender, race or class, and there are others that simply re-work those master narratives.

Of course, those who are routinely positioned on the margins of dominant discourse are certainly not powerless or passive. As Braidotti notes:

Let us remember, with Foucault, that power is a multi-layered concept which covers both negative or confining methods (*potestas*) as well as empowering or affirmative technologies (*potentia*). This means that the paths of transformation engendered by the 'difference engine' of advanced capitalism are neither straight nor predictable. They rather compose a zig-zagging line of internally contradictory options. Thus, human bodies caught in the spinning machine of multiple difference at the end of postmodernity become simultaneously disposable commodities to be vampirized and also decisive agents for political and ethical transformation. How to tell the difference between the two modes of becoming other is the task of critical theory. I consider it a political practice.

(Braidotti 2003: 2–3)

But here again it is possible to argue that rising public awareness of the transgressive potential of historically marginalised groups has, in itself, become an obstacle to the re-emergence of social justice agendas. After all, if 'we' know that 'they' aren't *really* 'powerless' and if we've known that now for a really long time then surely all the problems 'they had' must be pretty well solved? And if they haven't been by now, then maybe they actually *can't* be? And either way, is there anything else the 'average person' can do about it?

It is this kind of thinking – found in contexts as diverse as talk-back radio, federal parliament, and educational conferences – that fuels not only the consumption of carefully remediated forms of difference but also a kind of casual disinterest in the consequences – for disposable bodies – of traditional social and educational practices.

Some other points of view

> … man had always assumed that he was more intelligent than dolphins because he had achieved so much – the wheel, New York, wars and so on – while all the dolphins had ever done was muck about in the water having a good time. But conversely the dolphins had always believed that they were far more intelligent than man – for precisely the same reasons.
>
> Douglas Adams, *The Hitchhikers Guide to the Galaxy*

Given all of this it seems to me that educators today who wish to pursue a social justice agenda face three key challenges (well, all right they face many, *many* key challenges, but there are three that I want to foreground here). The first involves identifying the difficult context within which their work must now operate. This is relatively easy. The second and third, more challenging tasks, involve developing ways to work beyond the limits of this newly conservative, vampiric context in order to re-awaken public understandings of how educational marginality is experienced today whilst simultaneously generating new knowledge about what it might mean to be 'truly' innovative in a context where claims to innovation are as bountiful as SMS messages.

Central to all of these challenges is the ability to draw attention to the key issues that continue to be experienced by learners from diverse backgrounds. Developing this capacity – this new knowledge about new forms of educational injustice – is crucial for many reasons, not the least of which is the simple fact that educators – like every one else – have only so much time, energy and faith to invest in any kind of innovation. And if they're investing their effort in innovation X (which asks only that they do something with technology Y) then they are perhaps less likely to be interested in innovation Z which asks them to do something far, far, far harder relating to long-standing patterns of educational access and failure.

There are any manner of resources that can be drawn upon by academics to help us evaluate the extent to which any educational 'innovation' is likely to have an effect on those at the margins of the education system. And the value of many of these resources is that they can help take us out of our interpretive comfort zones. I have long been persuaded by Douglas Kellner's argument that 'constantly expanding one's theoretical perspectives and horizons helps to illuminate multiple dimensions of our cultural environment, providing richer and more complex understandings of our sociocultural life' (Kellner 2001: 3–4). He goes on:

> Against pluralism and eclecticism, we believe that it is important to challenge the established academic division of labor and to develop a transdisciplinary approach that contests both the bifurcation of the field of media and cultural

studies and the society that produces it. A transdisciplinary media and cultural studies will thus overcome the boundaries of academic disciplines and will combine political economy, social theory and research, and cultural criticism in its project which aims at critique of domination and social transformation… Such a transformative venture must also engage the new cultural, political and social forms of the present era.

(Kellner 2001: 28)

In this spirit, the work of philosophers such as Rosi Braidotti, Deleuze and Guattari, and Bruno Latour have much to offer.

Braidotti, as outlined above, reminds us of the multiple ways in which old patterns of cultural violence can be reinvented – remediated – every single day. Deleuze and Guattari and their oft-cited distinction between frames of references which they define as arboreal and rhizomatic are also useful companions. *Arboreal* structures reflect the vertical/hierarchical patterns of trees and can be understood as rigid, fixed, and clearly differentiated from other structures. A *rhizome*, in contrast, is a root that grows laterally across the surface of the ground: the function of the rhizome is to traverse arboreal structures and to interrupt oppositions and divisions: 'Unlike trees or their roots, the rhizome connects any point to any other point, and its traits are not necessarily linked to the traits of the same nature' (Deleuze and Guattari 1987: 21).

While arboreal structures seek to limit what it is that can occur within any particular framework – regardless how 'new' it may seem – rhizomes work against this limitation making connections outside of and across multiple frameworks: by connecting any point to any other point, the rhizome resists the order that would be imposed by working on one stratum alone (Deleuze and Guattari 1987: 503).

Arboreal structures represent what Deleuze and Guattari define as *majority* or *molar* positions. These positions are over-coded, legislated, authorised positions and ideas. *Rhizomatic* networks, by contrast, account for fluid, *minority* or *molecular* positions. Minority positions are unauthorised trajectories of thought that cut across molar lines. So educational innovations with a social justice trajectory might be conceptualised as rhizomatic lines of flight: lines of molecular activity that deviate and depart from molar codes; and serve to trouble and destabilise the rigidity of molar lines. The tension between the *molar* and the *molecular* is played out in a process of *reterritorialisation* and *deterritorialisation*. Reterritorialisation – the process by which lines of rigid or molar segmentarity confine movement within specific territories, codes and conventions – is the process that occurs when innovations – such as those I discussed at the start of this chapter – are brought back into the realm of the molar, and repositioned in a hierarchical relationship with 'classic' and 'traditional' practices.

Another helpful theoretical perspective comes from Bruno Latour – and others in the sociology of translation – who highlights the importance of attending to the processes through which innovations are introduced, modified, stabilised through negotiations between various actors in a network. Actor Network Theory (ANT) highlights the fact that the maintenance of a network is of crucial importance. A network becomes 'stronger' and more 'durable' the more actors that are attached to it who behave in the desired way. In other words, creating a durable network is a complex process of enrolling various actors, encouraging them to perform certain roles and to remain 'true to these roles', resisting, by extension, attempts to enrol them in other, competing networks (Simpson, 2000). In Latour's terms, this is a process that involves the on-going construction of a network's reality:

> ... anything can become more or less real, depending on the continuous chains of translation. It's essential to continue to generate interest, to seduce, to translate interests. You can't ever stop becoming more real.
>
> (Latour 1996: 85)

But regardless of the particular theoretical resources we choose to use, a key challenge is for us to translate the results of our theorising and analysis in ways that make it accessible to, meaningful for, and 'new' again, to a time-poor, critically fatigued population. As Michael Goldhaber (1998) has noted so clearly, we aren't really living in an information economy; it is, more accurately, an *attention* economy. One of the biggest challenges facing those of us with social justice agendas, then, is to re-capture the attention of educators, politicians, parents and community and to ensure that when we have it we put forward innovations most likely to effect some change. In the context outlined above, the development of sustainable, ethical responses by educators to the persistence of educational inequities in so-called 'new times' requires us to look critically at *every single dimension of our practices* to identify what understandings about 'students', 'learning', 'ability', 'success', 'society' and 'citizenship' are being produced, or reproduced, contested or transformed.

Conclusion

> Never miss a good chance to shut up ...
>
> Will Rogers

This chapter has aimed merely to open up some on-going discussion about the challenges associated with pursuing educational justice agendas in a world where significant amounts of time and energy go into the pursuit of forms of innovation that have little (or no) chance of disrupting the traditional relationships between difference and education. This leads me to the key, final point. Bearing in mind the contemporary proliferation of technologically based products and processes, the persistence of sociologically analysed experiences of marginality and risk, and the difficulties faced by anyone seeking to re-vitalise interest in issues of educational justice, it seems possible to argue that the label 'innovative' might now be most meaningful to educators if it was applied to those processes, products or interventions that have changed in some way the precise 'things' that have historically proven *most resistant* to sustained, sustainable change. To be 'innovative', in this sense, would require not only (nor even) some of the more traditional hallmarks of innovation – chronological 'newness', the addition of technology, or the creation of new market opportunities – but rather some fundamental transformation, interrogation, or interruption of long-standing patterns of educational access and success.

There is a key distinction to be made, in other words, between 'newness' or historically notable *inventions* and politically, ethically significant *innovations*.

Developing the capacity to make this distinction in a world – as acknowledged before – that is awash with so-called innovations, as Braidotti noted above, may indeed be the key challenge of critical practice into the twenty-first century. And working towards this goal, of course, requires those of us who seek to theorise innovation to be as innovative in our work as we would like others to be in theirs.

References

Appadurai, A. (1990) Disjuncture and difference in global cultural economy, in *Global culture: nationalism, globalization and modernity*, M. Featherstone (ed). London: Sage, 295–310.

Appadurai, A. (2001) *New logics of violence*. Retrieved 14 July 2003, from http://www.india-seminar.com/2001/503/503%20arjun%20apadurai.htm.

Braidotti, R. (2003) The return of the masters' narratives in *e-quality*. Retrieved 24 April 2004, from http://www.e-quality.nl/e-quality/pagina.asp?pagkey=21224.

Cummins, R.A. (1997) *Comprehensive quality of life scale: school version (Grades 7–12)*, Burwood: Deakin University.

Deleuze, G. and F. Guattari (1987) *A thousand plateaus: capitalism and schizophrenia*, Minneapolis, MN: University of Minnesota Press.

Department of Education, Science and Training (2004) *Backing Australia's ability*, Canberra: DEST.

Goldhaber, M. (1998) *The attention economy and the net*. Retrieved 22 July 1999, from http://firstmonday.dk/issues/issue2_4/goldhaber/.

Kay, A. (1996). *Revealing the elephant: the use and misuse of computers in education*. Retrieved 13 July 1999, from http://educom.edu/web/pubs/review/reviewArticles/31422.html.

Kellner, D.M. and M.G. Durham (2001) Adventures in media and cultural studies: introducing the key works. In M.G. Durham and D.M. Kellner (eds) *Media and cultural studies: key works*, Cambridge, MA, Blackwell Publishers: 1–30.

Latour, B. (1996) *Aramis: or the love of technology*, Cambridge, MA: Harvard University Press.

Lorde, A. (1990). Age, race, sex and class: women redefining difference. In R. Ferguson, M. Gever, T. Minh-ha and C. West (eds) *Out there: marginalization and contemporary cultures*, New York: New Museum of Contemporary Culture, 281–8.

Rushkoff, D. (1997) *Children of chaos: surviving the end of the world as we know it*, London: Flamingo.

Shenk, D. (1998). *Data smog*, revised and updated edn, San Francisco, CA HarperEdge.

Simpson, N. (2000) Diffusion theory and actor-network theory. In L. Rowan and B.A. Knight (eds) *Researching futures oriented pedagogy*, Brisbane: Post Pressed, 23–40.

Visvanathn, S. (2001) *The problem*. Retrieved 9 July 2003, from http:/www.india-seminar.com/2001/503/503%20the%20problem.htm.

Webopedia Computer Dictionary (2004) *Moore's Law*. Retrieved 15 April 2004, from: http://www.webopedia.com/.

Chapter 8

Narrations on democratic accountability[1]

*Jennifer C. Greene, Walter Feinberg,
Sarah Stitzlein and Luis Miron*

> Part of the attractiveness of the accountabilist ideology is its simplicity and reductionism: consequences (high stakes), easy to obtain evidence (testing), behavioralizing outcomes (or standards and performance…), and laying the whole of the responsibility on the doorsteps of schools as if they existed in a social, political, and economic vacuum.
>
> (Sirotnik, 2004a, p. 154)

During the last few years there has been a sea change in the politics and the procedures for evaluating public schools in the US. As part of the broad governmental shift to a "new public management" (Power, 1997) and its emphasis on accountability, the evaluation of public school performance has been narrowed to an intense focus on individual student performance on selected standardized tests. New federal education mandates, under the auspices of the national *No Child Left Behind (NCLB)* Act signed into law in 2002, require states to establish learning standards in multiple subject areas and to conduct annual assessments of student progress on these standards. In every school, students in each tested grade level and subject area must make satisfactory "annual yearly progress" or AYP so that *all* children pass their respective tests by the year 2014, or the school faces financial and other sanctions[2] and, ultimately, reconstitution or take-over by the state. Moreover, in schools with sufficient numbers of students in various sub-groups (demarcated by race/ethnicity, English language ability, socio-economic class, and disability status), test results must be disaggregated by sub-group, and *each sub-group* must make AYP or the school faces the sanctions enacted in this law.

The effects of this change on the long-range performance of schools are not yet fully known, although a number of highly respected educational researchers have suggested that the expectations laid down by the federal government are misplaced (Darling-Hammond, 2003; Stake, 1999) or unrealistic, especially the mandated timetable for improvement. For example, Robert Linn in his 2003 Presidential address before the American Educational Research Association, dramatically demonstrated that if schools in selected states were to continue to improve student test scores at their present rate:

It would take 57 years for the percentage of grade 4 to reach 100. For grade 8 it would take 61 years and for grade 12 it would take 166 years. Looked at another way, the average annual rate of gain in percent proficient or above would have to increase by factors of 4, 4.3, and 11.8 at grades 4, 8 and 12 respectively, to reach the 100 per cent [goal] by 2014. Such rapid acceleration would be nothing short of miraculous.

(Linn, 2003, p. 6)

Documented short-term school responses to *NCLB* mandates – in the media and in research studies – are simultaneously inspiring and frightening, though from our vantage point, substantially more frightening than inspiring (e.g., McNeil, 2000). On the inspiring side, states have indeed developed, for the most part, meaningful standards that incorporate high and appropriate expectations for students, in terms of both content and developmental considerations. And states have encouraged and supported significant alignment of these standards with curricula and assessment, so that children are, in fact, tested on what they are taught. (See, for example the standards and assessments established in the state of Illinois, http://www.isbe. state.il.us/ils/Default.htm.) Schools are also allocating significant resources to children who do not perform at acceptable levels on their tests – resources that are in most cases long overdue (James-Burdumy *et al.*, 2005). These resources include specialized tutoring and extra help in out-of-school programs, although the value of this additional academic time has been seriously challenged (James-Burdumy *et al.*, 2005) *and* although few of these resources accompany the *NCLB* legislation, leading to increasing state and local legal challenges that this is an unfunded mandate.

On the more frightening side, some states have employed strategies to beat the system, including fudging data on dropouts who otherwise would detract from the total scores (Lewin and Medina, 2003); ignoring or even encouraging district-wide teacher cheating (Dubner, 2003; Hoff, 2000); relaxing standards to avoid sanctions (Dillon, 2003); and buying time by setting timetables for improvement that load most of the gain onto the last few years of the deadline, in other words, betting on "the possibility that the law will be modified to make progress targets more realistically achievable" (Linn, 2003, p. 10). Some schools and school districts are also engaging in such extreme gymnastic contortions to fit the demands of *NCLB* that core ideas of teaching and learning are significantly distorted (Haney, 2000; Hursh, 2005). Moreover, educators of considerable renown are resigning from their posts, along with educators of more ordinary competence. Here is one such story.

Eighteen-year veteran high school mathematics teacher Kathleen Smith, an award-winning mathematics teacher, stunned [school] board members by resigning as a protest, she said, against district and federal policies that force teachers to "teach to the test." During Monday's school board meeting, Smith said she's resigning because she's at odds with current standards in the district and with methods imposed on teachers by George Bush's landmark *No Child Left Behind* legislation.

"I find myself constrained by a mentality that says all students will learn the same material at the same pace and prove it by taking the same multiple-choice test within a given time frame," she told the board. "I can't do that. I know all students don't learn at the same pace. I don't believe a student's understanding of mathematical concepts can be assessed by a multiple-choice test nor do I believe such a test is fair for all learners."

Further, "we've had to give up all integrated projects that tie together math, biology, English and reading," she said. "Now we teach those subjects in chunks so students are ready for tests. We used to pursue innovative teaching methods. Now there's no time." Smith figures she has lost 10 to 15 instruction days a year preparing students to take standardized tests and giving the tests.

Smith said, "I told my students, 'I don't want to teach you to take a multiple-choice test. I want to teach you that math is the language of the universe, the most powerful tool. With math, you can do anything.'"

"The supply of Kathleen Smiths is limited," said teachers' union President Greg Novak. "We can't afford to lose any of them."

(Taken from stories in *The News Gazette*, Champaign-Urbana IL, May 10 and May 22, 2005)

The modest project we report on in this chapter joins a number of other studies (e.g., Louis *et al.*, 2005) in seeking to better understand how US public school teachers are making sense of and responding to contemporary demands for accountability, particularly the *NCLB* mandates. Resignation is an extreme and dramatic teacher response. We wondered about the character and contours of other teacher responses to accountability pressures in their professional spaces of teaching and learning. We also wondered about teachers' views and interpretations of student performance on high-stakes accountability tests. And we wondered how well this kind of test-based evaluation of student learning was connected to or disconnected from teacher conceptualizations of meaningful evaluation of student learning and their own evaluative practices. This paper thus takes an evaluative lens on our project, focusing on the meanings and practices of evaluating student learning and, more broadly, school quality in the US today. We first reconsider meanings of accountability, with an emphasis on some of its democratic dimensions, and then briefly describe our procedures, followed by a narrative that captures some of what we have learned.

Reconsidering accountability

From an evaluative lens, educational or school "quality" under the *NCLB* approach to evaluating schools is equated with individual student standardized test performance, as sliced by conventional demography. And "accountability" means that public school educators are only responsible for student test performance, only answerable for an "account" comprised of student test scores. Moreover, others with responsibility for the quality and effectiveness of public education are nowhere held accountable for anything. In this chapter, we join the chorus of others who decry the exceptionally narrow conceptualization of educational responsibilities embedded in *NCLB* and the exceptionally narrow emphasis on very limited outcomes of what could and should be the most exceptional educational system in the world.[3]

Accountability as mutual, collective responsibility

Just as educators need to be held accountable, so do policy makers and the public as a whole. A society that is still marked by substantial racism and classism cannot expect just and equitable public schools not matter how much rhetoric is heard about better leadership, better teaching, and "closing the achievement gap."

(Sirotnik, 2002, pp. 664–5)

There is something both undemocratic and inefficient about holding students, parents, teachers, and principals accountable for test performance without any knowledge or concern about the conditions under which that performance was accomplished – conditions that ultimately are determined by officials in the state capital. A better accountability system would turn this system on its head and make state officials accountable to students and parents.

(Oakes *et al.*, 2004, p. 93)

Of major concern to many critics of *NCLB* accountability is "the decoupling of student achievement from the conditions in which students are expected to learn, [which] has led to accountability systems that represent failures of opportunity as failures of merit" (Oakes *et al.*, 2004, p. 83). "The assumption seems to be that differences in rates of academic achievement across schools are essentially a technical problem, and that the failure to resolve this problem is due primarily to a lack of will and expertise on the part of educators" (Beadie, 2004, p. 46). And so in *NCLB* accountability, "we now have high standards imposed on students but no standards for schools [regarding, for example] qualifications of teachers, the state of facilities, or access to learning materials" (Noguera, 2004, pp. 69–70).

In democratic societies, government is responsible to its citizens for maintaining the quality of our nations' highways and airplanes, the safety of our food supply, the cleanliness of the air we breathe and the water we drink. The lingering tragedies of the tsunami in southern Asia and of hurricane Katrina in the south of the US – of people with no homes, livelihoods, or even food and water – are understood as responsibilities of government. And so is public education. Yet, on matters of government responsibility, *NCLB* is silent. Needed, therefore, is a more democratic enactment of accountability, in which responsibility for the quality and effectiveness of public schooling in the US is mutual, collective, and shared by all actors in the system – government along with educators and the families they serve (Ryan, 2005). "Accountability and responsibility must go hand in hand" (Sirotnik, 2004a, p. 155).

Educational outcomes that matter (democratically and otherwise)

> Does anyone seriously believe that what a kid scores on an on-demand test really represents anything more than a small sample of highly contextualized paper-and-pencil behavior, ostensibly having something to do with teaching and learning …? Surely what matters more is … the future potential of each child and young adult in the care of our public schools.
>
> (Sirotnik, 2004b, p. 8)

> Responsible assessment and accountability must be informed and guided by our richest, deepest, and philosophically most defensible educational ideals.
>
> (Siegel, 2004, p. 63)

NCLB critics also vigorously deplore the narrowness of the educational outcomes that are commonly measured in standards-based state testing systems (Ryan, 2005). Not only is there a "striking 'disconnect' and incompatibility between our testing and accountability practices and our considered educational aims and ideals" (Siegel, 2004, p. 56), but the knowledge, skills, and dispositions so fundamental to the development of democratic citizenship are nearly completely ignored in such systems. These include critical thinking and the habits of mind that support deliberative engagement with reasons for acting (Siegel, 2004); opening of minds and overcoming provincialism (Siegel, 2004); and learning to respect, accept and understand difference. "Teaching students their moral and intellectual responsibilities as critical and informed citizens in a democracy … is arguably the central function of American schooling" (Soder, 2004, p. 101). And "public education must play a vital role in our pluralistic and democratic society. The very survival of a political democracy depends on a participating, educated, and critically minded citizenry" (Sirotnik, 2004a, p. 154).

Moreover, embedded in the NCLB conception of the evaluation of schooling is a highly instrumentalist view of education and of students as little more than future workers. NCLB focuses the school evaluation system on a very narrow slice of student learning *and* on a prescribed and very limited behavioral performance as demonstration of mastery. This signals considerable disrespect for students and their teachers, for the multifaceted character of teaching and learning, for the wondrous diversity of human expression, and for the basic agency of citizens in a democracy.

School setting

Our small window of understanding on teachers' experiences with contemporary forms of accountability and assessment comes from a series of engagements with 10 teachers at Evergreen Elementary School[4] during the 2004–5 school year, a school with about 400 students and 38 teachers in a mid-sized Midwestern school district. The population of the school has changed considerably over its 135-year history. For years, the school was locally known as one of the leading schools in the area and was populated largely by children of faculty and professional staff at a nearby college. More recently, a large working-class population moved into the area, including Spanish-speaking families mostly from Mexico. While this population began to trickle into Evergreen classrooms on its own, the greatest influx of Spanish-speaking students followed a controversial decision by the local school board in 1999. Due to overcrowding in a neighboring school, the board voted to move the district's bilingual program for Spanish-speaking elementary school students to Evergreen School. The Evergreen community strongly supported the board's decision; the opposition came from minorities elsewhere in the district concerned about the Spanish-speaking children's potential isolation in a school dominated by English-speaking faculty and students. At the time of our study, Evergreen's student population was about 12 per cent Latino/a, 15 per cent African American, 4 per cent Asian, and 67 per cent Caucasian students; and one-third (35 per cent) of Evergreen's students received free or reduced lunches.

Evergreen has long been guided by a tradition of strong educational leaders, from its founding namesake Frederick E. Evergreen to the 2004 National Distinguished Principal of the Year. The school's success has also been guided by highly trained teachers as well as a progressive school philosophy. Evergreen prides itself on devotion to three aspects of learning: active learning, process learning, and life-long learning. Moreover, the school is committed to the development of socially responsible students. These approaches to learning are guided by the school mantra, "the ability of a student to achieve determines the level of instruction to be utilized." Evergreen students typically perform well on standardized tests; the percentages of students meeting or exceeding standards on the State Test far surpass state averages – in most cases by at least 20 per cent.

Inquiry design and methods[5]

Sample

In the spring of 2004, we solicited volunteers from the entire school faculty for our mini-project, a tactic that yielded 12 volunteers, 10 of whom we ultimately worked with – all women. These 10 well represented the senior, highly experienced classroom teachers who had worked at this school for 30 some years (two teachers); the specialist faculty – also highly experienced – who worked with children with special needs (four teachers); and the relative newcomers to the profession and/or the school (four teachers). All teachers were paid for their participation in our project. To enliven this description of the teachers in this study, we offer three composite portraits representing the three main groups of teachers in our sample.

Donna has taught at Evergreen all of her 30 years of teaching, mostly in the upper elementary grades, but she also spent a few years in grade 2–3 classrooms. Most of the students at Evergreen have the same teacher for two years in grades K and 1 and then again in grades 2 and 3 and in grades 4 and 5, a practice called "looping". As the older students move on, the younger ones move up within the same classroom and a new group of younger students enters the loop. Donna's particular expertise is in math; she has a room full of math manipulatives and games for her students, along with a couple of well-used computers. She strongly believes that children must learn important mathematical concepts concretely before they can make sense of their abstractions. Donna also has a keen perceptive understanding of each of her students. She appears able to make many micro-decisions about their accomplishments and their needs on an ongoing basis, integrating what she knows about the family, the child's current stressors, and his/her academic profile.

Sally is a teacher of learning disabled children in Evergreen. Like Donna, she has been there all of her 25-year teaching career, except for her sabbatical leaves to the State Department of Education and to Cambridge, England for her own professional development. Sally is vehemently opposed to the current regime of high-stakes testing, because she has witnessed first-hand its devastating psychological and emotional effects on some of her students. When these effects are too extreme, Sally tells her students to just fill in the bubbles any way they want to. Like Donna, she also has the ability to make complex, integrative pedagogical decisions about her students all day long, distinguishing, for example, between a child's poor performance due to a specific vocabulary weakness or poor performance attributable to overall reading comprehension difficulties, including decoding and fluency.

Eunice is a decade younger than Donna and Sally, but newer to the teaching profession, having raised two children first. Eunice is also new to Evergreen School. At the time of our study, Eunice was in her fourth year of teaching, and her second year at Evergreen, also in a grade 2–3 class. She voiced admiration for the inner circle of veteran teachers at Evergreen, as they seemed so wise and experienced. Eunice's own teaching practice has a number of distinctive features, including use of a structured approach to teaching reading adapted from Reading Recovery, ongoing monitoring of students' learning via structured mini-assessments, and a preference for whole-class instruction over small groups and individual work. Eunice also strives to use multiple media in her teaching and to incorporate the arts, especially theatre and performance, into her planned activities for children.

Data generation, analysis, and representation

We first individually interviewed each teacher, focusing on the ways in which assessment and evaluation – both as externally imposed and as internally constructed – are present in her teaching practices. These interviews elicited rich descriptions of teachers' daily evaluative practices, highlighting the intensity and specificity of the micro-analyses and decisions they make all day long, every day. Each interview was conducted by two members of our team and was taped and transcribed. We then analyzed the interview data, using processes that were dialogic and iterative and that were thematically oriented towards representing these interview data in narratives. The logic of crafting narratives for our interview results featured the potential power of alternative representation to engage these teachers in meaningful dialogue about the issues and concerns presented in the stories. We were aiming less for a set of "findings" and more for a provocative set of scenarios that would invite further conversation about the assessment, evaluation, and accountability ideas, issues, and dilemmas that surfaced in the individual interviews (Abma, 2001). The four stories we crafted engaged four major themes from our interview analysis: curriculum compromises due to standards and assessment demands, the consequential character of *NCLB* failure, the complexity of each child's unique academic profile, and teacher-developed assessment alternatives to standardized testing. We present one of these stories in the next section of this paper.

We then shared all four stories with the teachers and scheduled three small group meetings to discuss them. We opened these meetings by asking teachers to react to the stories, starting with whichever one struck their fancy. We continued by probing both the extent to which the stories captured the experiences they had shared in the interviews and the further issues, vignettes, concerns that were provoked by the stories. These one-hour meetings were lively and full. Again, they were usually facilitated by two members of the inquiry team, taped, and transcribed.

Our final meeting with the teachers took place near the end of the school year. We invited all teacher interviewees to this one meeting, at which we shared highlights from the three group interviews about the stories and then several follow-up ideas about professional development within a framework of "democratic accountability" that we had generated. We sought teachers' feedback on these ideas. Refreshments were served, and we thanked our participants for their generous sharing of their time and expertise.

A narrative of teacher responses to accountability demands

In this section, we share one of the stories we constructed from the individual teacher interviews. Again, we constructed these stories as what we hoped would be provocative representations of what we learned in these interviews as well as authentic invitations to further dialogue.

A testing guide and the Oregon Trail (first author, Sarah Stitzlein)

Ms Hopper lets out a heavy sigh as she reviews the testing guide for the new series of standardized testing that will begin with her fifth grade class this spring. She looks down at her yearly lesson plan, remembers last year's students excitedly drawing pictures of Western mountains and counting up their pretend earnings after striking gold as they partook in her cross-curriculum unit on the Oregon Trail, and crosses out the unit. Every year since she began teaching four years ago her students have joined in a competition with other fifth grade classrooms that simulates the long trek across the nineteenth-century US. From planning for food provisions to constructing maps, the children re-enact the adventure with their own sense of exploration and anticipation in the present. She will miss the lesson dearly this year and she worries about both the enjoyment and the interdisciplinary learning opportunity her students will lose. She shares these frustrations with Ms Caldwell across the hall and while both are disappointed, they feel that, other than their caring principal, no policy makers or test writers will listen to their concerns. Both realize that the unit is time consuming and is based on content that will only appear in one or two test questions. They acknowledge that there are other goals and standards to be met, and Ms Hopper moves on with her lesson planning.

Ms Hopper pages through the testing guide, issued by the State Department of Education. While she generally believes the state standards are good, she feels distant and disconnected from the testing material. She scans the author information page to learn more about the creators of this test and its guide. Expecting to discover the biographies of master teachers who crafted these materials in light of their many years in the classroom, she reads about politicians, educational consultants, and university professors. Ms Hopper begins to wonder whether these authors have spent time in classrooms or talking to teachers. She wonders whether they know about the ESL (English as a Second Language) children struggling to learn English in her classroom. She wonders whether the authors are held to any standards of accountability in the way that recent policy holds her. She wonders whether their children attend a school not making adequate yearly progress, or perhaps a private school not required to undergo national testing.

Shaking herself, Ms Hopper decides that she must make the best of the situation. She reads through the guide carefully, adjusting her lesson plans and daily activities accordingly. She keeps the guide on the top of her desk and decides that she will view it as a motivator to do her job well and to ensure that the children are learning key information and skills. As the months pass, she turns to the guide often and, as it recommends, allocates a portion of each week to reviewing basic test-taking skills with her students. She encourages them to rest up, eat a good breakfast, and try their very best. As the testing week approaches the principal begins to make daily announcements about the test, telling students of its importance for measuring the achievement of each individual and the school. Parents begin to call Ms Hopper. A university professor asks about what content material will appear on the test, while a Latina homemaker asks what she can do to help prepare her child for the test the following week. Ms Hopper tries to confidently assure them that the students will be fine and explains the importance of the test, but she is aware that her voice falters at times and her tone is not entirely convincing.

On the first day of testing week, several children enter the classroom visibly distressed. One girl, who is usually tidy and neat, has managed to untuck her shirt and ruin her ponytail as she repeatedly and anxiously runs her fingers through it. Another girl asks to use the restroom again and again. Ms Hopper tries to calm and reassure her class as she passes out the test, but she realizes that the lengthy and detailed directions she is giving them only compound their anxiety. As students begin the test, the boy in the front row hurriedly grabs his pencil and fills in the bubbles as quickly as he can, seemingly without reading the test questions. Another girl, the star of the class, raises her hand and says she thinks there may be two correct answers to a question. Although curious to hear the student's rationale as she would usually request in class, Ms Hopper quiets her and urges her to choose one answer and move on to the next question. The following test day starts much the same way. As the children get deeper into the test, Ms Hopper picks up the guide and begins to worry that there may have been content items or test taking directions she has missed. When she looks back up at the class a few minutes later, the shy boy who sits on the edge of the class has disappeared. She scans the room and finally spots him underneath his desk crying. Ms Hopper throws the guide in her bottom desk drawer and walks back to the tear-soaked boy.

Democratically accountable teaching

This project generated a wealth of rich insights into how teachers are making sense of current demands for accountability as enacted in required standards and tests, and how their own assessment and evaluation practices intersect these external demands. This paper offers one story from amidst this wealth. Like our other stories, this one is grounded in the data we collected and includes some actual vignettes shared with us, but is otherwise constructed by the authors. It is primarily intended to illustrate some dimensions of "accountable teaching" that we perceive as consonant with democratic understandings of accountability.

Janice's math lesson

As soon as she completed her instructions in her grade 2–3 classroom for the math manipulative group work activities, Janice made a bee-line for Andrea's group. Andrea had spent the weekend with her father, as she did every third weekend, and she often returned from these visits distracted and unable to focus or concentrate. Janice perceived Andrea's father as well meaning. She had visited all of her new students' homes – including both homes in cases of divorced parents – at the beginning of the year, and the father clearly wanted to do well by his daughter. But he didn't seem to know how to enact his caring and, based on a few things Andrea had shared with Janice, seemed to mostly sideline or even ignore his daughter, often through an overabundance of material gifts.

When Janice reached the table where Andrea's group was working, she just stood quietly to one side observing. She noticed that Andrea was making eye contact with her peers, was smiling some, talking a lot (one of Andrea's characteristic traits), and was actively participating in the group task. Janice smiled to herself. Andrea seemed to be OK this time.

Janice moved on to the next table, and her attention first focused on Nancy. Nancy's worksheet for the group activity was characteristically sloppy, with handwriting that was almost undecipherable. And Nancy was just watching her peers as they engaged in the activity with some animation. When someone else shouted out an answer, Nancy would just write it down on the next available space on the worksheet. Like other struggling students, Nancy's peer relationships were strained and she had difficulty being a contributing member of a group. Understanding why this was so was a long-term project of Janice's. But, Janice knew Nancy had pretty good math abilities because she had worked individually with Nancy numerous times, both on problems and on diagnostic assessments. In particular, Nancy's spatial reasoning abilities were strong, and this math activity engaged just such abilities. Janice took a step closer and reminded the group to move the wand around the table. The wand – small and silver and made of plastic – when put at a child's place signified that that child was the leader for that problem. All groups were to move their wand around, taking turns at leading the group in problem solving. Janice had devised this strategy years ago in order to support her commitment to small group work with heterogeneous groups of students.

Janice stayed near Nancy's group, as she wanted to observe Nancy's turn at the leadership wand and ascertain Nancy's attention, engagement, and understanding. While waiting, she made a visual circuit of the classroom to check on how other groups were faring. Her gaze stopped for a moment on Francisco, and she inwardly groaned. Her encounter with Francisco's *abuela* (grandmother) last week was still painfully fresh. She had asked Francisco to stay in for recess on Wednesday to review the literacy lesson from that morning. Francisco was a wonderfully cheerful and happy child, and he gladly obliged. But he was beginning to falter in his reading progress and Janice, in coordination with Evergreen's bilingual and ESL teachers, was struggling to understand the specific character of the problem and to devise strategies to address it. It wasn't a language problem, as Francisco was displaying similar difficulties in his Spanish reading lessons. It seemed to be more an issue of decoding, in both languages.

Anyway, while working with Francisco last Wednesday, Janice had encouraged him to talk about his interests and dreams, as she often did with her students. All 8-year-olds have dreams! Francisco's dream was to be a soccer player; he dreamed of playing for his home country of Mexico's national team. Janice expressed enthusiasm and support for this dream, while also endeavoring to temper her response with some realism. She believed very strongly that sports offered real possibilities for only a tiny fraction of the young people who aspired to the status of a major league athlete, especially young people of color. And she wanted to insist that these young people develop their other skills and competencies, in case the sports didn't work out. To expect less of children of color was prejudiced and undemocratic, she thought. Well, Francisco told his grandmother about this conversation, and she came storming into Janice's classroom on Thursday morning, demanding an explanation and a retraction from Janice. "How could you deny this young boy his dreams?" implored the grandmother in a mix of Spanish and English. Janice's 10 months of Spanish classes had helped her understand what the grandmother was saying. But understanding was not the same as reconciliation. Janice remained worried about her relationship with Francisco and realized, once again, that a small bit of language facility could not bridge cultural divides.

As Janice waited for the leadership wand to come around to Nancy, she continued her visual review of the classroom. Again, her gaze paused – this time on Billy. Billy was a child with diagnosed learning disabilities, related to his difficulties in information processing and sequencing information tasks. Billy spent an hour every day with Sandra, Evergreen's learning disabilities specialist. Janice and Sandra had worked together at Evergreen for over 25 years! Janice was recalling what Sandra had shared during their last team meeting. State testing had happened – as it inexorably does every March – a few weeks ago. Billy had gone to Sandra's room to take the tests because he was eligible for testing modifications, including extra time. Sandra had reported that when Billy got to her room, he sat on the rug in the reading corner with his back to the classroom and wouldn't talk or move for anything. After 10 minutes of pleading and cajoling, Sandra decided to honor Billy's distress and not insist that he take the reading test scheduled for that day. Billy stayed in the reading corner and, after a bit of time, simply went to sleep.

Ah, the leadership wand was now at Nancy's place, and Janice returned her attention to this young girl. Nancy picked up the wand and started waving it through the air, although somewhat listlessly. Her three other group members stared at her, waiting quietly and, it seemed, respectfully. Janice, sensing Nancy's need for help, took a small step closer, bent down, and said, "Nancy, why don't you do a drawing of this problem for your group?" Nancy loved to draw and Janice had used this interest before in her individual work with

Nancy. In addition, Nancy had a special talent for representing mathematical issues in pictorial or graphic form. Nancy's eyes focused on Janice's, she gave a quick nod, and bent down to begin her sketch.

Reprise

Janice and many of her colleagues at Evergreen Elementary School engaged in evaluative practices quite different from those mandated by *NCLB*, and in our view, quite a bit more consonant with what educational accountability in a democratic society should look like.[6] These teachers' evaluative practices comprised ongoing, contextual, dynamic assessments of their students' progress – enacted primarily through keen observations of student learning activities and micro-decisions about appropriate pedagogical strategies for each child in their classroom, each day, all day long. These micro-decisions integrated teachers' knowledge of the students' individual characteristics and of their lives outside of school, and they focused on specific skills and content mastery while also supporting the holistic development of the whole child. Student work habits, relationships with their peers, self-discipline and self-confidence were all part of Janice's evaluative assessments of her students, as were dispositions like respect for others and acceptance of those who are different from you – thereby signaling that these dimensions of child development are themselves important and valued. Multiple forms of representation were also featured in Janice's ways of assessing her students' work and progress – thereby signaling a respect and valuing of diverse student talents and capabilities.

Janice further situated her evaluative self within a web of shared responsibility. At the center of this web were her Evergreen colleagues; close by were the families of her students. Janice actively involved her colleagues when multiple forms of expertise could better figure out what a particular child needed, either academically or socio-emotionally. Janice took the initiative in learning something about her students' families and in maintaining close communication with parents and guardians; she also aspired to partnerships and relationships of mutual respect and understanding with these families – all in service to her students' healthy development, academically and otherwise.[7] In short, in her assessments and evaluations, Janice treated her students and their families with agency and respect, thereby fostering these commitments throughout the strands of web.

Evergreen teachers also highly valued their collegial community and the inspired leadership of their principal. They all spoke about these. Yet Evergreen teachers took for granted the presence of well-resourced and well-maintained classrooms in which to work and, for many of their children, the active support and involvement of parents and families in the child's education. Not one mentioned the conditions under which they taught and their children learned either as important contributors to or impediments of their effectiveness as teachers. So, for most Evergreen teachers, the accountability and high-stakes testing demands presented by *NCLB* were experienced as disconnected from their own understandings of student learning and their own evaluative practices and as intrusive into some of their teaching practices, as illustrated by the Oregon Trail story, but otherwise just another external requirement to be endured. Recall that Evergreen students generally do well on the State Test. Recall that most of the Evergreen teachers we interviewed are seasoned practitioners, confident in their knowledge and judgment, well supported by their leaders and communities.

NCLB-inspired accountability assumes that all teachers and students toil in similarly well resourced schools in communities with similarly deep commitments to education. Of course, this is not so. And the *NCLB* legislation – which restricts the meanings of school quality to individual student test performance, devalues the professional judgment of teachers, and eschews the web of shared responsibility essential to a strong educational system in a democratic society – will not make it so. In counterpoint, democratic accountability, at root, aspires to provide all of our nation's children and the teachers who serve them with well-resourced and well-supported, taken-for-granted places for their work as teachers and learners.

Notes

1 The project on which this paper is based was funded by a grant from the University of Illinois Research Board, 2004–5. An earlier version of this paper was presented at the ICARE conference on "The social practice of an educational research community," Education and Social Research Institute, Manchester Metropolitan University, Manchester, England, September 2005. See also Feinberg *et al.* (2005).
2 These include mandating summer school for failing students and providing vouchers for students to attend different schools, including public, private, and religious schools, at the home school's expense.
3 There are many other criticisms of the notions of accountability embedded in *NCLB*, including, for example, its punitive rather than restorative character, its assumptions about radical homogeneity of student learning and performance, and its neglect of teacher professional development. Our work most directly engages the concerns stated about educational responsibility and outcomes.
4 All names used in this paper are pseudonyms.
5 More detailed information about our inquiry design and methods is available upon request from the first author.
6 In some important ways, *NCLB* accountability is eroding these teachers' commitments to ongoing, contextual, holistic student assessment. But that is another story (Feinberg *et al.*, 2005).
7 Within this framework of shared responsibility, Janice confessed, as did nearly all participants in this small study, that she repeatedly found it difficult to draw the line between her reach as a teacher and family matters. That is, there were some facets of working with children that were beyond her influence, beyond her authority, or both; but it was hard in the specificity of time and place to always know just what these were.

References

Abma, T.A. (ed.) (2001) Dialogue in evaluation. Special issue, *Evaluation*, 7(2).

Beadie, N. (2004) Moral errors and strategic mistakes: Lessons from the history of student accountability. In K.A. Sirotnik (ed.), *Holding accountability accountable: What ought to matter in public education* (pp. 35–50), New York: Teachers College Press.

Darling-Hammond, L. (2003). Standards and assessments: where we are and what we need, *Teachers College Record* (online, http://www.tcrecord.org/).

Dillon, S. (2003) States are relaxing education standards to avoid sanctions from federal law, *The New York Times*, May 22, p. A25.

Dubner, S.J. (2003) The probability that a real-estate agent is cheating you (and other riddles on modern life), *The New York Times Magazine*, August 3, p. 23ff.

Feinberg, W., Greene, J.C., McGough, S. and Miron, L. (2005) Illinois Project for Democratic Accountability. Unpublished paper. University of Illinois, Urbana-Champaign.

Haney, W. (2000) The myth of the Texas miracle in education, *Education Policy Analysis Archives*, 8(41).

Hoff, D.J. (2000) N.Y.C. probe levels test-cheating charges, *Education Week*, 19(16), 3.

Hursh, D. (2005) The growth of high-stakes testing in the USA: Accountability, markets and the decline in educational equality, *British Educational Research Journal*, 31(5), 605–22.

James-Burdumy, S., Dynarksi, M., Moore, M., Deke, J., Mansfield, W. and Pistorino, C. (2005) *When schools stay open late: The national evaluation of the 21st Century Learning Community Centers, Final Report*, U.S. Department of Education, Institute of Education Sciences, National Center for Educational Evaluation and Regional Assistance. Available at http://www.ed.gov/ies/ncee.

Lewin, T. and Medina, J. (2003) To cut failure rates, schools shed students, *New York Times,* July 31.

Linn, R.L. (2003) Accountability: responsibility and reasonable expectations, 2003 presidential address to AERA, *Educational Researcher*, 32(7), 3–13.

Louis, K.S., Febey, K. and Schroeder, R. (2005) State-mandated accountability in high schools: teachers' interpretations of a new era, *Educational Evaluation and Policy Analysis*, 27(2), 177–204.

McNeil, L. (2000) *Contradictions of school reform: Educational costs of standardized testing.* New York: Routledge.

Noguera, P.A. (2004). Standards for what? Accountability for whom? Rethinking standards-based reform in public education. In K.A. Sirotnik (ed.), *Holding accountability accountable: What ought to matter in public education* (pp. 66–81), New York: Teachers College Press.

Oakes, J., Blasi, G. and Rogers, J. (2004) Accountability for adequate and equitable opportunities to learn. In K.A. Sirotnik (ed.), *Holding accountability accountable: What ought to matter in public education* (pp. 82–99), New York: Teachers College Press.

Power, M. (1997) *The audit society*, New York: Oxford Press.

Ryan, K.E. (2005) Making educational accountability more democratic, *American Journal of Evaluation*, 26(4), 532–43.

Siegel, H. (2004) What ought to matter in public schooling: judgment, standards, and responsible accountability. In K.A. Sirotnik (ed.), *Holding accountability accountable: What ought to matter in public education* (pp. 51–65), New York: Teachers College Press.

Sirotnik, K.A. (2002) Promoting responsible accountability in schools and education, *Phi Delta Kappan*, 83(9), 662–73.

Sirotnik, K.A. (2004a) Holding accountability accountable – hope for the future? In K.A. Sirotnik (ed.), *Holding accountability accountable: What ought to matter in public education* (pp. 148–69), New York: Teachers College Press.

Sirotnik, K.A. (2004b) Introduction. In K.A. Sirotnik (ed.), *Holding accountability accountable: What ought to matter in public education* (pp. 1–17), New York: Teachers College Press.

Soder, R. (2004) The double bind of civic education: assessment and accountability. In K.A. Sirotnik (ed.), *Holding accountability accountable: What ought to matter in public education* (pp. 100–15), New York: Teachers College Press.

Stake, R.E. (1999). The goods on American education, *Phi Delta Kappan*, 80, 668–72.

Chapter 9

From 'human capital' theory to 'capability theory' as a driver of curriculum reform

A reflection on the educational implications of the work of Amartya Sen in the light of John Dewey's account of educational values

John Elliott

Introduction: capabilities, human capital and the development of society

Educationalists are beginning to explore the implications of Amatyra Sen's 'capability theory' for curriculum planning and pedagogy in educational institutions (see Saito 2003 and Walker 2005, 2006). This chapter is an additional contribution to an emerging interest by introducing a largely philosophical perspective that connects Sen's work to Dewey's account of educational values. The major thrust of Sen's work is to use philosophical tools to reconceptualize the relationship between economy and society in the context of development. He argues that development consists of 'the expansion of the "capabilities" of persons to lead the kind of lives they value and have reason to value' (1999, p.18). Capabilities consist of the substantive freedoms people have to do things they may come to value and, in so doing, enrich their lives. They presuppose both conditions of negative and positive freedom, i.e. freedom from external constraints on their opportunities to do things, and the development of capacities for doing them that are internal to the person (see Sen 2002, pp. 11–12). From Sen's capability perspective the end of development is the expansion of human freedom rather than economic growth at the societal level and income growth at the level of the private individual. He explicitly invokes Aristotle's contention in the *Nicomachean Ethics* that 'wealth is evidently not the good that we are seeking; for it is merely useful and for the sake of something else' (Sen 1999, p. 14). For Sen the linkage between economic wealth and people's overall capability to live lives they have reason to value is a contingent and complex matter that can vary in strength from society to society and depend on other circumstances. It cannot simply be viewed as a straightforward linear relation between cause and effect. Just as the expansion of people's capabilities or substantive freedoms may, at least in part, be a consequence of economic growth in society and growth in their individual incomes, it may also be the case that they contribute indirectly to such growth. The relationship is a reciprocal one.

An important distinction for Sen is that between the constitutive and instrumental roles of freedom in the development of society. The constitutive role relates to the intrinsic value of substantive freedoms in enriching human life, whereas the instrumental role relates to their contribution to economic progress. Capabilities are constitutive of a person's freedom to do things she has reason to value for their own sake, regardless of their contribution to economic progress and the accumulation of personal wealth. Capabilities may well possess 'commodity value' in labour markets, as a means of serving the economic ends of society and the individual, but such value will constitute extrinsic rather than intrinsic reasons for developing them. Sen does not wish to deny that economic benefits may be contingent upon peoples' capabilities to do things they value for their own sake. What he does deny is that the primary value of these activities or *functionings* resides in their instrumental value as means to some further end. Since capabilities are constitutive of a person's freedom to do and be what she has reason to value for its own sake, those who possess them cannot simply view them as commodities. This has important implications, as Sen has pointed out, for the role of education in the context of development. The primary aim of educational institutions is to establish conditions that expand people's substantive freedoms to do things they have reason to value for their own sake (Sen 1999 p. 41). For Sen such an aim is quite consistent with the view that educational provision may also indirectly serve economic purposes. However, in certain contexts, it does not have to be explicitly structured by such purposes as a condition of serving them. He argues, for example, that China's success compared with India in making use of market mechanisms to promote economic growth, depended on a well-educated and highly literate population that existed prior to efforts to move towards a more market-oriented economy.

Nevertheless, Sen acknowledges that contemporary economic analysis is reshaping perceptions of the role of educational institutions and systems. He argues (1999, pp. 292–3) that this analysis, based on empirical studies of economic growth in East Asia, Europe and North America, reflects a shift of emphasis from 'seeing capital accumulation in primarily physical terms to viewing it as a process in which the productive quality of human beings is integrally involved'. From this 'human capital' perspective, education is viewed as having an important instrumental function in promoting economic expansion through the formation of capacities that augment production possibilities.

How then does Sen view the relationship between his own 'capability theory' of development and the 'human capital' theory that is increasingly shaping educational provision in many countries, and rendering educational policy-making an integral part of economic policy-making? Do they not represent alternative perspectives on the role of educational institutions in the context of the development of society? Sen argues that although the two perspectives are distinct they are not incompatible and should not be treated as alternatives. He contends that, although 'human capital' theory presents a narrower view of development than his 'capability' perspective, it can nevertheless fit into the 'the more inclusive process of human capability' (1999, p. 293). This is because both place human qualities at the centre of attention, and therefore cannot but be related.

I find that Sen is somewhat ambiguous in the way he portrays the relationship between human qualities that can be employed as 'capital' in production and human capabilities. In the main, he portrays this relationship in terms of overlapping content. The difference in perspective is largely reflected in the 'yardstick of assessment' (1999, p. 293). The same content can be evaluated according to different standards of achievement. From the 'human capital' perspective, human capabilities are appraised in terms of their 'commodity value' within the processes of production, whereas from the 'capability' perspectives, they are appraised in terms of the expansion of people's freedom to lead lives they have reason to value and 'to enhance the real choices they have' in this respect (1999, p. 293). These different yardsticks for assessing the benefits that similar human qualities bring to both society and the individual rest upon the distinction Sen makes between *direct* and *indirect* benefits. The same human quality may be judged to be of value because of the way it directly enables a person to function in a way that enriches their lives or because of the way it indirectly contributes to the augmentation of production possibilities. It can therefore constitute both a substantive freedom and a productive capacity. Hence, education can make provision for the formation of human capacities that constitute both 'capabilities' and 'human capital'. However, for Sen, the capability perspective implies a much wider role for education inasmuch as it can provide for the formation of capacities that have little or no obvious commodity value, but can nevertheless directly enrich human life (see 1999, p. 294). By way of example, Sen writes:

> If education makes a person more efficient in commodity production, then this is clearly an enhancement of human capital. This can add to the value of production in the economy and also to the income of the person who has been educated. But even with the same level of income, many benefit from education – in reading, communicating, arguing, in being able to choose in a more informed way, in being taken more seriously by others and so on. The benefits of education, thus, exceed its role as human capital in commodity production. The broader capability perspective would note – and value – these additional roles as well. (1999, p. 294)

At times though he acknowledges a practical problem about integrating the two perspectives that revolves around the distinction between means and ends in making social arrangements for development. He points out that there is with respect to education:

a crucial valuational difference between the human-capital focus and the concentration on human capabilities – The acknowledgement of the role of human qualities in promoting and sustaining economic growth – momentous as it is – tells us nothing about why economic growth is sought in the first place. If, instead, the focus is, ultimately, on the expansion of human freedom to live the kind of lives that people have reason to value, then the role of economic growth in expanding these opportunities has to be integrated into that more foundational understanding of the process of development as the expansion of human capability to lead more worthwhile and free lives. (1999, p. 295)

I read Sen as saying that this integration is not simply something that has to happen at the conceptual level but also in the practical arrangements for education. At the practical level, is it not the case that the 'crucial valuational difference' between the two perspectives can culminate in a curriculum that separates the production of 'human capital' from the formation of capabilities, and treats the learning outcomes of the former as quite separate kinds of capacities to 'capabilities'? Sen appears to acknowledge such a possibility when he warns of the danger of treating human beings merely as a means of production rather than 'the end of the exercise'. In my view, he is not simply warning of the danger of narrowing the sets of capabilities developed through education, but also of separating out the content of 'human capital' from the content of 'capability'. Although he is far from explicit about the form this separation can take, I would argue that we have many examples of this happening in the guise of what is known as 'competency-based' education and training. A yardstick of assessment that is known as the 'standards methodology' drives the latter vision of the formation of productive abilities. The methodology involves analysing an occupation into its core functions as a basis for specifying the standards that have to be met in any competent performance of a particular function. The occupation is broken down into functional units and for each unit performance standards are specified to indicate precisely what a trainee must be able to do to achieve functional competence. From this methodological perspective productive capacities are defined as quite specific functional skills (competencies). The exercise of such skills will depend on underpinning knowledge of a largely instrumental kind, i.e. knowledge that can be usefully applied to selecting the best means of achieving the desired performance outcomes.

I want to argue that by defining productive capacities, viewed as 'human capital', largely in terms of 'competencies' the standards methodology delineates quite different sorts of capacities to what Sen calls 'capabilities'. In doing so it will be important to further clarify Sen's use of the term 'capability'. I will attempt to do this in the following section indirectly by viewing his conception in the light of two strands of philosophical thinking, which are themselves connected; namely, Aristotle's concept of *eudaimonia* and Dewey's concept of *appreciation value*. Sen (1999) himself acknowledges the connections between his capability approach to development and Aristotle's focus on human 'flourishing' and 'capacity' in the

Eudemian Ethics (p. 24). Since Dewey, in the course of developing his account of educational values, also draws on and critiques the ideas that Aristotle expounds in this work, I felt that it would be interesting to explore the connections between Dewey's account and Sen's notion of capability, and whether these cast any light on the implications of his work for education. Walker (2005, p.107) has argued that Sen's work can be located, if not explicitly, in many of Dewey's ideas. I am particularly interested in the extent to which Dewey's theory of experience throws light on a distinction I want to draw between 'capability' and 'competence' as educational aims. In showing the connections, between Sen's concept of 'capability' and certain strands of Aristotle's and Dewey's thinking, I hope to push the emerging educational discourse surrounding Sen's work a step or two further. In the final two sections of the chapter I will draw out the main implications of the capability approach for education, and in the process address a major issue posed by Saito and Walker respectively.

Capabilities, functionings, and values

Sen links his definition of 'capability' very tightly to the concept of 'human functionings'. He states:

> A person's capability refers to the alternative combinations of functionings that are feasible for her to achieve. Capability is thus a kind of freedom: to achieve various lifestyles. (1999, p. 75)

For Sen, a 'life-style' or 'way of life' will consist of a 'capability-set' – a set of functions – that a person has 'reason to value' as enriching their lives. This functional perspective acknowledges the Aristotelian roots of Sen's capability approach. For Aristotle *functionings* are activities which, when performed well, enable an organism to flourish in accordance with its nature. They are therefore activities connected to human well-being or flourishing. Human flourishing for Aristotle consisted not so much of being in a state of mind such as feeling happy or in love, but rather of doing something well in accordance with standards of excellence that are internal to the activity. Some of these functions would be common to all living beings, such as nutrition and reproduction, while others Aristotle viewed as distinctively human. The latter included practical social and political activity in accordance with excellences that he depicted in the *Nicomachean Ethics* as moral virtues. However, the highest *functionings* for Aristotle were depicted in the *Eudemian Ethics* as those 'activities of the soul' that gave expression to the faculty of reason, which he regarded as super-human and partaking of the divine nature. Human flourishing at its highest level consisted in the pursuit of activities in accordance with those standards of reasoning that he called 'excellences of the intellect'. Aristotle assumed that this higher level of functioning demanded a life of leisure that was detached from the practical pursuits of everyday living. Intellectual pursuits at their best and in their proper functioning culminated in a contemplative appreciation of things in the form of theoretical knowledge (*episteme*) that is valued for its own sake rather than for any further end. Indeed Aristotle regarded knowledge that was simply useful for the purposes of productive enterprise (*techne*), although necessary to provide human beings with the necessities of life, as intellectually inferior. Such knowledge did not issue from activity in accordance with the excellences of the intellect, since it did not free the mind from the conditions of bodily existence. This view effectively restricted access to the higher levels of human flourishing to a leisured class of males, and thereby rationalized much of the existing social order in the Athenian city-state at the time.

It is not difficult to see how Aristotle's hierarchy of functionings is reflected in western educational systems. The traditional role of the university, for example, as an educational institution is to cater for higher-order functionings that only an elite is capable of achieving. The traditional distinction between academic and vocational subjects also reflects Aristotle's distinction between *episteme* and *techne* as domains of knowledge, and the presumed inferiority of the latter as the culmination of human functionings.

Sen clearly links his idea of capabilities to the Aristotelian notion of human functionings. Capabilities are capacities to perform functions, that contribute to human flourishing, well i.e. in accordance with standards of excellence that are internal to that activity. However, he does not organize functionings in terms of Aristotle's hierarchical scale of values running from 'higher-order intellectual' to 'practical' to 'technical' functionings. On the other hand he does appear to differentiate functions that meet basic human needs and constitute common conditions of human flourishing, from those which might make up a freely chosen way of life. The former he links to basic human rights, such as 'elementary capabilities linked with basic survival needs e.g. being able to avoid starvation, under-nourishment, escapable morbidity and premature mortality' and 'those associated with literacy and numeracy, enjoying political participation and freedom of speech' (Sen 1999, p. 36).

In my opinion this is a far cry from establishing an evaluative hierarchy of functionings and capabilities. If Sen had organized *human functionings* along Aristotle's scale of values then a person's most important capabilities would refer to a combination of functionings of a purely intellectual kind that it was feasible for her to achieve. This would largely restrict the conditions of human freedom to opportunities for achieving an intellectual life-style, as opposed to opportunities for choosing between various life-styles. From Aristotle's perspective human freedom consists of capacities to achieve functionings in accordance with standards of reasoning that culminate in theoretical knowledge. It is 'freedom' understood as the liberation of the mind from the conditions of bodily existence and practical living rather than a person's freedom to choose their own good. If Sen shared Aristotle's conception of human flourishing he would have to accept the mind–body dualism it presupposes, and be unable to claim any overlap in content between capabilities and those productive abilities that constitute human capital. From Aristotle's perspective, the excellences of the intellect and productive abilities fall unambiguously into the separate functioning realms of *episteme* and *techne* respectively.

The importance Aristotle attributes to 'excellences of the intellect' in his account of human flourishing is not irrelevant to attempts to clarify Sen's concept of capability. I will show this by drawing on Dewey's critique of Aristotle's ideas and the way they have shaped the structure of the school curriculum in western societies, and his attempt within this critique to acknowledge some of Aristotle's insights and their enduring significance for education.

Aristotle was permanently right, argues Dewey (1916, pp. 255–6 of Macmillan paperback edition 1966), in his belief that 'any occupation or art or study deserves to be called mechanical if it renders the body or soul or intellect of free persons unfit for the exercise and practice of excellence,' and in assuming 'the inferiority and subordination of mere skill in performance and mere accumulation of external products to understanding, sympathy of appreciation, and the free play of ideas'. Inasmuch as all mercenary occupations simply involve the operation of mechanical skills then Aristotle was once again permanently right, Dewey contends, in believing that they deprived the intellect 'of the conditions of its exercise and so of its dignity'.

Aristotle's error, according to Dewey, lay in assuming 'that there is a natural divorce between efficiency in producing commodities and rendering service, and self-directive thought; between significant knowledge and practical achievement". For Dewey such a divorce is socially constructed and what Aristotle described was simply 'the life that was before him' (p. 255). He argues that in spite of all the social changes since Aristotle's time – the abolition of legal serfdom, the spread of democracy, the extension of science and of general education – 'there remains enough of a cleavage in society into a learned and an unlearned class, a leisure and a labouring class, to make his point of view a most enlightening one from which to criticize the separation between culture and utility in present education' (p. 255). The idea still prevails, argued Dewey nearly a century ago now, that an education that is fit for the masses as opposed to an elite 'must be useful or practical education in a sense which opposes useful and practical to nurture of appreciation and liberation of thought'. As a result 'our actual system is an inconsistent mixture' of liberal and practical studies (p. 257).

Dewey was writing in 1916 but even today, in the first decade of the twenty-first century, in spite of the development of comprehensive schooling in many countries, curriculum planners are still making a distinction between academic and vocational subjects that enable students to follow different curriculum pathways before leaving school. The persistence of this distinction, and the difficulties of securing parity of status for vocational subjects, reflects a continuing divorce between conceptions of the skills linked to the production of commodities and conceptions of intellectual excellence. This divorce amounts to a failure at the level of curriculum and pedagogy – in spite of the increasing political and social emancipation of the masses – to transcend the Greek philosophy of life. It is deeply embedded in the standards methodology that shaped the development of national vocational qualifications (NVQs) in the UK, and the expansion of its 'post-compulsory' learning and skills agenda outside the confines of the 'higher education' sector. Dewey set out a vision of educational transformation that fused the two conceptions cited above by dissolving the mind–body dualism inherent in the Greek philosophy of life. It is to this vision and its connections with Sen's notion of capability that I now turn.

For Dewey, the dynamic nature of contemporary society poses practical problems for education that could only be resolved by transcending the Greek philosophy of life. The practical activities of everyday life, including those linked to gainful employment, can no longer in the main be viewed as matters of routine carried out under the supervision of others (p. 258). Job-specific skills associated with routine tasks cannot 'be made useful beyond themselves', argues Dewey. What is needed in dynamic social and working environments are skills that can be put to use in new situations and are under the personal control of the individuals who use them. These kinds of skills cannot be achieved without a 'deepening of knowledge and perfecting of judgment' (p. 259). Activities that involve such skilful performances constitute expressions of a 'trained intelligence' and are carried on 'because of a personal appreciation of their meaning'. They differ significantly from those activities that characterize rule-of-thumb occupations 'that are engaged in for results external to the mind' of the worker and over which she may have little control. The ends she pursues through her activity become *her ends* rather than simply those provided by others.

Dewey argues that the intellectual and social context of work is very different now to that which obtained in ancient Greece (p. 259). The elements due to custom and routine are increasingly subordinate 'in most economic callings' to elements derived from the study of mathematics, science, geography, politics and other subject-matters. There is an increasing economic dependence on science and mathematics, and as the area of the world 'influenced by economic production and influencing consumption' expands so there is a greater need to incorporate geographical and political considerations into the exercise of skill and judgment in many occupations. Changes in the context of work have opened up uses for what was once regarded as useless kinds of knowledge. Dewey concludes that as the social uses of traditional academic subject-matters widen and expand in response to the changing intellectual and social context of work their intellectual value and practical value 'approach the same limit.' His argument dissolves any tight distinction between academic and practical subjects in the curriculum and implies that social and economic change imposes limits on our ability to predict and demarcate which kinds of academic subject-matter will have the greatest utility for the production of commodities. Inasmuch as notions of a common core curriculum demarcate studies that are predicted to have the greatest economic commodity value as human capital, they may well prove to be dysfunctional in the face of economic changes that arise from the globalization of markets. In responding to such changes societies may need to have a much more open view of which areas of study will yield human capital for the purposes of production.

Dewey's views echo the current acknowledgement that economies are increasingly knowledge-based, and that the 'higher order' skills increasingly demanded by employers are similar to the 'intellectual qualities' the universities have claimed to foster through the traditional academic curriculum. There are now indeed attempts at the present time in a number of countries to reshape the organization of educational systems, particularly at the upper secondary school and post-compulsory levels, to allow for a blurring of the boundaries, between curricula that cater for the acquisition of productive skills and those that nurture what Dewey calls 'appreciation and liberation of thought'. However, Dewey was quite clear that institutional change alone was not sufficient to complete the process of educational transformation. What was needed were curriculum and pedagogical interventions that are grounded in a coherent vision of the link between the development of productive and practical abilities and the cultivation of what Aristotle called the 'excellences of the intellect'. He attempted to provide it, and I shall now attempt to connect elements of this vision with Sen's concept of capability.

Dewey's distinction between 'to value' and 'to valuate or evaluate' throws light on Sen's view of 'capabilities' as constitutive of a person's freedom to choose a way of life she values, and has reason to value. For Dewey 'to value' refers to a direct appreciation of the quality of an experience, unmediated by the use of words and symbols, while 'evaluation' refers to the passing of a reasoned judgment 'upon the nature and amount of its value as compared with something else' (p. 238). Seen in this light, 'capability' refers to both capacities for appreciative realizations of value, and a capability for evaluating the relative worth of different functions in choosing a way of life. I will first focus on Dewey's account of 'appreciative realizations of value' (pp. 232–8) and its significance for understanding what a 'capability' consists of in the context of a particular human functioning. Following this, I will focus on his account of evaluation as 'reasoned judgment' (pp. 239–43) and its significance for having a reason to value particular functionings as part of a way of life or chosen 'capability set'.

Dewey views appreciative realizations of value as the outcome of an imaginative engagement with a situation involving 'a warm and intimate taking in of the full scope of a situation' for enriching life. The imagination is the medium for appreciating the value of experiences in themselves – their intrinsic value – in every sphere of activity that is not simply mechanical, since 'the engagement of the imagination is the only thing that makes any activity more than mechanical'. Although such engagement is an intensely personal response, he regards it as part of the work of the intellect or understanding, arguing that such work cannot simply be confined to the use of language to represent experience. However, appreciative experience can be enlarged and given deeper meaning by connecting it to things that are absent and remote and which can only be presented symbolically. Dewey argues that linguistic media can only truly represent the absent and remote if they are used in a way that makes it enter into a present experience. The use of language to represent connections between direct experience and the absent and remote, and thereby give it deeper meaning is the process of thinking and reflection. For Dewey, there can be no authentic thought and reflection in the medium of language that is dissociated from contexts of immediate and direct experiences, and a personal need to make sense of them. Hence for Dewey, the construction of 'knowledge', conceived as representations of experience, is not the end of thinking and reflection. Such representations are not ends in themselves. Their role is to educate the imagination in its search for personal meaning.

In order to clarify Dewey's view of the relationship between experience and thinking, it is important to understand how he dissolves the dualism between mind and body (pp. 139–51). Experience for Dewey is never a purely passive affair. It is both active and passive. Experience is always doing something to change a thing, and therefore involves the use of the body. The passive aspect of experience relates to the consequences of 'doing' something. The changes made by a person's action reflect back into changes in her. Experience, for Dewey, always involves doing something and then suffering the consequences of doing it. Sometimes these consequences bring satisfaction to the agent and at other times dissatisfaction. In the former case what is done *works,* while in the latter case a problem arises in experience. If this alone constituted the totality of experience then, argues Dewey, learning from experience will simply consist of 'learning *what works*' on the basis of trial and error, and education would be reduced to training in mechanical and habitual routines underpinned by a knowledge of *what works*. On such an account of experience we would get nothing out of it 'to foresee what is likely to happen next, and no gain in ability to adjust ourselves to what is coming – no added control' (p. 140). In order to exercise personal agency and control over our actions we need to understand the connections between our actions and the consequences that flow from them and back into our experience. This is the task of thinking and reflection, which involves us stepping back from our immediate experience in order to give it a deeper and wider meaning. It is only in this context of making sense of our experience – of the personal hunt for connections – that theoretical representations of the world will convey any sense. Dewey argues that 'in just the degree in which mental activity is separated from active concern with the world, from doing something and connecting the doing with what is undergone' words and symbols come to take the place of ideas (p. 144).

The mind–body dualism has plagued western education since the days of Plato and Aristotle, and appears to have been transferred across the globe. Dewey's resolution links thinking and reflection to experience through a form of experimental inquiry in which the doing of something becomes 'an experiment with the world to find out what it is like' and the undergoing of consequences becomes 'the discovery of the connections of things' (p. 140). He claims that all thinking is a form of research that enables us to learn from our experience and to direct and control our actions in the service of our practical ends. As such, thinking is not an end in itself. Its role is to enhance our capacity for imaginatively doing the things we value in life. In Sen's terms its role might be couched as fostering our capabilities to realize valued functionings.

Dewey argues (p. 236) that the imagination, as the medium of appreciative realizations of value, is not to be identified with 'the imaginary', which leads to an exaggerated estimate of the role of 'fairy tales, myth, fanciful symbols, verse and something called 'Fine Art,' as agencies for developing imagination and appreciation'. Such an estimate leads to a segregation of the imagination to areas of the curriculum like literature and the fine arts to the neglect of imaginative vision in other areas where 'instruction is reduced to an unimaginative acquiring of specialized skill and amassing of a load of information'. Hence, the cultivation of the imagination as the medium for appreciative realizations of value should be an aim of education across all areas of study. Dewey argues a similar case with respect to all those intellectual powers that are valued in education and which he regards as involved in the development of a full appreciative valuing of experience. These include what are now fashionably regarded as 'higher-order thinking skills'; powers of reasoning and judgment – whether in relation to abstract, concrete or social entities – that have been traditionally segregated as the province of specialized academic disciplines, each serving a distinctive mental function. Dewey links such a segregation of studies in the curriculum to the organization of society into interests that are themselves regarded as the pursuit of quite distinct and isolated functions, such as 'politics, business, recreation, science, the learned professions, polite intercourse, and leisure'. Each course of study, he argues, is deemed to correspond to a particular interest and the specialized knowledge and skills that mark it off as distinctive and separate. Such interests may contribute to one another only externally and accidentally (p. 247). From this standpoint, Dewey contends, it appears to be unreasonable for a particular interest to acknowledge the unity and integrity of all experience and the role of education in fostering it. 'How unreasonable,' he exclaims, 'to expect that the pursuit of business should be itself a culture of the imagination, in breadth and refinement' (p. 248).

We must not, Dewey argues, 'divide the studies of the curriculum into the appreciative, those concerned with intrinsic value, and the instrumental, those which are of value for ends beyond themselves' (p. 249). Hence, in the case of Arithmetic, if it has never 'been realized or appreciated for itself, one will miss something of its capacity as a resource for other ends'. If there is a tendency to view the value of Arithmetic largely in instrumental terms, Dewey argues that the reverse is often the case with respect to literature, music and the fine arts. They are not, he contends (p. 238) the exclusive agencies of appreciation as they are often regarded. However, they are the chief *agencies* of an intensified and enhanced appreciation of human experience. This is because they 'select and focus the elements of enjoyable worth which make any experience enjoyable' for its own sake. As such they can provide resources for the pursuit of ends beyond themselves. In this sense functions are not discrete but overlapping, and enable elements developed in one context of activity to be transferred to another. Dewey cites the industrial arts as an example. Here the activities of production will call upon the exercise of capacities for aesthetic and artistic appreciation. In this respect, a person who draws on elements of enjoyable experience in this context to augment an industrial function will come to experience her activity as more than simply a contribution to economic productivity or personal income. It will also provide her with intrinsic enjoyment and satisfaction. From this perspective the arts can provide human capital for industry and commerce,

The inclusion in the curriculum of studies explicitly designed to serve particular economic and social interests (e.g. citizenship education) should not, Dewey argues, be regarded as activities that serve quite separate ends to forms of appreciative experience. The realization of the instrumental value of an activity, inasmuch as it takes a non-mechanical form, will depend on an appreciation of its intrinsic value. However, when the socially or economically serviceable aspects of studies are emphasized there are limits on the extent to which the quality of appreciative experience involved can be intensified and enhanced. Hence, there is an important role in the curriculum for studies that are primarily concerned with the intensification and enhancement of appreciative experience, not simply for its own sake but as a resource for sustaining more overtly instrumental activities as a medium for enriching the lives of their participants.

We are now in a position to see how Dewey's account of appreciative experience illuminates Sen's notion of 'capabilities' and its implications for education. Inasmuch as 'capabilities' consist of capacities for achieving particular functionings that intrinsically enrich human experience, they may be regarded as conditions that make appreciative realizations of value possible. From a Deweyan perspective, these functionings do not have to correspond with traditional curriculum subjects, or with the specialist knowledge and skills that have come to be associated with them. For example, a course of study may be explicitly designed to serve the interests of an occupation in the field of business and commerce, without denying or neglecting the opportunity it provides for an appreciative valuing of occupationally relevant experience in its own right and irrespective of its outcomes for production. From Dewey's perspective, the pedagogical process of inducting people into activities that serve the interests of production should also have regard for the integrity and unity of human experience. 'Capabilities' on this view will not refer to a set of discrete abilities or skills that have been isolated from a context of appreciative experience in terms of their purely productive functions. The achievement of a particular productive function will involve the combined use of a variety of specific abilities and dispositions. Viewed in this light a person's 'capability' will refer to a combination of elements exercised in the context of a particular functioning. In this respect it will have both a generic and context-bound aspect. The generic aspect refers to the fact that 'capabilities' may draw on similar powers of the intellect and imagination regardless of the particular context of functioning. The context-bound aspect refers to the fact that the use of these powers will shape up in rather different configurations across different functional contexts. Educationally this implies that the development of 'capabilities' is a very context-bound affair. They should not be confused with the notion of 'transferable skills'. The development of a person's 'capability' to achieve a particular functioning will, however, involve an enhanced capacity to transfer knowledge and skills acquired in other contexts to a new situation. As such, 'transferability' refers not so much to what is transferred as to a quality manifested in a person's increasing capability to improve their level of functioning in a situation.

The above account of 'capabilities' is relevant to Sen's view of their often overlapping relationship to human capital and its role in augmenting production processes, inasmuch as it implies that they are not skills or dispositions operating in isolation from a capacity for imaginative appreciations of situations. Such a use of skills, conceived largely as 'competences' in terms of their instrumental effectiveness for augmenting production, will as Dewey points out take a mechanical form. Although 'capabilities', when viewed as human capital, will involve the use of productive skills such a use will stem from the operation of an appreciative intelligence.

Dewey's account of evaluative judgment also throws further light on Sen's notion of capability. He depicts the formation of evaluative judgment as a mode of reasoning, which comes into play in a concrete practical situation where an agent is faced with a choice of ends that are themselves equally worth pursuing for their own sake, but conflict with each other. Faced with a concrete situation of choice, the agent seeks a reason for preferring one end to others in the light of her understanding of what is needed in the situation. Finding a reason for judging the relative worth of things as ends is a very context-bound affair. 'In the abstract, or at large' Dewey argues 'there is no such thing as degrees or order of value' (p. 239). There are no context-free standards of reasoning.

In addition to choosing an end in a concrete situation, the agent also has to deliberate about the instrumental value of alternative means of pursuing it, each of which may again be worth pursuing simply for its own sake. Instrumental valuing is a matter of discerning a connection between an activity and some further end. As I argued earlier, Dewey believed that unless the activity is appreciated as worth pursuing for its own sake, its instrumental value is limited and impoverished. This is because its value as a means of enriching the agent's experience in a situation depends upon the extent to which it manifests intrinsically valuable qualities that can be utilized as a resource for achieving the desired end. Reasoned judgments about means are context-bound estimates of the utility of the resources of imagination and intellect that alternative possibilities provided. Dewey also believed that forming a reasoned judgment about ends could not in practice be separated from reasoned judgments about means, since the former depended on what it was feasible for a person to achieve in a situation given the possible means available to her. Hence it is not wise in particular situations of choice to abstract reasoning about ends from reasoning about means.

Dewey's notion of evaluative reasoning is relevant to Sen's notion of capability as the freedom to choose between alternative combinations of functionings to construct a way of life that one values and has reason to value. Evaluative reasoning can be understood as the process by which a person finds 'a reason to value' some functions rather than others, all of which she will have experienced as intrinsically worthwhile, as part of her chosen way of life. The situated form such reasoning takes implies that choosing a way of life will not be a one-off event. It will be a gradual and deliberative process that integrates and synthesizes specific evaluative judgments across a range and variety of concrete situations of choice into a coherent way of life. This situated form of reasoning also implies that choosing a way of life will be open to new situations that arise in the context of everyday life. Judgments will be flexible and open to change in the light of further experience, rather than fixed and closed.

This interpretation of Sen's concept of capability in the light of Dewey's concept of evaluative reasoning, is particularly relevant to the former's distinction between 'the opportunity aspect' and the 'process aspect' of freedom (see, for example, 2002, p. 506). The *opportunity aspect* is 'concerned with our actual capability to achieve functionings that we value'. The *process aspect* relates to autonomous choice, 'having the levers of control in one's own hands (no matter whether this enhances the actual opportunities of achieving our objectives or not)'. Autonomous choice, for Sen, is a matter of opening up one's choices to a process of *rational self-scrutiny* that bears marked resemblances both to Aristotle's *practical reasoning* or *phronesis* (as distinct from *episteme* and *techne*) and to Dewey's *evaluative reasoning*. It involves a person being able to rationally assess both her goal values and the best means of pursuing them. The latter type of assessment will not only take the form of instrumental reasoning, weighing up the consequences of different alternatives, but also involve a consideration of reasons for restricting her choice of means on the grounds that some are more consistent than others with non-goal values, e.g. moral obligations towards others. This is consistent with Aristotle's conception of 'phronesis' as a deliberative process for determining, in particular concrete situations, those actions that are in accordance with virtue. Sen might also have included Dewey's conception of appreciative values as non-goal values.

Sen's distinction between the 'opportunity' and 'process' aspects of freedom tends to echo Dewey's distinction between 'to value' and 'evaluation'. Freedom of choice is enhanced by both an expansion of capabilities '*to appreciate*' a wide range of different functionings for their own sake, and the development of a capability for autonomous judgment and reasoning about which of these functionings make up a worthwhile way of life, either as ends or means, when faced with concrete situations of choice. From Dewey's perspective a chosen 'way of life' will consist of those patterns of judgment that have emerged from a process of evaluative reasoning across a range and variety of concrete situations that a person has experienced. It is this kind of process that Sen refers to as 'rational self-scrutiny'. It is the invariant and fundamental element in his account of freedom as capability, whereas specific capabilities under the opportunity aspect of freedom may vary. This is because what constitutes valuable functionings will vary as societies adapt to changes in their social and economic environment (1999, pp. 240–2). Changes in social and economic circumstances will result in the emergence of new forms of appreciative experience and the demise of old forms. Hence, the options people have available to them in choosing a way of living that they have reason to value cannot be fixed.

As Walker has pointed out (2005, pp.106–7), Sen resolutely resists pressure to produce lists of valuable capabilities because this would constitute a 'theory of capabilities'. Again he echo's Dewey's view (see above) that there are no context-free, transcendental, standards of reasoning against which to determine what would count as the 'good life'. With respect to one such principle proposed by economists, that of the *maximization of utility,* Sen argues (see 2002, pp. 39–42) that it restricts 'rational scrutiny' to having one's choices assessed solely in terms of their instrumentality for maximizing the desired end. The principle leaves no space for opening up discussion about one's goals and values and whether there are reasons for self-limiting one's choice of actions for the sake of non-goal values. Sen shares Dewey's pragmatic and Darwinian perspective on the cultural dimension of human experience (see Sen 1999, p.241). It is the need of people to discover the best way of coping with the actual problems of living in a changing human environment that shapes their evaluative reasoning and judgment. In this context it is important that the options open to them are rationally assessed through participation in public discussion (1999, p. 242).

For Sen, the social dimension of a person's capability to engage in rational self-scrutiny is important. Such scrutiny is not so much a matter of private reflection based on introspection as one of opening up her reasoning to the scrutiny of others. It is in the context of a discursive and democratic process that she is prompted to reflect on reasons for valuing certain ends and means rather than others in the light of other people's views. A conception of capability that falls under the process aspect of freedom implies a reciprocity and affiliation with others. Viewed in these terms rational self-scrutiny opens up the possibility of achieving an overlapping consensus of view about what ways of living there are reasons for people to value, yet also carries the implication that any level of consensus that is achieved should be provisional and free of power restraints. Nor can rational self-scrutiny involve the imposition of some favoured formula or set of *a priori* principles for rationally resolving differences of view (2002, p. 46). Values and choices are rationally established and validated through free and open discussion alone (2002, p. 287). In this respect Sen's position follows on from Dewey's conception of 'democratic rationality'. This has been eloquently articulated by one of Dewey's major contemporary interpreters, Richard Rorty. There are no wholescale constraints on inquiry, Rorty argues (1982, p. 165), 'derived from the nature of objects, or of the mind, or of language'. The only constraints are conversational ones, 'those retail constraints provided by the remarks of our fellow inquirers'. He argues that those of us engaged in inquiry 'have a duty to talk to each other, to converse about our views of the world, to use persuasion rather than force, to be tolerant of diversity, to be contritely fallibilist' (1991, p.67). Such are the democratic virtues that Dewey associated with the scientific method (see Dewey 1974, pp. 182–92), which he extended beyond the substantive focus of its traditional subject matter to cover all inquiry, including the study of values.

Sen appears to be in tension with Dewey's account of evaluative reasoning, in one respect, when he argues that capability refers 'to the alternative combinations of functionings that are feasible for her to achieve' (1999, p. 75). This suggests that the process of autonomously choosing a life-style involves a choice *between* socially pre-determined capability-sets. One might ask of Sen, 'Why should people's choices of life-style be restricted to alternative and tightly bounded combinations of functionings that appear to be presented to individuals in advance of any democratic and deliberative process of rational self-scrutiny? Do not such combinations restrict a person's options and freedom of thought, by preventing her from freely selecting valuable functionings to make up her own personally constructed way of life?' In reply Sen might argue that such combinations will simply reflect the major patterns of choice that have evolved in society to date. This implies that they are contingent upon social arrangements, and as Sen himself argues, from a capability perspective there is a need for all individuals in a society to participate in decisions about which combinations of functionings to preserve and which to let go of (1999, p. 242). If this is the case then such combinations cannot simply be regarded as 'givens' that stand over and against the individual as objects of choice. Sen implies as much when he argues that a person's achievements, when viewed as capabilities, 'can be judged in the light of her own values and objectives, whether or not we assess them in terms of some external criteria as well' (1999, p. 19).

In viewing autonomous choice as a matter of choosing between socially pre-determined capability-sets, Sen appears to be contradicting his general view that rational assessments of choices should be open to the possibility of forging new ways of living. In this context pre-determined configurations of valuable functionings will not so much circumscribe people's choice of life-style as provide resources for reflectively constructing their own in discussion with others. In doing so they may well leave certain established 'ways of life' behind, while at the same time drawing on some of their elements. Hence, a rational assessment of choices need not restrict a person's choice of life-style to certain pre-determined options. Dewey is less ambiguous than Sen about what is involved in rationally assessing choices. His account of evaluative reasoning clearly implies that a person is capable of configuring, through discussion with others, her own combination of functionings as a way of life.

The implications of capability theory for the curriculum

Sen's idea of capabilities as constitutive of human freedom, implies a major role for educational institutions in expanding 'equality of opportunity' for all by expanding and intensifying the range of 'capabilities' that enhance an individual's freedom of choice. However, does it also imply a major role for educational institutions in developing a capability for practical reasoning about the relative value of different functionings as ends and means in the context of everyday life? In other words should educational institutions not only provide students with equal opportunities to expand their capabilities, but also enable them to make autonomous judgments about which capabilities they have reason to weave into a coherent way of life? This is a question that is relevant to a question that Saito (2003, pp. 25–9) posed to Sen himself in relation to the applicability of the capability approach to the education of children. She did so because Sen's conception of freedom appeared to conflict with the generally accepted view 'that children need support from parents, teachers or societies in choosing what is best for their lives'. It implies that restrictions on children's freedom to decide what is worth learning might be justified, and appears to limit the relevance of the capability approach for education. Saito addressed the following question to Sen:

> How can we apply the capability approach to children, since children are not mature enough to make decisions by themselves? (p. 2)

She reports (pp. 25–8) that Sen's response constitutes an argument for applying the capability approach to the education of children in two respects. First, he emphasizes the importance not of the freedom a child has now, but of the freedom the child will have in the future. Second, he argues that 'the capability approach is relevant when it is viewed from the perspective of functionings it is feasible for the child to achieve, as opposed to her freedom to choose which functionings make up a worthwhile way of life'. Education has an important role, Sen argues, in opening up a 'functioning space' for the child. Hence, compulsory education can be justified in terms of giving a child much more freedom when grown up.

Sen's response to Saito's question reflects his distinction between the 'opportunity aspect' and the 'process aspect' of freedom. I feel that her question conflated these two aspects, by locating the latter largely at the point of choosing which things are worth learning, rather than at the point of choosing in the everyday situations of life, which of these things there is reason to value as part of a coherent way of life.

Saito claims, rightly in my view, that Sen's response (see pp. 25–6) supports White's view (1973, p. 22) that 'Letting children learn what they wanted – might well restrict the range of possible things that they might choose for their own sake' later, and therefore that freedom of choice must be viewed from a lifelong perspective. However, I would argue, on the basis of one quotation from Sen's response (p. 26), that the conclusion she draws about the applicability of the concept of freedom to the education of children is rather too straightforward. He writes:

> The functioning space is still appropriate to think about, even the well-being of the child. The freedom aspect is affected, but even the freedom aspect may be important for the child because: A) child makes some decisions, like

whether he or she is being unhappy, wants milk and so on; and B) a child's future involves the time when the child will actually exercise some freedom.

I understand this to mean that in creating functional space within the curriculum it is not only important to consider the child's freedom to choose a way of life she has reason to value in the future, but also to an extent in the present. With respect to the future Sen implies that it is important to design this space in a form that will enhance rather than restrict children's capability in the future to autonomously choose a way of life *they* have reason to value. The implication of this is that the 'functioning space' shaped by the curriculum for the child should not be restricted to a narrow set of capabilities. The provision of a narrow capability-set will tend to leave little space in the future for the grown adult to make autonomous and reasoned choices between alternative functionings. With respect to enhancing the child's capability for *making* autonomous choices in the present, Sen regards this as a relatively weak aspect of education for capability in comparison with the future-orientated aspect (see Saito 2003, p. 26). Nevertheless, he does not deny its importance, as Saito's interpretation of his position appears to imply. In the passage quoted above he argues that there is a space for decision-making by children in the context of their everyday lives. Hence, 'the functioning space' provided by education should also to an extent be experienced by children as enriching their present lives and enhancing their capability to make choices within the space for freedom available to them.

Dewey's account of experience can illuminate Sen's response to Saito, with respect to his argument that the child's educational experiences should provide her with a context for extending and deepening her appreciative understanding of their significance and meaning. Dewey is making a pedagogical point here about the importance of teachers being able to help children connect their studies to their direct experiences in everyday life. Viewed in the context of the development of specific capabilities it implies that such development involves helping children to make such connections as a condition of developing their capability 'to value' the things that formal education requires for their own sake. Dewey's account is also relevant to Sen's response when he argues that appreciations of the intrinsic value of activities is a necessary condition for making reasoned estimates of their relative value in choosing a course of action in the context of the concrete situations encountered in life. Since, as Sen argues, children have some space for exercising freedom of choice in their lives, their capability for making reasoned estimates about the relative value of different activities or functionings, will be enhanced by an expansion of their opportunities 'to value' and enjoy (for their own sake) the things that education requires of them.

However, Sen's point about children having space for choice in their present lives, also has an implication that he seems to neglect. Does it not imply that the functioning space enshrined in the formal curriculum should also make direct provision at its core for engaging children in a process of practical or evaluative reasoning about the concrete situations of choice they encounter in their lives?

The development of a capability for practical or evaluative reasoning is, I argued earlier, fundamental to the process of choosing a way of life one has reason to value, and Sen's point is consistent with the view that the education of children should not simply expand their opportunities for choice, but also develop their capability for *making choices* in the process sense of 'freedom'.

I would argue that Sen weakens the relevance of the 'process aspect' of freedom when it comes to the education of children, because he tends at times, as I suggested earlier, to have a 'supermarket' conception of what is involves in making autonomous judgments and decisions. This is reflected in his view that capability refers to a person being able to choose between alternative sets of functionings it is feasible for them to achieve. It is as if they can only become fully capable of exercising their freedom, in the 'process sense', once they have 'stored up' a comprehensive range of specific capabilities from which to choose. However, as I argued earlier, Dewey's account of evaluative reasoning and judgment implies that choosing a way of life a person has reason to value is a more gradual and ongoing process. It is personally constructed in the process of estimating the relative value of activities – that a person has come 'to value' at the time – in relation to the particular concrete situations of choice experienced in life, and which may change and vary in the course of their life history. From a Deweyan perspective, the development of a person's capability for autonomously choosing a way of life she has reason to value is an ongoing process from cradle to grave. Education should therefore make space in the curriculum for its development at every stage from compulsory to post-compulsory education. In Dewey's terms the 'process aspect' of freedom would not be viewed, in comparison with the 'opportunity aspect', to be the weaker aspect of a capability approach to the education of children. Both would be equally important dimensions of the capability approach when applied to basic education. They would not only be held in balance within the curriculum but allowed to interact, so that increasingly children were able to define their own learning needs and create their own curriculum pathways or functioning spaces. The fact that Sen views the 'process aspect' of freedom to be weaker then the 'opportunity aspect', with respect to the education of children, may well be explained in terms of the blinkering effect of a somewhat 'supermarket' model of autonomous choice.

Whereas Walker appears to endorse Sen's view that the 'process aspect' of freedom is significant but weaker than the 'opportunity aspect' in relation to the education of children (2005, p. 107), she appears to have changed her mind about his general refusal to specify a list of capabilities beyond the baseline of elementary capabilities cited earlier. In her 2005 paper she expresses an appreciation of Sen's reasons for wanting to leave his framework 'deliberately open, even vague'; namely, 'because of the importance for him of communities deciding what capabilities are of value' (pp. 106–7). However, in her later book on *Higher Education Pedagogies* (2006) she produces a list of 'capabilities', having been influenced by Nussbaum's disagreement with Sen on the issue (pp. 128–9) and her list of ten universal capabilities that are essential for living a good human life. Walker selects seven of these as being intrinsically important for education and articulates them in a form that she believes, in the light of her experience and research, can inform teaching and learning in a higher education context. I am afraid the line-up at this point in my chapter is going to look very gendered, since I have reasons to align myself with Sen rather than Nussbaum and Walker on the issue of capability lists. This is in spite of the fact that the latter both argue that their lists are not set in stone but open to revision in the light of further discussion.

What is at issue for me relates to Sen's functional perspective on capability. Walker's list, and Nussbaum's before her, assumes that capabilities can in the main be specified independently of their functional contexts. For Sen on the other hand capabilities are bound to particular functionings. This implies, as I argued earlier in the light of Dewey's account of the unity and integrity of experience, that capabilities are complex capacities. They are particular configurations of elements of experience that shape up differently in relation to particular functional contexts. Although they will share certain qualitative similarities across contexts, any attempt to specify these generic qualities as 'capabilities' will change the meaning Sen gives to the term. This I believe is what Walker, following Nussbaum, has done. With the exception of 'practical reasoning', which both identify as a fundamental capability linked to human agency and choice, all the other items on their lists refer to generic elements that have been disaggregated as parts of the unified wholes that make up particular capabilities. These elements are couched in terms of categories that variously refer to attitudes towards 'self and others', to dispositions and virtues, to mental capacities, and to social skills. I would argue that they refer to *common dimensions* of capabilities rather than to specific 'capabilities' as such, at least not in Sen's use of the term.

Walker uses the term 'multi-dimensional' to characterize her list and point out the range of objectives that a capability approach to planning for teaching and learning in higher education might pursue. She also points out that 'multi-dimensionality' implies that the dimensions listed should not be treated as discrete, since 'each capability shapes and influences the development of others' (p. 129). Here lies the problem. If the major purpose in producing her list is to translate the capability approach into a tool for specifying learning objectives, which is what I understood her to be saying, then how can one avoid treating the items listed as discrete? Surely, an 'objective', in the sense in which this term is used in instruction design, is a discrete intention? I will gradually return to this issue about the educational purpose of Walker's list in what follows.

Walker argues that the items on her list are not simply to be understood as opportunities, but also 'as skills and capacities that can be fostered ... in higher education'. I would contend that they cannot be understood as 'opportunities' in Sen's sense at all, since they do not refer to functionings. Any education that set out to provide such opportunities would start by defining the 'functional space' in the curriculum, and resist breaking down the capabilities that occupy that space into categories of objectives. Walker collapses the distinction between specific capabilities and their common dimensions in an attempt to translate capabilities into categories of learning objectives. It would be difficult to think of any other explanation. The cost of this endeavour is to marginalize Sen's functional perspective on 'capabilities', and to encourage pedagogies that have scarce regard for the unity and integrity of different forms of appreciative experience.

Walker appears to intuitively acknowledge, when referring to the multi-dimensionality of her list, that there is a problem, from a capability perspective, about using the list for the purpose of planning by objectives. Conflating 'dimensions of capability' with 'capabilities' obscures the problem. When the items listed are simply viewed as qualitative dimensions manifested in the achievement of functionings generally, then the problem with treating them as learning objectives is that in the process of achieving a particular functioning they will be configured differently as complex wholes. This suggests a different educational use for Walker's list. It provides a set of criteria that educators might use to inform their diagnostic judgments about, and pedagogical interventions to improve, the quality of learning-in-process as it relates to the achievement of particular functionings. Using the list as criteria in this context requires educators to bear the holistic quality of learning in mind.

A functional perspective on education for capability implies a *process model* as opposed to an *objectives model* of instructional design (see Stenhouse 1975, Chapters 5–7). When learning is placed in the context of functionings that learners can come to value for their own sake as forms of appreciative experience, the unity and integrity of learning will be undermined by the use of the objectives model. However, such learning can be supported by a process model of instructional design that specifies a functional space for learning, and criteria to orientate teacher's judgments as facilitators of learning within this space. It is in the context of this model that lists of the kind produced by Walker can be pedagogically useful. However, to treat them as lists of capabilities rather than dimensions of capability will be counterproductive, and reinforce the tendency of human capital theory to treat human qualities as discrete items of knowledge and skill.

The implications of the capability approach for educational reform

Both the 'opportunity' and the 'process' aspects of freedom, in my view, tend to be neglected in many educational systems across the globe. The content of the curriculum tends to be divided into academic and vocational/practical subjects, each shaped by intended learning outcomes cast in the form of discrete and measurable items of knowledge and skills that lack respect for the unity and integrity of any educationally worthwhile experience. In these terms, pedagogy becomes a technology of instruction designed to maximize such discrete outputs rather than a process of inducting students into an appreciative valuing or cherishing of different forms of human experience for their own sake. The latter process will engage the learner in a personal search for meaning in their experience, through thinking and reflection about the connections between her actions and their consequences. There can be no development of capabilities from a Deweyan perspective without experiment and inquiry on the part of the learner. This implies a pedagogical process that provides a space for experimentation and inquiry. When curriculum and pedagogy are cast in terms of a technical rationality, there is little space for the development of capabilities, and therefore for securing through education a socially just distribution of opportunities and processes that enable people to enrich their lives.

The globalization of markets has intensified the need of nation states to secure competitive advantage as a condition of economic growth. Educational reform across the world is in the main being driven by human capital theory that has not been reconstructed and integrated with a capability approach of the kind depicted by Sen. National curriculum frameworks are increasingly emphasizing the development of discrete abilities that are conceived largely in terms of their productive functions and commodity value on labour markets, rather than as components of human functionings that may have intrinsic as well as extrinsic value. From a capability perspective, specifications of such abilities as measurable learning outcomes abstract and isolate them from the actual contexts of their use in the world of business and commerce. Key indicators of the extent to which a national curriculum is shaped by unreconstructed human capital theory is indicated by:

1   A common core curriculum that defines worthwhile content solely in terms of its 'commodity value' for the labour market.
2   Learning outcomes that are defined in terms of 'measurable outputs' of the educational system as a whole.
3   A pedagogy that is evaluated largely in terms of its instrumental effectiveness at maximizing the desired level of output established by national standards and targets. It is 'standards-driven'.

These indicators are ideologically underpinned by a picture of rational planning, that Martha Nussbaum (1990, pp. 56–7) characterizes as 'the science of measurement'. She argues that this picture embodies four claims. First, there is the claim of *metricity*, that 'in a particular choice situation there is some one value, varying only in quantity, that is common to all the alternatives'. The rational chooser is one who uses this single standard as a metric to weigh each alternative and thereby determine which will yield the greatest quantity of value. Secondly, there is the claim of *singularity*, that one and the same metric or standard applies in all situations of choice. Thirdly, there is the claim of *consequentialism*, that the chosen actions only have instrumental value as a means of producing good consequences. Fourthly, by combining each of these claims, we have the principle of *maximization* 'that there is some one value, that it is the point of rational choice, in every case, to maximize'.

Policy-making and research in the field of education has become increasingly shaped by this so-called 'scientific' picture of practical reasoning (see Schwandt 2005, pp. 294–5 and Elliott and Doherty 2001, pp. 209–21 in relation to the US and UK respectively). Hence, the educational reforms initiated by many governments are viewed as devices for 'driving up standards' conceived in terms of *metricity* and *singularity*. Research increasingly takes the form of school and teacher effectiveness research aimed at determining how schools and teachers can 'add value' to students' learning. The *maximization principle* is embedded in the idea of 'value added', which presumes that the practices of schools and teachers only have value if they produce good *consequences* that can be quantified in terms of a single metric that applies generally across the system. Hence, the widespread use of standardized testing in educational systems and international comparisons of performance.

The 'science of measurement' embodies a very different conception of practical reasoning to the one that underpins Sen's notion of a person's freedom to choose a way of life they have reason to value (in its *process* aspect). Its dominance as an approach to educational planning constitutes a major obstacle to curriculum development based on an integrated conception of human capital development and education for capability. As such, one might anticipate that many educational reforms will prove counter-productive by creating the conditions of capability deprivation and thereby diminishing human freedom, irrespective of whether they achieve their economic goals. Indeed the hegemony of the 'science of measurement' in educational planning is the outcome of a global tendency of governments to abstract economic from social ends. It is only when they come to recognize that the human good cannot simply depend on people's economic productivity that they may come to recognize the need for a capability approach to educational planning, and the limitations of 'the science of measurement' in this context. They may also come to recognize that the use of such a 'science' is indicative of a capability deficit in the policy-making context. A capability approach to educational planning will require a different kind of planning process, one that embodies a more democratic and deliberative kind of practical reasoning of the kind depicted by Aristotle, Dewey and Sen. It will also need to be orientated by such broad principles as:

- The curriculum should be designed to expand capabilities and thereby extend the range of opportunities students have to choose a way of life they value and have reason to value.
- Curriculum frameworks should not restrict the set of capabilities given space for development, simply to those that are perceived to be instrumentally significant for economic progress at the societal level or income growth at the private level.

In other words, human capital theory and a concern to alleviate income deprivation should not be the exclusive drivers of reform:

- Since the instrumental relation between lowness of income and capability deprivation *varies* across communities, so also should the extent to which human capital theory shapes the curriculum vary.
- The process aspect of freedom implies that the curriculum should not only provide students with opportunities to expand their capabilities, but also to develop their capability for autonomous reasoning about which of the functions they are capable of achieving they have reason to choose (as ends and means) in the concrete situations they encounter or are likely to encounter in life.
- Since the process aspect of freedom also relates to freedom of thought at the level of developing specific capabilities, a curriculum for capability should make explicit the pedagogical implications of this for teachers, and their responsibility to foster 'learning from experience' through inquiry.

References

Dewey, J. (1916) *Democracy and Education*, New York: Free Press (Macmillan 1966 edition).

Dewey, J. (1974) 'Science as subject-matter and as method', in R.D. Archambault (ed.) *John Dewey on Education: Selected Writings*, Chicago and London: University of Chicago Press.

Elliott, J. and Doherty, P. (2001) 'Restructuring educational research for the "Third Way"?', in Fielding, M. (ed.) *Taking Education Really Seriously: Four Years' Hard Labour*, London: RoutledgeFalmer.

Nussbaum, M (1990) 'An Aristotelian Conception of Rationality', in *Love's Knowledge*, Oxford: Oxford University Press.

Rorty, R. (1982) *Consequences of Pragmatism*, Minneapolis, MN: University of Minnesota Press.

Rorty, R. (1991) 'Pragmatism without method', in *Objectivity, Relativism and Truth: Philosophical Papers Volume 1*, Cambridge: Cambridge University Press.

Saito, M. (2003) 'Amartya Sen's capability approach to education: a critical exploration', *Journal of Philosophy of Education*, 37(1), 17–33.

Schwandt, T. (2005) 'A Diagnostic Reading of Scientifically Based Research for Education', *Educational Theory*, 55(3), 285–305.

Sen, A. (1999) *Development as Freedom,* Oxford: Oxford University Press.

Sen, A. (2002) *Rationality and Freedom*, Cambridge, MA: Harvard University Press (Belknap).

Stenhouse, L. (1975) *An Introduction to Curriculum Research and Development*, London: Heinemann.

Walker, M. (2005) 'Amartya Sen's Capability Approach and Education', *Educational Action Research*, 13(1), 10310.

Walker, M. (2006) *Higher Education Pedagogies*, Maidenhead: Open University Press.

White, J. (1973) *Towards a Compulsory Curriculum*, London: Routledge & Kegan Paul.

Chapter 10

Rethinking doctoral writing as text work and identity work

Barbara Kamler and Pat Thomson

Universities play a key role in the new knowledge-based economies through the provision of research and research education, and the production of highly skilled graduates through doctoral programs of many kinds. This role is more significant than ever given the dramatic expansion in higher degree enrolments in recent years. As Neumann (2002) notes, between 1991 and 2000 doctoral enrolments in Australian universities virtually doubled from 19,000 to over 37,000 (DETYA 2001).

This expansion has been accompanied by an increase in the diversity of students in terms of age, gender, ethnicity, nationality and discipline area (Pearson 1999; Johnson *et al.* 2000). The number of international students has increased rapidly, as many universities in Western countries now actively seek large numbers of students from developing countries for income generation, rather than aid, purposes. Part-time candidature has grown (Evans 2002) and increasing numbers study at a distance (Evans and Pearson 1999; McWilliam *et al.* 2002).

Doctoral candidates in the social sciences are now equally likely to be mid-career professionals, as young students straight from undergraduate work. They are joined by increasing numbers of older candidates who may be seeking a career change, a post-retirement option, or simply to further an area of interest (Leonard *et al.* 2005). Doctoral researchers also have more diverse motivations for undertaking study. They arrive at university with a wider range of work and life experiences and include numbers of university staff in both academic and administrative positions seeking to increase their qualifications.

This increasing diversity and the addition of students with various English language demands, histories of under- and postgraduate experience and different cultural norms and expectations, creates new pressures on supervision. While many universities recognise the need to support supervisors in their work, this concern is generally couched in terms of quality assurance and training, rather than pedagogy. Universities require supervisors to keep detailed audit trails of their interactions with students, but this is primarily to avoid student complaints and litigation. The inclusion of PhD completion rates in government measures of research performance has placed a new emphasis, in countries such as Australia and the UK, on 'getting students through'. But the press by universities for documentation and smooth passage from enrolment to graduation does not necessarily enhance what actually happens in pedagogical practice.

While most universities in Australia now target completion rates and supervisor efficacy as key arenas for institutional improvement, such measures tend to bypass complex questions of knowledge production; of pedagogy; of scholarly identity formation and writing. Many scholars are arguing for new kinds of research and thinking on doctoral education that attend to this complexity (see for example, special issues of the *Australian Universities' Review* (38, 2) in 1995 and (43, 2) in 2000; *Higher Education Research and Development* (21, 2) in 2002 and (24, 2) in 2005; *Australian Educational Researcher* (29, 3) in 2002). Pearson highlights the need to develop

> a research-based conceptual framework of doctoral education to guide quality management, improvement, and innovation. It is timely to consider that the (necessary) stress on institutional quality assurance on the one hand, and individual supervision, on the other, has led to insufficient attention to the way doctoral education proceeds within particular contexts and settings, and insufficient attention to the lived experiences and perceptions of participants in specific research and learning environments.
>
> (Pearson 1999: 270)

Boud and Lee (2005) similarly interrogate recent policy-driven preoccupations with doctoral completions, funding and contributions to the economy. They argue that current emphases on supervision and the training of supervisors are inadequate and they make the case for a new focus on pedagogy. They theorise the research education environment as before pedagogical space and foreground the importance of peer learning to facilitate student entry into communities of research practice.

It is in this context of increasing diversity of students, increasing pressures on supervisors, and increasing policy imperatives to improve the quality of research, that we situate our discussion of doctoral writing. Like Boud and Lee (2005), our concerns are pedagogical. Like Pearson (1999), we think it is crucial to attend to the lived experiences of doctoral students. Thus we ask: To what extent have the intensified pressures to improve performance in research education actually improved the doctoral student's experience of writing and research? What has been done to build pedagogies of supervision that address the central work of dissertation writing?

From our perspective, research *is* a practice of writing. Writing shapes a text – the dissertation – the object which is examined and judged as the basis of awarding the degree. But it also shapes a scholar, the person who is judged in and though the text. And for the most part, the relationship between writing and research and writing and identity is overlooked, misunderstood, or ignored in universities – to the peril of the quality of research and the production of buoyant academic writers who know the game and can play it with confidence.

A recent experience at the ICARE[1] forum in September 2005 suggests how fragile doctoral identities can be, and how at risk in the current climate. The occasion was the presentation of a version of this chapter at ICARE. The response was positive – nothing controversial or heated. Some senior academics commented on the utility of our text-work identity-work framework; others discussed their own practices of supervision in relation to questions of doctoral writing. But the silences of that conversation were not evident until afterwards, when Barbara entered the ladies room. She was approached there by three early-career researchers, all recent or current doctoral candidates in their institutions in the UK, who wanted to talk about the paper.

One by one, they talked with great intensity about their own experiences of writing the doctorate, their struggles, their passions, their fears. They resonated with the identity struggles Barbara had spoken about. But they said they were too frightened to admit their struggles in the company of 'expert' scholars. The conversations with these young women were engaged and invigorating, more lively than those in the forum proper, but Barbara was struck by the fact that such concerns could only be spoken in the space where women carry out their intimate and private business. These diffident and emerging scholars were ashamed of not writing well enough. The senior scholars in the room had no idea of their younger colleagues' unspoken concerns – which had they been articulated, would have enlivened the ICARE conversation. Instead they remained private, uttered in confidence in a private space, construed as personal failing, as a problem of isolated individuals.

Our aim then, as now, is to bring the textual practices of scholarship into the public arena – to discuss pedagogy – to imagine a writing-centred supervision. We want to relocate the problems doctoral writers face and reconnect them to the complexities of dissertation writing and broader threats to the preparation of educational researchers. In this chapter we rethink doctoral writing as text work and identity work, foregrounding the anxieties that both students and supervisors experience in relation to writing the dissertation.

The invisibility of doctoral writing

Writing the dissertation lies at the centre of doctoral education. It is through writing that students make their findings known to the public and develop a sense of themselves as authorised scholars. Yet, in many universities, writing is treated as ancillary to the real work of research – as the invisible and taken-for-granted labour of the doctorate (Kamler and Thomson 2001). While failure to successfully complete the doctorate has been linked to student writing problems (e.g. Torrance and Thomas 1994), even this obvious connection with matters of efficiency has failed to put doctoral writing on the map.

Nevertheless, writing the dissertation remains a major site of anxiety for students and often, for their supervisors. It is not uncommon to hear frustrated conversations at conferences and faculty meetings about turgid prose, badly structured arguments and laboured literature reviews. Yet graduate students are rarely offered systematic instruction in high-level academic writing (Rose and McClafferty 2001); and when writing support is given, it often misunderstands the profound interrelationships between writing and identity (Lee 1998; Richardson 1994), treating academic writing rather as a discrete set of add-on skills that are effectively context free.

There is a burgeoning literature on doctoral pedagogies, supervision and examination (e.g. Delamont *et al.* 1997; Bartlett and Mercer 2001; Dias and Paré 2000; Green *et al.* 2001). But little attention has been given in this work to the processes of writing the thesis, through which professional identities are formed and reconfigured. There is also a rich research tradition that examines academic writing as discipline-specific practice: studies that explore rhetorical differences across academic disciplines (Bazerman 1988; Myers 1985); and the way graduate students learn to appropriate discourse conventions in disciplinary communities (Paré 2002; Prior 1998; Berkenkotter and Huckin 1995; Kamler and Maclean 1997). But this research rarely addresses the doctoral arena. Unfortunately, those texts that most directly address questions of doctoral writing are written in the pedestrian self-help, advice genre: the how-to-write-your-dissertation manual. Such manuals reduce writing to a set of procedures and rules that can be learned in a mechanical way.

For a number of years we have been addressing this gap in scholarship by examining questions of doctoral writing, pedagogy and identity. In our recent book *Helping doctoral students write: pedagogies for supervision* (Kamler and Thomson 2006) we examine thesis writing in the pedagogical space of supervision, treating doctoral writing as research (Richardson 1994) – a complex, institutionally-constrained social practice. We pay attention to the genres and conventions of scholarly writing. We examine an array of doctoral writing practices that seek to support the production of both scholarly writing and the scholar.

In this chapter, we explore a central tenet of our pedagogy: our conceptualisation of doctoral writing as text work and identity work. We explicate this framework by examining the work of reviewing literatures, one of the most anxiety-provoking tasks doctoral writers face. We consider the issue of criticality, the difficult task of helping students take an evaluative stance in writing about literatures. We examine an interactive text-work strategy to illustrate how supervisors might better support doctoral researchers to produce more authoritative writing and a more authoritative scholar.

Reviewing literatures as text work and identity work

Work with literatures is vital to doctoral research. When students sketch out the nature of the field or fields relevant to their inquiry; when they identify major debates and define contentious terms, they are not simply conducting an 'academic exercise'. They are mapping a field of knowledge production (Kamler and Thomson 2006). They are establishing which studies, ideas and/or methods are most pertinent to their own study in order to create the warrant for the study in question, and identify the contribution the study will make. As such, it is not something that they can ignore, no matter how badly they feel about it. Nor is it something that doctoral education can ignore in preparing researchers.

In a recent review of dissertation literature reviews, Boote and Beile (2005) deplore both the poor quality of student reviews and the lack of serious pedagogical attention given to this act of scholarship in doctoral education. A thorough, substantive literature review, is they argue, 'a precondition for doing substantive, thorough, sophisticated research' (Boote and Beile 2005: 3). Yet, many of the doctoral candidates they survey espoused naïve conceptions of literature reviewing or seemed to perceive it as of relatively low importance.

Our work in Australia and the UK suggests that doctoral candidates understand its pivotal importance, but are plagued by an excess of anxiety and expectation about literature work. There are many reasons for this angst. There are writing myths which complicate and make writing about literatures a task to be endured, rather than enjoyed. And there is a lack of recognition of the intensity of identity work involved at this site of text production. We would go so far as to say that literature reviews are *the* quintessential site of identity work – where the novice researcher enters what we call occupied territory – with all the immanent danger and quiet dread that this metaphor implies, including possible ambushes, barbed-wire fences, unknown academics who patrol the boundaries of already occupied territories.

It is difficult to write confidently in dangerous territory. It is difficult to be a 'novice' seeking entry to a community of 'expert' scholars, and at the same time 'critically review' these experts. Unfocused reviews, slavish mechanical summaries, clumsy attempts at creating links to the work of expert scholars are rarely just 'writing problems'. What often looks like poor writing, we suggest, is also a textual struggle to take on a scholarly identity and become authoritative.

It is our argument that there are two sides to reviewing literatures: knowing the genres, conventions and textual practices; and assuming what we call a 'hands on hips' subject position. When doctoral researchers write about literatures, they are constructing a representation of the scholar and her scholarly practice. The struggle with writing occurs because of the difficulty of negotiating text work and identity work simultaneously. The challenge is to learn to speak and write with authority, to critically survey and categorise texts and the field with 'hands on hips'. In the remainder of this chapter we outline some strategies we've used with students in order to illustrate our larger argument – that doctoral education needs to take up a more complex view of dissertation writing as text work and identity work in order to facilitate not only thesis production, but the production of more confident, enabled scholars.

Adopting a critical stance

Most supervisors, advice books and university websites suggest that the literature review needs to be critical. On the surface, the term *critical* positions the doctoral researcher powerfully, as judge and evaluator of the research that has preceded her. But this is where many students come undone. They take critical to mean *critique*, to find what is *wrong*. They feel intimidated, sometimes paralysed by the prospect of critiquing (esteemed, elevated) scholars who are senior, more powerful and acknowledged experts in their fields.

The seemingly innocuous and common-place phrase *a critical review of the literature* carries with it a set of presuppositions that create a difficult subject position for the doctoral writer, which makes the task of writing more difficult. Doctoral researchers often revert to writing summaries, we believe, because they are nervous about taking on the subject position of 'critic'. They may be cautioned a hundred times that the literature review is not a summary, that it involves making a case for their work and finding which research literatures are like/unlike/ connected to what they are doing. But such advice is often not sufficient.

We can capture the dilemma by considering a text written by a doctoral researcher who has difficulty achieving a critical stance. The writer Gina (a pseudonym) is a senior school administrator who is researching what is 'known' about school reform. She writes:

> Fullan (1993) proposes some paradoxes about change that would help one to understand and deal with the complexities of change. He claims that you can't mandate what matters since the more complex the change, the less you can force it. He also explains that change is a journey, not a blue print and that we will encounter problems. However, we should see problems as our friends. Can one ever regard problems as good? This could be the most feared thing and could become an obstacle for some, knowing the stress and headaches that problems can cause. Nevertheless, the author is of the view that because they are inevitable, we can't learn without them. In this light, I share the author's view because the old adage goes 'experiences are our greatest teacher'.

There are many things we can say about this text. Certainly it is characteristic of diffident scholars who lack authority and feel somewhat overwhelmed by the work of 'experts'. Here Gina shows a grasp of the issues and debates about school change, but has difficulty positioning herself in relation to the writer Fullan, a senior scholar in the field of educational reform. She talks of herself as 'one' and 'I' and addresses the audience somewhat awkwardly as 'you' and 'we'. She is critical of the proposition Fullan is making, but in order to make the critique she resorts to rhetorical questions. She then absents herself from the text to make a critical comment based on her own considerable professional experience, but which she is reluctant to assert, saying 'knowing the stress and headaches that problems can cause'. She does not produce counters from other literature. She reasserts herself, as the 'I', only when in agreement with the author.

It would be easy to respond to this text as a piece of 'bad writing', but a closer reading shows the problem is not primarily about style and expression. Some of the tongue-tied-ness and lack of inter-textuality derive from Gina's inability to find a comfortable 'hands on hips' stance. To move forward, she needs strategies that can help her connect with and evaluate the work of 'expert scholars' in relation to their own. She requires an expanded notion of what it is to be critical – beyond praise and blame – and the adoption of a stance we might characterise as appreciative.

Becoming critical

To be critical is not just about praising and demolishing the work of others. Being critical involves making judgments and decisions about which literatures to engage with, and which to ignore, which aspects of texts to stress and which to omit or downplay. Adopting a critical stance to a text means paying attention to: definitions; underpinning assumptions; theoretical resources mobilised; epistemology and methodology; method (who, what, where, how); and findings. These perspectives can be brought together to establish points of similarity and points of difference. It is through such focused interrogation and inter-textual work that students come to identify major debates in the field.

But to be critical is also to be respectful of what others have done, to look at what they have contributed, rather than going on the attack. A key question to ask is: what does this work contribute? rather than: what does it fail to do? This creates an evaluative frame which helps developing scholars enact 'criticism' as more than negative or destructive behaviour.

Some students arrive at a generous and generative criticality by themselves. Others benefit from a more direct pedagogical strategy. We have found the work of Wagner (1993) useful in establishing an analytic framework for criticality that moves beyond liking or disliking, agreeing or disagreeing. Wagner distinguishes between what he calls the 'blind spots' and 'blank spots' in others' research. What we 'know enough to question but not answer' are our blank spots; what we 'don't know well enough to even ask about or care about' are our blind spots, 'areas in which existing theories, methods, and perceptions actually keep us from seeing phenomena as clearly as we might' (1993: 16).

So, for example, surveys typically give a broad snapshot of a phenomena using respondent's perceptions. What they cannot do is to provide in-depth reasons about why those particular answers are the way they are. This requires a different kind of investigation. These in-depth reasons are a blind spot of this type of research (and indeed, are typically why mixed methods are seen as preferable to single surveys). To identify the blind spots in others' research, students need to focus on the things a particular methodology or method does not do, that is, areas that have been overlooked because of theoretical or methodological reasons. Identifying blank spots, by contrast, involves asking what this research could have seen or done that it does not. That is, what are the shortcomings of the research? So, if a survey omitted questions or failed to take up opportunities for informative cross-tabulations, these are arguably blank spots. This distinction clarifies the difference between research that is poorly executed, and research that can only provide a limited data set.

Combining the notion of blind spots and blank spots with an appreciative stance allows doctoral researchers to focus on what the research contributes and how/where/why more might be required. The combination also provides evaluative detail beyond summarising content and themes. In workshops we encourage doctoral researchers to assess the individual texts of other scholars by asking such questions as:

- what is the argument?
- what kind/aspect of x is spoken about in this article?
- from what position?
- using what evidence?
- what claims are made?
- how adequate are these (blank spots and blind spots)?

Working with blank and blind spots across many texts provides important understandings about the gaps and spaces in the field, one of which the doctoral researcher will occupy. This is analytic text work that can build students' sense of place in a field of scholarship. But we suggest a more 'hands on' textual approach is also required to help students develop criticality in reviewing literatures. We conclude by illustrating one such strategy which we call joint texting.

Joint texting

Joint texting is one of several textwork strategies we've developed (Kamler and Thomson 2006) to foster more authoritative doctoral identities. The term joint texting signals that this is not *correcting* writing, but working with doctoral researchers at the computer to revise their draft writing. Remaking text and manipulating it until it speaks more assertively is a tangible activity. It makes the process of knowledge production more 'hands on'. The supervisor takes the lead and models revision-in-action, often with powerful effects on doctoral researcher identities.

To illustrate, we consider an interaction between doctoral researcher Mia and her supervisor Andrew (pseudonyms). Mia is reviewing literatures for her dissertation proposal. She has summarised trends in the field of homework research as a foundation for her own qualitative study on the effects of homework on families in diverse sociocultural contexts. She consolidates a large number of studies into a short space, but starts most sentences by naming previous studies and reviewers of homework. We highlight this syntactic pattern in bold type and number her sentences to facilitate our analysis of the text.

Mia LR 1

(1) **All reviewers of the homework literature agree** that much research into homework has been poorly designed, short term, experimental and narrowly focused on academic achievement (Cooper, 1989; Coulter, 1979; Paschal, 1984). (2) **Further, studies** have been premised on partial or commonsense definitions which either assume an understanding of homework or narrowly define homework as time spent in completion of school assignments (Hoover-Dempsey, 1995). (3) **Many studies** have been based on self-reported quantitative data alone; such data is inevitably limited in its potential to provide insights into the relationship between homework and achievement.

(4) **Several scholars who have reviewed the academic literature on homework** (Hoover-Dempsey, 1995; Coulter, 1979) suggest that the equivocal nature of the findings into the effects of homework, despite a century of research, reveals more about the methodological challenges of researching this complex subject than can be stated **conclusively** about the relationship between homework and achievement. (5) **Apart from the quantitative studies previously discussed, many studies** have used evidence from interviews with children, parents and teachers. (6) **There has also been little research evidence** derived from classrooms which explores teachers' framing of homework or children's understandings of their tasks. (7) **Further, the majority of studies** have concentrated on homework practices of adolescent secondary students. (8) **Scholars who have reviewed the academic literature on homework** (Hoover-Dempsey, 1995) have directed little research attention to primary school students' homework, with the exception of the role of parents in the development of child literacy. (9) **Few observational studies** have examined the webs of social interaction between children and their parents, siblings, friends and schools within which homework is constructed (Coulter, 1979: 27). (10) **A few influential studies** have looked at the family interactions around homework in diverse socio-cultural contexts (Breen *et al.*, 1994; Freebody *et al.*, 1995; Lareau, 1987) and will be discussed in a later section of this review.

Mia's writing is competent in terms of fluency, syntax and clarity. She is neither drowning in the literature nor overwhelmed by it. But she is absent from the text. She succinctly summarises the equivocal findings of the homework research, but her own opinions and evaluations are backgrounded or attributed to other researchers. As a result, a critical and authoritative stance is missing.

To interrupt this way of writing, her supervisor Andrew put Mia's text on the computer screen. His aim was to model how Mia might foreground her own point of view. It is important that this text work occurred in her presence, rather than as red-pen corrections in her absence. She was part of the process, not simply a recipient of teacher judgement. Andrew talked out loud about what he was attempting. His manner was tentative, exploratory. He tried things on the screen and deleted them. Mia was both witness and participant, making suggestions and seeing the text change before her eyes. The interaction was punctuated by Andrew asking Mia questions about the text.

His first move was to make visible how Mia attributed everything (every idea, trend, opinion) to other researchers. So, for example, he looked at sentence 1 where Mia begins *All the reviewers of homework agree.* He asked whether *she* agreed. When she said yes, he shifted her sentence structure so that the assertion came first, and the citation last.

> In sum, it appears that much research into homework has been poorly designed, short term, experimental and narrowly focused on academic achievement.
> (Cooper, 1989; Coulter, 1979; Paschal, 1984)

This is a subtle shift, but one that lets Mia assert *with* this community of scholars, rather than exclude herself. Andrew used a similar strategy in the second paragraph. He looked, for example, at sentence 4 where Mia begins: *Several scholars who have reviewed the academic literature on homework suggest.* He again shifted the pattern of attribution from the start of the sentence to the end, so Mia owns the claim.

> It seems, then, that despite a century of research, the equivocal nature of the findings say more about the methodological challenges of researching this complex subject than about any definitive relationship between homework and achievement itself.
> (Hoover-Dempsey, 1995; Coulter, 1979)

He then created a third paragraph, missing altogether from the first draft. His aim was to model how Mia might highlight the gap her own research was addressing. He looked, in particular, at sentence 10, where she refers to *a few influential studies* without making any link to her own work. He asked: What is the link between this work and what you will do? How do you plan to use these influential studies?

On the basis of this conversation, he started adding phrases and sentences, asking: What will you say here? How do we mark your contribution? Gradually he inserted Mia's words, acting as her scribe and text-worker. This conversation provided a scaffold for Mia to learn syntactic conventions for staking a claim. Mia worked *with* Andrew to make textual connections between her work and the wider scholarly community, thus locating her place more firmly in the field of knowledge production. Her revised literature review constructs a more authoritative stance for Mia as doctoral researcher. We use bold print to highlight the new syntactic pattern at the beginning of sentences and the change in writer stance it achieves.

Mia's Revised LR 2

(1) **In sum, it appears that much research into homework** has been poorly designed, short term, experimental and narrowly focused on academic achievement (Cooper, 1989; Coulter, 1979; Paschal, 1984). (2) **Studies** have been premised on partial or commonsense definitions which either assume an understanding of homework or narrowly define homework as time spent in completion of school assignments (Hoover-Dempsey, 1995). (3) **The over-reliance on self-reported quantitative data alone** has lead to limited insights into the relationship between homework and achievement.

(4) **It seems, then, that despite a century of research, the equivocal nature of the findings** say more about the methodological challenges of researching this complex subject than about any definitive relationship between homework and achievement itself (Hoover-Dempsey, 1995; Coulter, 1979). (5) **The qualitative research evidence to date** has relied heavily on interviews with children, parents and teachers, that is, on what people say they do. (6) **There has been little attention** given to the practice of school homework as it occurs in the family context. (7) **There has been little classroom-based research evidence** which explores teachers' framing of homework or children's understandings of their tasks. (8) **Further, little research attention** has focused on primary school students' homework, with the exception of the role of parents in the development of child literacy.

(9) **In this proposal I** attempt to address these methodological gaps by designing an observational and interview-based study which examines the webs of social interaction between children and their parents, siblings, friends and schools within which homework is constructed (Coulter, 1979: 27). (10) **I focus** on the primary secondary school nexus and work with a more complex understanding of homework as a social practice. (11) **A number of influential studies which have examined family interactions around homework in diverse socio-cultural contexts** (Breen 1994; Freebody 1995; Hill 2002) provide a foundation for my study and will be discussed in Section 3.3 of this review.

In this revision, Mia takes a 'critical' stand on the trends she identifies. She incorporates evaluative comments at the start of sentences: *The over-reliance on self-reported quantitative data alone has lead to limited insights* (3). She identifies gaps: There *has been little attention given to* (6); *There has been little classroom-based research* (7); *Further, little research attention has focused on* (8). And she acknowledges her debt to previous scholarship: *A number of influential studies... provide a foundation for my study* (11).

The textual outcome is a more assertive, less descriptive construction of the field of knowledge production. Importantly, the identity work was profound. Mia was not only pleased with the revision, but astounded at how little it took to make her sound more authoritative. The joint texting with Andrew affected her deeply and almost seemed to be written into her body as she left the supervision session seemingly taller. She spoke later of the session as a pivotal event in helping her 'get how to become critical'.

This collaborative strategy was certainly more powerful than just explaining or correcting Mia's draft. As supervisor and student remade the text together, they also remade her identity and capacity for a textual authority she desired but was unable to create on her own – particularly at this early stage of her candidature. There was also something pleasurable about the sociality of this joint texting. It created a different subject position for the doctoral researcher, not just as novice but as text worker, working collaboratively with her supervisor to strengthen the text.

What differentiates this approach to doctoral writing is a conscious attention to both the text work and identity work. Our emphasis is on repositioning doctoral writers as text workers and using supervision as a space to make explicit how to construct the genres of scholarly writing. Our aim is to foster student agency in the process of reviewing literatures, and in writing the dissertation more broadly. Central to this work is a reconceptualisation of supervision pedagogy as a space for treating doctoral writing as both text work and identity work.

Of course, if we return to our concerns at the start of the chapter about the increasing pressures supervisors now face, it is also important to think beyond the supervisory space. The responsibility for fostering good writing and authoritative scholars cannot lie with supervisors alone. There needs to be adequate institutional support. By this we don't mean that institutions start 'training' supervisors about writing. Rather, that universities themselves must take up the question of research writing. They must establish what we call institutional writing cultures (see Kamler and Thomson 2006: chapter 9 for an extended discussion).

A writing culture is one in which questions of writing are foregrounded and not confined to the realm of a pre-dissertation technical fix. It is one in which writing initiatives are linked to policy priorities and wider institutional aspirations (Lee and Boud 2003). It is one in which writing is not narrowly connected to productivity, but linked to fostering research capacities, practices and 'know how'. It is a culture in which the hitherto private pleasures and pain of writing are made public through institutionally-resourced writing groups, courses and collectives. Such a writing culture is not remedial. It recognises that research practices are writing practices and that all university staff and students benefit from systematic attention to writing.

Such writing cultures do not simply happen. They must be consciously produced. As universities continue to monitor the quality of doctoral education and ensure that all university teaching staff are cognisant of a range of teaching and learning strategies appropriate to adult learners, it is timely for them to also consider how to provide support for writing-oriented research practices.

Note

1   The International Centres for Applied Research in Education (ICARE) is an international research and evaluation collaboration between Deakin University, the University of Illinois, Manchester Metropolitan University and the University of East Anglia.

References

Bartlett, A. and Mercer, G. (eds) (2001) *Postgraduate Research Supervision: Transforming Relations*, New York: Peter Lang.

Bazerman, C. (1988) *Shaping Written Knowledge*, Madison, WI: University of Wisconsin Press.

Berkenkotter, C. and Huckin, T.N. (1995) *Genre Knowledge in Disciplinary Communication: Cognition/Culture/Power*, Hillsdale, NJ: Lawrence Erlbaum.

Boote, D.N. and Beile, P. (2005) Scholars before researchers: On the centrality of the dissertation literature review in research preparation, *Educational Researcher*, 34(6), 3–15.

Boud, D. and Lee, A. (2005) 'Peer learning' as pedagogic discourse for research education, *Studies in Higher Education*, 30(5), 501–16.

Delamont, S., Atkinson, P. and Parry, O. (1997) *Supervising the PhD: A Guide to Success*, Buckingham: Open University Press.

DETYA (2001) *Students 2000: Selected Higher Education Statistics*, Canberra: Department of Education, Training and Youth Affairs.

Dias, P. and Paré, A. (eds) (2000) *Transitions: Writing in Academic and Workplace Settings*, Cresskill, NJ: Hampton Press.

Evans, T.D. (2002) Part-time research students: are they producing knowledge where it counts? *Higher Education and Research and Development*, 21(2), 155–65.

Evans, T.D. and Pearson, M. (1999) Off-campus doctoral research in Australia: emerging issues and practices. In A. Holbrook and S. Johnston (eds), *Supervision of Postgraduate Research in Education*, Coldstream, VIC: Australian Association for Research in Education, pp. 185–206.

Green, B., Maxwell, T.W. and Shanahan, P. (eds) (2001) *Doctoral Education and Professional Practice: The Next Generation*, Armidale, NSW: Kardoorair Press.

Johnson, L., Lee, A. and Green, B. (2000) The PhD and the autonomous self: gender, rationality and postgraduate pedagogy. *Studies in Higher Education*, 25(2), 135–47.

Kamler, B. and Thomson, P. (2001) *Talking down 'writing up' or ten emails a day is writing and play*, Paper presented at Australian Association for Research in Education, December 2001, Fremantle.

Kamler, B. and Thomson, P. (2006) *Helping Doctoral Students Write: Pedagogies for Supervision*, London: Routledge.

Kamler, B. and Maclean, R. (1997) 'You can't just go to court and move your body': first year students learn how to write and speak the Law, *Law/Text/Culture*, 3, 176–209.

Lee, A. (1998). Doctoral research as writing. In J. Higgs (ed.), *Writing Qualitative Research*, Five Dock, NSW: Hampden Press, 121–36.

Lee, A. and Boud, D. (2003) Writing groups, change and academic identity: research development as local practice, *Studies in Higher Education*, 28(2), 187–200.

Leonard, D., Becker, R. and Coate, K. (2005) 'To prove myself at the highest level': the benefits of doctoral study. Special issue, (ed.) B. Kamler and T. Evans, *Higher Education Research and Development*, 24(2), 135–49.

McWilliam, E., Singh, P. and Taylor, P. (2002) Doctoral education, danger and risk management, *Higher Education Research and Development*, 21(2), 119–29.

Myers, G. (1985) The social construction of two biologist's proposals, *Written Communication*, 2(3), 219–455.

Neumann, R. (2002) Diversity, doctoral education and policy, *Higher Education Research and Development*, 21(2), 167–78.

Paré, A. (2002) Genre and identity: Individuals, institutions, and ideology. In R. Coe, L. Lingard and T. Teslenko (eds), *The Rhetoric and Ideology of Genre: Strategies for Stability and Change*, Cresskill, NJ: Hampton Press, 57–71.

Pearson, M. (1999) The changing environment for doctoral education in Australia: implications for quality management, improvement and innovation, *Higher Education Research and Development*, 1 (3), 269–87.

Prior, P. (1998) *Writing/Disciplinarity: A Sociohistoric Account of Literate Activity in the Academy*, Mahwah, NJ: Lawrence Erlbaum.

Richardson, L. (1994) Writing: a method of inquiry. In N. Denzin and Y. Lincoln (eds), *The Handbook of Qualitative Research*, California: Sage Publications.

Rose, M., and McClafferty, K. (2001) A call for the teaching of writing in graduate education, *Educational Researcher*, 30(2), 27–33.

Torrance, M.S. and Thomas, G.V. (1994) The development of writing skills in doctoral research students. In R.G. Burgess (ed.), *Postgraduate Education and Training in the Social Sciences*, London: Jessica Kingsley, 105–12.

Wagner, J. (1993) Ignorance in educational research: or, how can you not know that? *Educational Researcher*, 22(5), 15–23.

Chapter 11

Politics, knowledge, identity and community

Methodologist as hitchhiker, skateboarder, ...

John Schostak and Jill Schostak

Laying a mathematical grid over the universe enables travellers to get from specified places to specified places, measure distances, time arrivals, coordinate activities. It is an image of perfect control. Mastery. Everyone and everything is countable, measurable, locatable, trackable. Everyone knows where they've come from and where they're going. The ambition to locate and manipulate is central to technology and the scientific mind, engineered during that intellectually and politically revolutionary time by such contributors to the emergence of contemporary science as Bacon, Descartes, Galileo and Newton and to the emergence of contemporary politics and governance such as Hobbes, Machiavelli, Spinoza and Hegel. Right away there is a tension that methodology has to get to grips with: the coolness of scientific reason, and the heat of politics as different worlds make claims about what is right, wrong, included, excluded. Methodology is not naively about knowledge but about love, death and subjection. It is there in the birth of the modernist mind and its multiple implications for the political, the social, the personal. It won't go away. And research methodology needs to contend with it.

Subjectivity: the god's-eye view and the wanderer

Standing at the roadside, map in hand, there is nowhere without an address, not a god-given address, but a rational address, an address that is humanly, wilfully constructed. That is the ambition of Modernity to leave no space uncovered, unnamed, unsubjected. With such a map there is implicitly a point at which everything can be seen, as if from a god's-eye view. For the Enlightenment philosophers all was to be subjected to the laws of reason and thus all could be planned according to the rules of reason. Metaphorically, the desire is for a god's-eye view of everything, where human beings, not gods are those who survey all and rule all through reason. However, without an appeal to some religious revelation from an all-seeing god, human subjectivity can only encounter reality through experience, based upon whatever happens to be encountered, contingently. Without the possibility of a book of revelations concerning reality and the meaning of the universe, reason has only experience and imagination to work with. For Rancière (2004a) this aspect of the modern subjectivity entailed by Enlightenment philosophy was expressed poetically in Wordsworth's rambling subject who 'wandered lonely as a cloud'. Alone, the privileged subject glimpses, notices, is conscious of, reflects upon whatever chances by, whatever attracts the eye. There seems to be a freedom here from any imposed order, any prior regulation. There is only the reason of the singular subject to create some desired order, some sense of unity for the individual out of the multiplicity of chance meetings. Like a ghost, with the inauguration of such a singular subject appears the imposing figure of Hegel's Absolute Reason seeking to master, and so encompass from within the field of subjectivity a whole universe of differences under its dialectical progression towards coverage and closure. On the one hand, there is the single figure of the individual free to wander and encounter others – things, creatures, people – haphazardly freely creating whatever sense possible. On the other, there is the desire to master, to order, to cover all eventualities and call it Reason. Figure 11.1 visualises this in terms of a triangular relationship.

From point 'X' in the diagram all can be seen. If reason can make a map that covers everything, then all the points between 'y' and 'z' can be seen. Everyone and everything can be located, named and described in terms of their relationship one with another. The architect, Tschumi (1996) writes of the pyramid and the labyrinth as alternative architectural models. Each entails different subjective 'mentalities'. The architect as master planner constructs the designs of a building, a cityscape, or a communications network in a way where everything can be seen to fulfil some architectural purpose. However, when walking through the streets of a city, you cannot see the whole plan, you do not necessarily know what is around the corner – and without a map, the city takes on the aspect of the labyrinth where

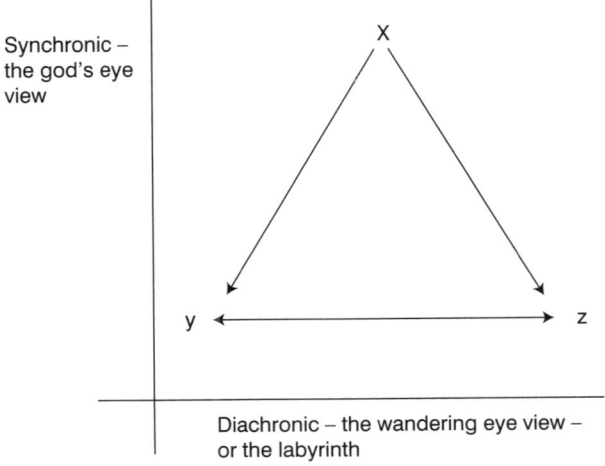

Synchronic –
the god's eye
view

X

y

z

Diachronic – the wandering eye view –
or the labyrinth

Figure 11.1 Towards an architecture of the mind and its realities

entrances and exits are confused, and promising directions can lead to dead ends or dangerous places.

In each circumstance, the god's-eye view of the architect or the wandering-eye view of the city dweller, it is the human grasp of the world about that is in play. For the Wordsworthian or Rancièrean wandering subject, at the level of the labyrinth, it is to create a poetic or political engagement with the contingent, in ways that are both personal and universal but not necessarily completable. Under the desire for mastery, at the all-encompassing level of the architectural designer, it is to generate a map of all possible addresses: the ultimate in knowledge, the book of all written by Reason. In each case, the subject that takes its leave to wander freely, to make connections, to formulate views and worlds that are dependent only upon human reason and will, is freed from any pre-ordained, god-given map. The revolutionary import of the modernist mind was in its rejection of anything outside the human ability to think, to will, to feel, to act. This is both the freedom to wander, to de-construct, to imagine as well as to impose, construct, reify and totalise. It is the impossible synthesis of an emancipatory and a totalitarian logic (Schostak 2006; Schostak and Schostak 2007). Something of this logic is explored in Box 1.

Escaping the light of reason

The figures of the hitchhiker and the skateboarder slip between the imposed logics of modernity to evoke the freedoms that to the rational logics of the authoritarian, and indeed, totalitarian mind appear irresponsible at best, dangerous at worst. There is an implicit tension as they escape the logics of control, the logics of rational expertise of the prevailing orders and so evoke the 'irresponsibility' and 'danger' of a desire to exceed the normal behaviours. Yet this tension between 'rational order' and the irresponsible and dangerous is at the core of modernism. It cannot be sucked from the equation leaving one side 'pure'. We use the figures of hitchhiker and skateboarder as a kind of condensation of all figures that slip between and evade the logics of control, measurement and the proper use of space. But this is both metaphor and more than metaphor. It is a rhetoric through which the subjective organisation of experience takes place, leaving its traces in the material practices of people in everyday life. This process in its political dimensions has been well described by Laclau (2005). Simply, in a heterogeneous world the wandering subject comes across people, objects, places and so on, contingently. There is no necessary order or relation. Subjective organisation may begin simply with noticing what is next to something else, what is like something else, what goes with something else. There is this and this and this within my sight. When we think back to some place we wandered through we recall the things that we saw when looking around. One thing goes with another in our memories. The rhetorical process is that of a kind of metonymy as one thing mentally associates with another. There is the ice cream placed in the ice cream cone which associates also with fond recollections of childhood at the seaside. The image of the ice cream metonymically stands for the whole seaside context in our minds. At some

Box 1: An example from the training of specialist medical staff in a hospital

Senior House Officers (SHOs) often talk resignedly and despondently about what they call "going through hoops" during their training process. Whilst a few recognise something positive in this as contributing to a rite of passage, all of them find the jumping through hoops a repetitive activity they can't wait to leave behind. Indeed these very frustrations pervade their perspective of this part of their training and colour their thinking of the job. Airing this data to a group of five consultants from four different specialties at a core team evening discussion meeting (an integral part of the research project entitled "Consultants as Educators" [CasE]), evoked quite a different response from them as trainers. One consultant explains "You see I think going through hoops is the fact that you've actually become competent at the procedure and think you are but what you actually need to do is another ten, or another twenty, really to get properly accustomed to the odd [unexpected] or something will go wrong." S/he goes on to suggest that perhaps the trainee will see the process of going through hoops in quite a different light at the end of the training process. This suggestion receives unanimous support from the other four consultants.

Research comment

The consultants'-eye view is that of seeing the 'whole', whereas the trainees (Senior House Officers – as they were called in the UK at the time, January 2002) could only see the events as repetitious and tedious. What was merely 'going through hoops' for the trainees, was seen as having major significance in terms of learning to become an 'expert' by the consultants. From the 'expert' viewpoint each contingent and 'useless' event has a purpose within the whole. Knowing all the possible variations that can only be abstracted from the contingent experiences of individual events is what constructs the position of 'mastery' – the subject position of the consultant. Seeing only individual, repetitious events, unable to 'complete the picture' is the subject position of the trainee, the one who is still wandering through the experiential labyrinth. However, the wandering of the trainee is not purposeless and is already subsumed under a guiding logic; one day they will see this process 'in a different light', the light of reason.

point in time it may be that this image of the ice cream does not merely call up an image of the seaside, but condenses a whole range of experiences to do with youthfulness, romantic episodes, feeling free, … In short, the image is not simply a part conjuring up the particular whole of which it is a part, but metaphorically stands for youthfulness and so on in general. The 'ice cream' is not associated with, nor simply like, it *is* freedom. Of course, the example is trivial, unless one thinks of the similar processes through which coca-cola signifies metaphorically 'the real thing' (Zizek 1992), or the ways in which advertisements associated cigarettes with health, sophistication or youthful rebellion in the twentieth century, or how political propaganda is employed to demonise organisations or ethnic groups. The methodology involves (a) a heterogeneous reality through which (b) the subject who wanders, and thus is contingently conscious of phenomena, rhetorically or subjectively constructs objects, features, qualities through processes of association which form the basis of metonymic relations between objects or qualities found in particular contexts (like fire associating with smoke) which in turn, (c) through the strength of the associations experienced in multiple contexts can condense, unify or universalise what was originally contingent, heterogeneous and particular so that the fire in being associated with heat, destruction, the consuming of forests, the speed with which an area is consumed, its impossibility to control and also its association with an excited state can be applied metaphorically to a person as *being* fiery. Rather than fire, think of a flag: people have died for it; not because of the cloth but because of the universal values it metaphorically signifies for them. Now, this process through which the dissimilar, subjectively transforms into the similar (the fire is like the person who shows destructive, all-consuming yet exciting passions) and then the identical (fire and person become identical) can of course be reversed, or de-constructed. When the process is applied to the process through which disparate individuals, collect together, organise and produce a unified sense of a 'community', a political organisation or a 'people', it becomes a methodology that both explores and constitutes the possibilities of the political, of knowledge(s), of identity(ies) and of community(ies). It is a methodology that focuses upon and has its method in the heterogeneous and thus the possibilities for conflicting views, disagreement, and yet equality in the face of ignorance and the gift that is no-one's to give or to receive. It is a methodology that is at once anti-essentialist and productive of claims based on the celebration and realisation of difference(s). Such methodologies (see Box 2) abound in social practice, keeping in play both the universalising politics of 'the system' and the resistance to the system or a yearning for play, spontaneity and freedom.

Box 2 describes the aspiration of educational action research, to bring change that will improve the quality of social relationships as a basis for decision making, learning and undertaking action. However, by encouraging the decision-making capacity of children a degree of uncertainty was introduced into classroom processes. It is the introduction of this degree of freedom that encourages a creative re-framing of 'normal' behaviours and the use of the world about that the metaphors of the hitchhiker and the skateboarder provide a way of thinking about what is at stake.

Box 2: An example from action research in a primary school

Research to promote change and development is typically professed to be the motive behind many 'action research' and 'evaluation' projects carried out by professionals. In a discussion, a recently appointed headteacher of a primary school was concerned at the numbers of children sent to her for punishment by her staff. She was further concerned about the general level of violence in the playground and wanted to do something about it. She was attracted to the idea of action research as a way for staff to research their own practice as a basis for formulating courses of action through which to bring about changes. It was noticed that children very often were able to resolve their own differences and it was speculated that this might provide insights into a way of dealing with such problems generally. Hence, the 'talking and listening project' was born which led to such typical scenes as:

> Scene: it is a first school classroom, there are just under 60 children in a large room which has been used as two classrooms. There are two teachers and one welfare assistant. It is nearly dinner time and the children have just cleared up their work. One of the teachers has just praised them and the excellence of their work and clearing up their work quickly and neatly. She goes on to say:
>
> T: Before we have our lunch … could I just speak to for a moment…
> P: Yes
> T: Um … Quite a few people have come and said that other people are bothering them. I think people came and said me that Alan was bothering them and people came and said to me that Mary was bothering them. What do you think you should do in that situation? What do you think is the best thing to do, Jill?
> JILL: Go on the carpet.[1]
> T: Go on the carpet and sort it out. You can just say to the person "You are bothering me, please come with me on the carpet and we can sort it out." Now, what are you going to do if you can't sort it out, it's too hard? What do you think you could do then? Jane?
> JANE: Come and fetch you.
> T: Yes, come and fetch some help and then we'll, we'll help. There's no point in coming and saying to me "Alan did this and Mary did that", because I'm not going to sort it out for you. … OK? So, let's try that and see how it goes. Alright?

(http://www.enquirylearning.net/ELU/Issues/Education/democratic.html)

Research comment

There is a displacement of hierarchy regarding who is able to 'sort out problems'. The teacher does not profess to have a god's-eye view over what is to count as the right solution. This, in itself, subtly changes the relation between teacher and child as the school realised over time. This is not like the 'going through hoops' of Box 1. There only the identity of the trainee changes over time as he or she comes to adopt the 'expertise' required to become a consultant. The teacher, as ultimate authority, has changed. In the above scene the teacher undermines her own position as the final arbiter of issues. This in turn changes the identity of the child as becoming one who takes on responsibility by going through the procedures of 'sorting it out'. Both teacher and child are in the labyrinth with no escape to a higher authority who can put everything into the right order. At this point two communities implicitly emerge, the one the traditional, hierarchically organised form of the traditional school, the other the community of equals who must sort out their problems by taking into account the needs and concerns of each in ways that each party agrees as being just.

1 In the UK the area at the front of a primary classroom is known as 'the carpet' and this is where children gather, sitting on the floor, for formal whole-class teaching.

The freedom to ride and the reconfiguration of urban space

Two worlds emerge, seductive, alluring with just a cosmetic hint of romanticised danger:

> Clifford Popp, a 49-year-old public relations professional working in Pittsburgh, hitchhiked throughout high school and college. What was the allure?
> 'The freedom of being on the road, man,' Popp said. 'Jack Kerouac was one of our idols, and "On the Road" was our bible.' It was thrilling to climb into a car with a perfect stranger and chat. 'It often provided inspiration for short stories, songs, and poetry,' he said.
>
> http://msnbc.msn.com/id/6576347/

There is a poetics of the ride that initially involves the recognition of contingent conjunctions (metonymic relations) so that after a period of time one signifies the other, the thumb signifying the hitchhiker requesting a ride. But there is a metaphorical dimension too, where much more is condensed into these images of the thumb, the hitchhiker, the backpack, the road, the car: a sense of freedom, and the sense of identifying with others, that is, a community of hitchhikers who had a bible to unify their sense of being and proclaim their values, beliefs and way of life. But what could that freedom, that vision, that community mean?

In the above extract, there are two visions of community and the identity(ies) that in a sense were able to negotiate both and were capable of hitching a ride and providing the ride as a 'gift' to each. Community in each case could be defined as a summation of addresses, as that totality which provided the matrix of locations that enabled each identity to engage with each other. In the one community there are the fixed and named locations, and with each location there are the places where named individuals reside and where they work and shop and go to pass their leisure time. Everything is covered. Everyone has their place as a member, as a part of a whole. Here all is counted and accounted. Then there is that other world, that romantic loosening of the boundaries, of identities, of the means of exchange where not all is counted and accounted.

There is an aesthetics, a distribution of the visible (Rancière 2004a), that is, what can be seen, heard, said, felt, done is made visible by acts of discrimination, naming, locating. There is the off-road and the on-road: the freedom of the road and the freedom of the off-road. Implicit in the hitchhiker account is the multiplicity of politics attendant on the multiplicity of ways of configuring the visible: the politics of the on-road, the off-road and the politics that orders the relations between them. On the road the motorist is part of a system of property rights through which he or she owns or rents the car, is able to road tax it, pay for petrol. The hitchhiker stands at the roadside, outside this system, wanting a free ride. What is free, what is scrounging, what is ownership all become visible parts of this configuration of the world(s) of the road. As in Box 1, what is visible from a god's-eye view is not visible from that of the trainee. In Box 2 the carpet becomes visible as a place of 'sorting it out' and with it, the child who has suffered 'injustice' and the one who is accused, alongside the issue in dispute, the procedures through which it is to be 'sorted' as well as the new roles of teacher and pupil during the 'dispute'. Thus, identities, places, objects and their temporal phasing all become part of the aesthetics through which some seeable, sayable, actionable 'real' emerges. Without this aesthetics of the real what could be seen, said, done? Its data arises only as an already configurable domain of the sensible and the imaginable. It is thus aesthetic in form drawing upon the creative poetics and fictions through which realities are composed as communicable, negotiable, exploitable texts and images. This aesthetics is neatly figured in reference to Jack Kerouak. The road and the dream coalesce in imagination to produce an aesthetics of adolescent freedom. This imaginary of the road provides an enveloping architecture of addresses and possible connections but in their subjective wanderings heterogeneous people and objects engage contingently in events which can retrospectively be named and drawn into other imaginaries for other agendas. The innocent dream of free encounters has for many ended as other agendas and other dreams or nightmares took over, as described in the following web article.

> "The interstate highway system took over as the principal route of long-distance travel, and hitchhiking was forbidden on these well-patrolled throughways," Thompson said. "Law enforcement in many communities began taking a less casual approach to hitchhikers." And finally, he said, "a generation of paranoid horror tales of what can happen if you hitchhike scared the bejesus out of most people who might otherwise have taken up this unique form of ad hoc carpooling."
>
> http://msnbc.msn.com/id/6576347/

However explained, the hitchhiker as perhaps the 'floating signifier' to the more fixed routines of the person who provides the lift, provides a way of thinking about the methodologist who, in a sense, hitches a ride with subjects met 'in the field' and 'opens up' views into their worlds, their lives and writes accounts that 'explain' the 'underlying basis for' relationships between apparently different 'communities', or 'world views'. As in Box 3, the methodologist, however, may only describe and glimpse the lives of others but not formulate the conditions and the actions that generate change.

The schism described in Box 3 is implicit in the metaphor of the hitchhiker and the car owner and is implicit too in the image of the city. The city is a focus for change, demolition and redevelopment as needs and interests change. It is the focus for the contests that people have with each other as well as their needs for cooperation and mutual security through the creation of communities which address needs. Rather than merely hitching a lift from one place to another, merely changing scenes of action, the city is about the creation of the conditions for social and political life.

From the beginning two images of the city vied with each other: the harmoniously ordered city of Plato with the democratic city state of Aristotle. In each case, the space of the city is configured differently. For the Platonic, as it were, all addresses are counted. Each part of the city is a well-defined part of the harmonious whole, there are no gaps. For the Aristotelian, there are the places where disputes take place, alliances sought and grievances aired. In this latter image, the city is always a fragile compromise, made and remade through the decisions of those whose voices can be counted. In contemporary terms, there are two architectural images that express metaphorically, materially the distinctions. The first is the city built to be as compact and functional as an egg, the modernist ideal of Le Corbusier. For him, there should be no frivolous meanderings, simply the straight line as the expression of the will, the rational ideal that imposes its logic as the rule of law on the world to achieve its goals. For the Situationists, Le Corbusier's compact egg should be broken and scrambled. This alternative image of the city which coagulates around lines of connection, spreading in all directions, never focusing on a centre aspires to embed free, democratic association in its material structures,

Box 3: An example from research which interviewed children about smoking and alcohol

According to Laura lots of children and young people smoke; "all the school" she says. The anti-smoking campaigns of recent years have had no impact at all: "people in the school do it now. They hide up everywhere. 4th and 5th years don't seem to care less if they get caught". The attraction of smoking lies in the fact that it "makes you feel big. There's not a lot of other reasons". Laura says that is why she started; it made her feel "grown up". A lot of people have friends or would like to be friends with people who are older than them. This effects their behaviour. Anyway, she says "You just like to be older than you are". In some ways this is a reaction to the constraints of being treated "like a little kid…. your mums worry if you go out to see a friend and that's a boy. They don't like you to go to parties with them. If I say, like, I'm going to a party and there's loads of boys they won't let me go."

(Profile 2 in: Schostak and Davis 1989)

Research comment

In a project researching 'alcohol cultures' there were interviews with young people about their experiences that became the basis for writing profiles giving narrative glimpses into their lives. As well as talking about alcohol, some talked of the role of smoking as a signifier of 'feeling big'. Hitching oneself to a key signifier impacts upon identities, and thus how an individual is addressed by others. What is attractive about a particular signifier also seems to involve its potential to signify resistance, or indicate a reaction against a sense of wrong or injustice like being treated 'like a little kid'. The role of an act like 'smoking' is not about the particular material content – although the addictive powers of tobacco as a drug together with its impact on health and its use by powers of capital to create profit adds another dimension – but about how that content can be marshalled in relation to a signifier of universally desired values like being 'grown up', smart, strong, free. Perhaps from a god's-eye view, the 'correct' view concerning what is 'right' and 'healthy' behaviour might become obvious. Immersed within the everyday circumstances of everyday life, things are more confused. How does one increase ones sense of freedom under conditions of restraints that feel unjust? Zizek (e.g., 1992) in his many writings has called attention to the role of commercially made objects of desire – whether soft drinks, cars or drugs – as representing valued universals such as freedom of choice, innocence, love… and so on. If, as in Box 2, the desire is to bring change in the circumstances under which people conduct their lives simply hitching a ride on objects and acts that are manipulated to appear as if they realise such desired values is illusory. Instead of soft drinks, cars or drugs what if these objects are replaced with such 'things' (or social products/processes) as Randomised Controlled Trials as the 'gold standard' of research evidence, or 'performance indicators' defined by government bodies, or concepts of 'orderly behaviour'? Through such symbols of 'expertise', of 'good' management, or a 'safe' society one community of interests can attempt to manipulate and control another. However, the objects of desires through which one community of interests attempts to escape the controls of another may be produced by that very controlling community. There is thus a conflict, a schism at the heart of such a social 'order'.

its uses of space (Sadler 1998). However, the architecture of a city evolves rather than being planned according to some overall vision (Johnson 2001). To that extent, the buildings and other features of a city are, for all, whether architects, residents or passers by, found objects. It is with these objects that the multiple visions of the human are played out, contested, built, demolished, transformed. For Tschumi, architecture is not a static form but an interaction between the materiality of constructions, ideas, and the impact of social uses and physical forces. In one of Tschumi's adverts for architecture he displays a photograph of a ruin with the explanation:

> Architecture only survives where it negates the form that society expects of it. Where it negates itself by transgressing the limits that history has set for it.
>
> (Damiani 2003: 30)

This dynamic notion is made explicit in Tschumi's formulation of architecture in terms of space, movement and use (Damiani 2003: 19). It is this reformulation of architecture, of city spaces, that evokes our next figure of the methodologist as skateboarder as described by Borden (2001) which:

> has a history, but is unconscious of that history, preferring the immediacy of the present and coming future. It requires a tool (the skateboard), but absorbs that tool into the body. It involves great effort, but produces no commodity ready for exchange. It is highly visual, but refutes the reduction of activity solely to the spectacle of the image. It began in the suburbs, but has come downtown to the core of urban conflicts. It is seen as a child's play activity, but for many practitioners involves nothing less than a complete and alternative way of life. It is, therefore, architecture, not as a thing, but as a production of space, time and social being.
>
> (Borden 2001: 1)

Like the figure of the hitchhiker there is a transgressive dimension to that of the skateboarder. But there is a different use of space. There is a conflict between city citizen as property owner and the skateboarder who transforms the buildings, the passageways, the walls, the rails, the steps, the curbs of the built environment into alternative uses. Borden sees this as an architecture of space, time and social being. It is not about going anywhere as such. There is no use of the enveloping system of addresses to get somewhere. Rather, there is a seizure of space, space that is produced through action, space that is experienced. Perhaps here there is a clue to an alternative methodology? Not a methodology that must be subsumed harmoniously under the powerful laws of mathematical science, nor a methodology that is irreducibly conflictual. It is perhaps an echo of the surrealism that sees in art a joyful purposelessness, a subversion of the practices of markets and the seriousness of the experts who impose their logics, their knowledge, their laws upon all the urban spaces of life. Perhaps it is a kind of détournement, the strategy of the Situationists, to divert, hijack, reroute (corrupt, abuse) the processes, structures and objects desired and employed by the powerful. Here any presupposition of such 'expertise', 'knowledge', 'laws' and 'rights' is suspended. Thus it cannot be a methodology reducible to figures, limited and recuperable under totalising systems of thought and action. Yet, it is so easy for contemporary capitalistic market forms and governmental administrations to draw every form of resistance back into its systems of ownership, exchange, value and profit. As in Box 3, resistance and rebellion is re-packaged and sold as cigarettes. The image of the hitchhiker is the theme of Hollywood films, television, books bought and sold. Skateboarding has its manufacturers, distributors, retailers, magazines and skateboard parks. And as pointed out during a discussion of the figure of the skateboarder as methodologist, it is quintessentially male, a sport of the lads. Yet, that is the point. Every figure collapses under its own weight. Like Tschumi's ruin that expresses architecture, by negating expected social forms, the methodology to be drawn from considerations of such figures as the hitchhiker and the skateboarder first negates then is negated in an unsettling process where negation of negation continues without a final recuperation into a homogeneous system. It is, in the broadest sense of the term, an educational process where possibilities for the expression of freedoms through negation are drawn out (educated) in an open, unending series: '…'.

'…'

What does the '…' of the title mean? The methodologist as educator of differences, spaces, addresses, boundaries, identities, events draws from the found objects of experience possibilities for otherness, deconstructing identities framed as compact as an egg into their heterogeneous constituents. There is no way of sucking from the egg – the pure image of totalitarian space – its impurities without also destroying its nature. The imaginary of totality, of compactness, of identity – whether expressed mythically under the all-powerful eye/I of a god, or politically under the Leader or technologically as Globalisation – cannot fully negate the realities of difference, heterogeneity that provide the condition both for the possibility of identity and its dissolution into multiplicity, difference. Thus this precarious imaginary depends for its continued existence on a process of vigilance where each party that is a member of the whole is accorded rights that are regulated, policed:

> The police is, essentially, the law, generally implicit, that defines a party's share or lack of it. But to define this, you must first define the configuration of the perceptible in which one or the other is inscribed.
> The politics is thus first an order of bodies that defines the allocation of ways of doing, ways of being and ways of saying, and sees that those bodies are assigned by name to a particular place and task; it is an order of the visible and the sayable that sees that a particular activity is visible and another is not, that this speech is understood as discourse and another as noise.
>
> (Rancière 1999: 29)

For Rancière, then, the 'order of police' is not identical to the state apparatus, and hence no opposition emerges between state and society. Rather Rancière suggests considering politics as 'a meeting of the heterogeneous, as an encounter of the police order and the equality principle' (Dikeç 2003: 4). The equality principle, as expressed here is not about each individual being identical to the other. Rather, it is that each individual is equal only to the extent that no one is master, no one has greater rights than another. As in Box 2, no child or teacher is accorded greater right than any other when 'sorting it out'. It is at this point where the marginalised, the invisible (and pupils in the authoritarian order of traditional schooling are invisible in this sense) – those not included in the compact totality of the egg, the globalised envelope – say 'our concerns, ideas and interests are equal to anyone else's'. It is upon this that demands may be made that cannot be accommodated within the prevailing 'police system' or 'school order'. Such demands become dangerous to the system, threatening to overthrow it, to smash the egg, or at least, the imaginary that is sustained only through the police order as Rancière defines it. Thus, the 'order of police' is always contested and riven with tensions; it remains an open system in flux. For Rancière (2004)b the cry of the dispossessed/poor is 'I'm one more, take me into equal consideration too.' But this one more is difficult for the prevailing order to assimilate since it involves a change in the prevailing order. For the school of Box 2 the prevailing order changed under the impact of 'sorting it out' to produce increasingly democratic effects. More typically, rather than accommodation and change, forces of suppression and recuperation are unleashed – indeed, the introduction of the National Curriculum alongside closer controls over the school system introduced from the 1980s eroded the ability of the school to maintain democratic changes. However, the policed order remains vulnerable to challenge from alternative methodologies for the production of space, the naming of events and the formation of 'bodies' that envelop without reducing all to the same. The '...' (in the case of the school of Box 2, 'sorting it out') represents a kind of threshold to 'spaces' or 'bodies' that are yet to be formed, defined. It is a kind of preface to a body of work yet to be produced by those methodologies capable of encompassing differences without reducing them to what had gone before. But the preface does not act as a simple opening to the body of work, a mere representation of the reality to come, but in effect acts upon the work.

Derrida explains how the Preface is 'outwork', on the edge, 'simultaneously exergue and *parergon*' (Derrida 2002: 32), and 'the more it keeps alive and simultaneously ruins [*pedre*] the (be)loved body [*corps*] of the work [*oeuvre*], or *ergon*, which lives, then, only from this *parergon* – essential and inessential at the same time, vital and mortal, faithful and unfaithful' (Derrida 2002: 31). In fact, '[i]t cannot help but skid off its path' (Derrida 2002: 32). In *par-ergon* an against and a beside exist alongside each other plus collapse into one another – it is 'neither simply outside nor inside' (Derrida 2002: 54). Recall the process of sorting it out described in Box 2. The carpet, a mere piece of floor covering, takes on the meaning of being the location of a new kind of work (ergon) that is a preface to (a parergon of) a new framework of relationships, a new reality (constructed through the logos, the word of reason), that developed between children and teachers (cf., Dunkelsbuhler 2002: 43). The carpet symbolically separates off – places into a kind of conceptual box – one way of doing things from another, one space of interaction from another, one framework of discourse, from another. However, this space is not somewhere outside of the reality to come, nor is it the reality itself but somehow represents the reality to come. If the *parergon* belongs to the outside as well as to the inside, then in some senses it touches on desire, that is, the desire for the reality that is not yet fully realised. It is a place of uncertainty. The children who have to resolve their problems on the carpet have no recourse to certainty, no authority who will save them from the problem of deciding. As such, the symbolic space of the carpet is 'something like a "para-site", a site as what is alongside a *site*, but also – parallel to the prefix of para-dox – *against*' (Dunkelsbuhler 2002: 68). Its effects are the setting of limits but also the lifting of them off their hinges. The binary of inside/outside has been unsettled such that 'the frame, as a "*forme en process*", initiates a paradoxical movement that draws and removes boundaries' (Dunkelsbuhler 2002: 71). On the carpet, within its boundaries, the usual boundaries that prevent children from making decisions on their own behalf have been removed.

However, on what basis can the children decide? There is a conflict of interests, of desires, of needs, which is not necessarily susceptible to resolution by 'knowledge', by knowing all the facts of a case and weighing up the merits of one case against another. The carpet symbolises a space of undecidability. 'Undecidability' is quite distinct from 'indeterminancy' since the latter is a 'negativity' or 'nothingness' (Derrida 1988: 149). In this terrain of in-between-ness that is *parergon* – the place of weaving between – Derrida advises glimpsing 'only on the bias' (Derrida 1982: 275) to avoid killing, that is, confining things to coffins through pigeon-holing (Derrida 1987). In other words, a moment of decision is precipitated. That is, a decision is not made coolly but under conditions of haste – precipitously – because all the facts cannot be known. A decision is thus always too soon (Derrida and Ferris 2001). Tension thus exists: why this decision and not that? Moreover, as 'the structure is undecidable', a decision, any decision, 'cannot be ultimately grounded in anything external to itself' (Laclau 1996: 52). So, in Derrida's view there is 'the experience of that which, though heterogeneous, foreign to the order of the calculable and the rule, is still obliged' and he further insists that it is 'of obligation that we must speak – to give itself up to the impossible decision, while taking account of law and rules' (Derrida 1992: 24). This 'moment of *decision, as such*, always remains a finite moment of urgency and precipitation, [...], a madness, says Kierkegaard' (Derrida 1992: 26). This very moment of decision, its eruption into the well-policed scene where only the following of pre-prescribed rules, adopting the well-policed identity of the part submitting to the objectives, performing the functions demanded by the administrations, achieving the outcomes desired by the policies – this very act of decision is a madness inaugurating methodologies that play at the edges, hitch rides with universals, skate the borders, transform space, and create new architectures for the emergence of social being. It is, as Derrida describes, a double writing, at once a writing that employs the terms of the policed order and those of each decision and its madness, that open up the spaces ...

In the school described in Box 2 the research brought about deconstructions of previous practices, the generation of differences, new spaces, edges, weaves, addresses, boundaries, identities. Like Rancière's (2004b) 'ignorant schoolteacher', Jacotot, the teachers inaugurated a principle of equality where no individual whether teacher or pupil could impose a decision through authority to settle an argument. The children had to come to a resolution by talking out their problems. This effectively ran counter to the principle of inequality typically existing between teacher and pupils where the teacher is the final arbiter, the source of knowledge. Once inaugurated, the principle opened up decisions about curriculum matters as well as behavioural issues to children (Schostak 1988). They, along with their teachers, discovered that:

> It is always a question of relating what one does not know to what one knows, to observe and to compare, to say and to verify. The pupil is always a searcher. And the master is first of all a human being who speaks to another, who tells stories, restoring authority to knowledge only on the poetic condition of every verbal transmission.
>
> (Rancière 2004c: http://multitudes.samizdat.net/article.php3?id_
> article=1714)

For Rancière, to count in the public arena is to have a voice. But to have a voice one has to be able to appear in the public arena, that is, to be visible. The teacher, philosopher, Big Business as Master, as the subject source of knowledge and decision making always has as the other, the Poor (2004) as the subjected who do not know, the ones who have to be guided, who have to be supervised, controlled, policed. The always already urgent question is: how can people take on the means of 'becoming their own expert' as equals one to another in order to search/research as a basis for informing judgement, making decisions and taking action in world(s) of equals? In a paradoxical world of increasing globalisation and fragmentation, perhaps it is a matter of hitching, of skating, of surfing, of improvising the edges, the boundaries, the surfaces, the spaces by means of which provisional, playful identities and communities can emerge, facilitate, become entwined and then fray, subside into new ways of creating the spaces for the expression of self, community, difference – but most of all, it begins with children making decisions …

References

Borden, I. (2001) *Skateboarding, Space and the City*, Oxford and New York: Berg.

Damiani, G. (ed.) (2003) *Tschumi*, London: Thames and Hudson.

Derrida, J. (1982) *Margins of Philosophy*, trans. Alan Bass. Chicago, IL:Chicago University Press: Chicago.

Derrida, J. (1987) *The Truth in Painting*, trans. Geoffrey Bennington and Ian McLeod. Chicago: University of Chicago Press.

Derrida, J. (1988) *Limited Inc*, trans. Samuel Weber and Jeffrey Mehlman. Evanston, IL: Northwestern University Press.

Derrida, J. (1992) 'Force of Law: The Mystical Foundation of Authority', in Drucilla Cornell, Michael Rosenfeld and David Gray Carlson (eds) *Deconstruction and the Possibility of Justice*, London: Routledge.

Derrida, J. (2002) 'How to Translate – The Skidding of a Preface', in U.O. Dunkelsbuhler *Reframing the Frame of Reason*, trans. Max Statkiewicz. New York: Humanity Books.

Derrida, J. and Ferraris, A. (2001) *A Taste for the Secret*, trans. Giacomo Donis. Cambridge: Polity.

Dikeç, M. (2003) 'The "Place" of "Space" in Rancière's Political Thought', paper presented at conference entitled *Fidelity to the Disagreement: Rancière and the Political* at Goldsmiths College, London, 16–17 Sept. 2003.

Dunkelsbuhler, U.O. (2002) *Reframing the Frame of Reason*, trans. Max Statkiewicz. New York: Humanity Books.

Johnson, S. (2001) *Emergence: The Connected Lives of Ants, Brains, Cities and Software*, London: Allen Lane, Penguin Press.

Laclau, E. (1996) 'Deconstruction, Pragmatism, Hegemony', in C. Mouffe (ed.) *Deconstruction and Pragmatism*, London: Routledge.

Laclau, E. (2005) *On Populist Reason*, London and New York: Verso.

Rancière, J. (1999) *Dis-agreement: Politics and Philosophy*, trans. J. Rose. Minneapolis, MN: University of Minnesota Press.

Rancière, J. (2004a) *The Politics of Aesthetics*, with an afterword by Slavoj Zizek, trans. Gabriel Rockhill, London and New York: Continuum; first published in 2000 by La Fabrique-Éditions.

Rancière, J. (2004b) *The Philosopher and his Poor*, Durham, NC and London: Duke University Press.

Rancière, J. (2004c) *Sur "Le maître ignorant"* Mise en ligne le lundi 1er novembre 2004 [Uploaded Monday, 1 November 2004], http://multitudes.samizdat.net/article.php3?id_article=1714.

Sadler, S. (1998) *The Situationist City*, Cambridge, MA and London: MIT Press.

Schostak, J. (1988) 'Developing More Democratic Modes of Teacher–Pupil Relationships: The Early Years Listening and Talking Project, Conference of the Northern Ireland Action Research Association; archived at: http://www.enquirylearning.net/ELU/Issues/Education/democratic.html.

Schostak, J. (2006) *Interviewing and Representation in Qualitative Research Projects*, Maidenhead: Open University Press.

Schostak, J.F. and Davis, R. (1989) *Final Report: The Culture of Alcohol in Relation to Secondary Age Pupils*, CARE mimeo and AERC, London.

Schostak, J.F. and Schostak J.R. (2007) *Radical Research: Designing, Developing and Writing Research to Make a Difference*, London: Routledge.

Schostak, J.R. and Schostak, J.F. (2001–2) 'Consultants as Educators – CasE', Project funded by NANIME charitable Trust, Norfolk and Norwich Medical Education.

Tschumi, B. (1996) *Architecture and Disjunction*, Cambridge, MA and London: MIT Press.

Zizek, S. (1992) *Enjoy Your Symptom! Jacques Lacan in Hollywood and Out*, London and New York: Routledge.

Chapter 12

Last words

Speculative knowledge

Bridget Somekh

> Do not use thought to ground a political practice in Truth; nor political action to discredit, as mere speculation, a line of thought. Use political practice as an intensifier of thought, and analysis as a multiplier of the forms and domains for the intervention of political action.
>
> (Foucault in his Preface to Deleuze and Guattari's *Anti-Oedipus*, 1983)

In Chapter 2 of this book Marilyn Strathern writes, 'There is much to be gained from acknowledging uselessness – and today's world of knowledge producers and knowledge managers might benefit from knowing why.' She challenges the common-sense view of policy-makers that research should generate knowledge that is relevant, and should be judged in terms of productivity. Her keynote lecture was delivered at a conference whose theme was 'The Social Practice of an Educational Research Community' and she challenges us, too, as authors of this book and educational researchers, to look at our own assumptions about the relationship between research, knowledge generation and human action. What are the values and beliefs that drive our community's practices? How do we position ourselves as researchers in a contemporary world which is ruthlessly challenging the traditional practices of social science researchers and universities? In terms of the book's title, what is our research work *for* and how is it constructed by the interesting times in which we live?

In this final chapter I want to use my position as co-editor to address these questions and go beyond them to ask, further, how could we reconstruct our research practices and reposition ourselves as researchers to act 'politically' and have an impact by promoting human flourishing? I will do so by arguing the case for developing and using *speculative knowledge*. The term speculative knowledge draws on the quotation from Foucault's Preface to *Anti-Oedipus* at the start of this chapter, and suggests that speculation is at the heart of the process of analysis and knowledge generation. In belittling 'a line of thought' as 'mere speculation', political activists (in terms of this chapter, policy-makers and the media) overlook the key role that curiosity, insight, imagination and speculative theorising play in analysis and knowledge generation. By suffocating the researcher's speculative impulse we are in danger of reducing research knowledge to technical, unactionable information. I will argue that educational research communities, such as ours, have been socially constructed as powerless in the contemporary world, and have colluded in this process of construction through an impetus to conformity rather than transgressive speculation.

What are the fields of practice we write within? How does our habitus construct personal and professional knowledge? This chapter argues for a deeper understanding of the ways we position ourselves as researchers, and of how our social practices as a community construct what we give ourselves permission to know. It asks if our community can open up new ways of knowing and support us in braving the paths to epistemological outposts, or in looking for new meanings in yesterday's well-trodden highways. Social fields, as described by Bourdieu, are constructed by historical practices and regulated by rules of their own making (Bourdieu 1992), but they are open to development and change through situated action (Shilling 2004). Our knowledge is physically embodied (Mol 2002; Cheville 2005) and inscribed by our positioning within race (Walker 2005) and social class (Bourdieu 1980), but we have the possibility of disrupting these cultural templates by engaging in discursive reinscriptions of how we come to know. This chapter suggests that we can go about this through engaging in the process of building speculative knowledge.

Foucault, in the quote with which this chapter opens, refutes the politics of knowledge in which thoughts that pursue a new line are 'discredited as mere speculation'; and then mobilises this link between politics and knowledge into a call for 'political practice' to intensify thought, and analysis to become 'a multiplier' for 'the intervention of political action' (Foucault 1983, p. xiv). For me, the anarchic creativity coupled with the practical utility of Foucault's own writing is inspirational for action. In the Preface I am delighted by his capacity to encapsulate the 'schizoanalytic' visions of Deleuze and Guattari into a conclusion which he calls, 'a summary … to make this great book into a manual or guide to everyday life'. Speculative knowledge, as a discursive turn, deconstructs the disconnection between speculation, knowledge and imagination embedded in traditional epistemologies. Speculative knowledge is engaged, opportunistic and political.

Marginalisation: the deligitimisation of social science researchers

Knowledge is power and what counts as knowledge is always politically contested. The power and importance of research in generating knowledge has been challenged during our lives as professional educators and researchers, because universities' core function as producers of knowledge and models of the process of coming to know has been challenged and delegitimised. This has disturbing implications for our society's ability to educate to the highest level. What Brown and Duguid call 'the warrant' of the university has traditionally given space within degree programmes 'to serve both students and society with more than they know to ask for', by encouraging 'diversity' and 'versatility' of mind. The increased level of quality control and inspection, resulting from deligitimisation of the warrant, fundamentally undermines the quality of higher education in Brown and Duguid's view, because this 'neglects the importance of serendipitous news – news that people didn't set out to find – to the way people understand the world' (Brown and Duguid 2000, pp. 216–19). The word 'academic' has become synonymous in popular culture with inertia and irrelevance, labelling us with the stereotype of the desiccated scholar, Casaubon, in *Middlemarch*. George Eliot was portraying the stultifying, inward-looking practices of a particular kind of theology, but nowadays all academics, and perhaps particularly social scientists, are similarly discredited by those who pride themselves in being guided, not by scholarship and expert knowledge but by 'common sense'. In an article that is forceful in its condemnation of sociologists, Davies (2004) supports his claim that the government social research service (GSR) he leads 'has some of the best social researchers in the UK' by telling us that 'GSR recruits graduates with at least an upper-second class undergraduate degree and, in many cases, a Masters qualification'. Thus he undermines the professional status of researchers by discounting the need for their qualifications to be at doctoral level. Policy-making in England under New Labour has turned away from 'conviction politics' to 'evidence-based policy and practice', but embedded in this discourse is a rejection of the value of knowledge and knowledge-generation through research. Evidence is part of a common sense discourse, and allows politicians and the media to ignore the methodological knowledge gains of the last 100 years and claim, on a narrow evidence base, the generalisability of findings across contexts, regardless of culture, social class, race, gender and religion (MacLure 2005, reprinted as Chapter 4 of this book). High quality in social science research is being marginalised. There is, therefore, great need for us to give a high priority to Foucault's call to make engagement in 'the intervention of political action' part of the normal practices for our 'everyday life' as researchers and scholars.

Engagement or detachment? the relationship between social science and policy

A powerful intervention to reorientate sociology towards political action among the community of researchers was made by Lauder *et al.* (2004) in an article in the *British Journal of Sociology*. The journal's status, the high standing of the authors including Halsey, one of Britain's most eminent sociologists, and the deliberate reification in the article of 'the tradition of political arithmetic' in a nostalgic glow of the great social reform policies to which Halsey contributed in the 1960s and 1970s, are all claims to symbolic power (Bourdieu 1991). Loveman (2005) describes symbolic power as 'the ability to make appear as natural, inevitable, and thus apolitical, that which is a product of historical struggle and human intervention'. To open up the widest possible debate, Lauder *et al.* were no doubt active participants with the journal's editors in inviting the responses to their article from the Chief Economist in the DfES and the Chief Scientific Adviser in the Home Office, published in the same issue of the *British Journal of Sociology* (Johnson 2004; Wiles 2004). It is an indication of the politicised struggle for power in defining 'what counts' as knowledge that Lauder *et al.*'s article – and presumably also the responses – attracted the attention of the Deputy Director of the Government Chief Social Researcher's Office, within the Prime Minister's Strategy Unit; he published in a later issue in the same year (Davies 2004, already quoted) a response which, after damning with faint praise, indulged in reiterating negative stereotypes of social research and concluded with settled gloom: 'Being detached, conceptual, taxonomic, and theoretically abstract may be the contemporary *modus operandi* of academic sociology. In which case, LBH's vision of sociology playing such a central role in policy science is misplaced' (ibid., p. 450).

The Lauder *et al.* article argues for 'a policy-oriented sociology' which will also 'hold governments to account' (op. cit., p. 20) and proposes managing the tensions between the two by engaging in 'democratic debate'. It can be seen as arguing the case for Foucault's vision of using research as 'a multiplier of the forms and domains for the intervention of political action'. It is interesting to compare this approach with that of Cecil Wright Mills. In an article tracing the origins of Mills's *The Sociological Imagination* (1959) in the contested relationships between Mills and other sociologists of his day, Brewer contends that 'in Mills's view it was the relationship between sociology and biography that helped to make sociology distinctive' (Brewer 2004). Knowledge-generation for Mills was personal and productive, and the sociologist's responsibility was to explain large-scale social phenomena and allow individuals to understand how their lives are constructed by them, so that they do not become trapped into apathy or anxiety through a sense that their experiences are arbitrary and meaningless. Mills was a journalist and communicator, who was concerned to embed sociological knowledge in his own practice and make a difference to the lives of ordinary people. *The Sociological Imagination* attacks his opponents for their detachment and locates his sociological theory in his own biography.

The separation of research from action, which Mills opposed, is still a common construct for researchers, not merely in the stereotypical views of civil servants like Davies, but as performed in the writings of contemporary sociologists. For example, the prime responsibility of the social scientist is sometimes characterised as 'speaking truth to power' (Wildavsky 1993) or 'holding government to account' (Lauder *et al.* op. cit.), which places the emphasis on discovering unintended consequences of policy rather than measuring its successes. Johnson, in his response to Lauder *et al.*, points out that this has the unfortunate effect of leading to a proliferation of policies based on guesswork rather than evidence, since 'when they know there is a problem, inaction is rarely an option for policy makers, particularly for politicians' (Johnson 2004, p. 25). The routine operation of this passive, analytical construction of the sociologist's work is exemplified in a very large number of articles. For example, in mainstream journals of sociology the main focus is often on the elaboration of existing theoretical knowledge, in order to claim the adding of a new brick to the overall structure of 'normal science' (Kuhn 1970), *viz.* the many articles elaborating and refining Bourdieu's concepts of habitus, field and cultural capital. Another recognisable trend is for data relating to an innovation such as the use of the internet in education to be analysed in relation to existing organisational structures, using well-established analytical frameworks, without considering that the problem might lie in the need for radical structural reform rather than a failure of policy vision (see for example, Robertson *et al.* 2004; Hope 2005). In the latter case, the research process of knowledge generation reinforces the 'culture lag' that McLuhan notes is typical of the introduction of technological innovations into existing infrastructures (McLuhan 1964). The problem is delineated and reported from a detached stance, without using the research generatively and moving beyond analysis to the production of speculative knowledge as the basis for intervention.

Since a university career normally entails being a teacher as well as a researcher it may be useful to think of teaching as key to enriching the process of research. So often the assumption is that the gains are the other way around. Teaching has a natural orientation towards having an impact on the thinking of others; it mobilises knowledge and often inspires further inquiry; it focuses always on how to make conceptual understanding communicable to other minds, so it entails empathy and the foreseeing of likely blocks to understanding. I like to conceive of my role as a programme evaluator in terms of its educative function, not merely in reporting formally but more importantly in communicating knowledge and understanding to sponsors and programme directors at meetings of various kinds and in unpublished interim reports. This entails educative work in relation to the constraints that existing structures and cognitive/social tools place on policy implementation (Somekh and Saunders 2007). The pragmatist philosophy of Dewey, with his orientation towards engagement in democratic processes in education (Dewey 1944) provides a good model for the concept of researcher-as-teacher. Symbolic interactionists, particularly Mead (1934), provide us with understanding that human interactions are constituted by a kind of continuous playing-out of socio-culturally constructed performances, and can be modified through deliberate intervention. In terms of Aristotle's five kinds of knowledge (Aristotle 1955, p. 206), this aspect of my own research consists of building *phronesis* (knowledge which combines reason and moral understanding as the basis for action) and *nous* (intuitive knowledge that draws on understanding). Both of these 'kinds' of knowledge are action-orientated and socially-powerful, particularly if *nous* is conceptualised as a form of knowledge that draws on situational understanding – that is that decision-making in situations of uncertainty and complexity is based on intuitive knowledge built up over time through reflexivity rather than 'judgement and opinion' (ibid., p. 206) which Aristotle says 'are liable to be quite mistaken' and I think might better be rendered in contemporary discourse as 'common sense' (Somekh 2006, p.29).

Transgressing the orthodoxies of research paradigms

Dewey, Mead and Aristotle are voices from the past, and in citing them as powerful influences on my research practice I am in danger of positioning myself as a traditionalist among the competing paradigms which construct *social fields* in the world of research. Mills, Mead – and Aristotle for god's sake – are white males and yesterday's men. The authorities we reference in our writing are taken to signify narrow allegiances. There is a tacit conformity of view that packages us in paradigms, according to our own discursive self-presentation. Marxists and modernists are categorised as quite separate from post-structuralists and deconstructionists. Sociologists are kept apart from psychologists, so that post-Vygotskian cultural psychologists have little or no cross-fertilisation with sociologists who follow the work of Bourdieu – despite the enormous and obvious overlaps in their theoretical frameworks (e.g. 'communities of practice' – Wenger 1998 – and 'social fields' – Bourdieu 1992). In recent reading I have come across two articles in which researchers struggle to come to terms with the fact that theorists whose work has been seminal to their thinking have been superseded – perhaps one might say have gone out of fashion. The first of these is Lather's (2003) paper in which she engages in reformulating the notion of praxis within a deconstructionist framework. Through her reading of Derrida's *Specters of Marx*, she recounts discovering 'that my mourning in relation to Marxism is for a certain praxis characterised by salvation narratives, consciousness-raising, and a romance of the humanist subject and agency' (Lather 2003, p. 262). The paper contains a re-analysis of both 'ideology critique' and 'deconstruction' and reaches a resolution between deconstruction and engagement that is interesting and persuasive. But in a sense, I cannot empathise with the problem. Why the need for reconciliation? My instinct is to agree with Haraway's solution of living with the tension of holding two epistemological positions at the same time – in her case: '*simultaneously* […] a critical practice for recognising our own "semiotic technologies" for making meanings, and a no-nonsense commitment to faithful accounts of a "real" world' (Haraway 1991, p. 187). There is no need to throw away a life-time's knowledge, so intimately embodied in the working practices of being a researcher if, instead, new epistemological understandings can be layered over the old ones to build a more intricate and complex set of understandings. Lather is clearly committed to her new project and has found a way of fitting a working model of praxis into deconstruction so that she can engage in practical work with women living with HIV/AIDS. By comparison, Nancy (1996) seemed on first reading to be seriously disturbed by the incompatibility of the bygone days when, 'I still practised philosophy as a contemporary of Sartre and Bergson, and even of Hegel or Kant' (ibid., p. 108) and the new world incorporating the 'virtual philosophy' (ibid., p. 110) of the 'Deleuzian fold'. On re-reading however, his metaphor of these two philosophies as 'two massifs, two continents, two tectonic plates' of which 'the one slides over the other or against it, the one folds on the other – without passage from one to the other, without a synthesis of the two' seems more like a detached acceptance of his positioning through his life's work as 'other' to the contemporary. He finds himself inescapably positioned in a tension. He identifies, between the Deleuzian fold which 'is also a leap' and what he calls 'my tradition',

> ... something very precise and even very pointed: the indication of a contemporary necessity, or *our* necessity of thought, which would persist within the fold itself, or within the leap. Philosophy folded in two, at right angles to itself: thus in some way discontinuous or straining against itself, in debate with its own proceedings, with its own subject.
>
> (Nancy 1996, p. 109)

There seems to me to be something sad about his sense of dislocation, and his metaphor of tectonic plates suggests the earthquake force of the folding. I prefer to seek a way of holding differing concepts together in a creative tension, through a process of working with layered and shifting epistemological understandings to find points of fit or friction.

I am certainly *not* saying that the great methodological movements of our time, such as symbolic interactionism, ideology critique, post-Vygotskian psychology, poststructuralism and deconstruction are *merely* (there is that 'put down' word again) a matter of fashion, though I *am* saying that allegiances to these various ways of understanding the world become 'regimes of truth' (Foucault 1972, p. 131) for social fields among researchers. That is why it was possible for a recent paper by colleagues (Stronach *et al.* 2007) to be rejected out of hand by *Educational Researcher* and shortly afterwards accepted for publication in *Qualitative Inquiry*. The process of aligning with one or other tradition is *de facto* a significant politicised choice for a researcher. But this is what I understand Foucault to mean by 'using thought to ground a political practice in Truth'. I want to resist this classification of my own work by spanning these boundaries; to draw as a researcher on more than one way of understanding truth and reality; to mobilise the notion of 'bricolage' (Levi-Strauss 1964) not so as to build 'new forms of rigour and complexity in social research' (Kincheloe 2005, p. 323), but 'to be provocative and even promiscuous in [my] approach to theory construction (...) weaving a polyvocalic web of meaning from the theoretical resources which are to hand' (Pearson and Somekh 2006). In the paper from which this quote is taken, Matthew Pearson and I draw on various writers to defend this position including, as well as Levi-Strauss's notion of the pragmatic and creative 'bricoleur', Stronach and MacLure's (1997) notion of 'transgressive validity' which resists the grand narratives of any orthodoxy, even its own. Questions of epistemology and ontology will always be foundational to research, but cross-fertilisation of insights across boundaries is productive. Nancy says at the end of his article that freedom of mind is crucial: 'There is no philosophy, there are philosophies – but that there are philosophers, dissimilar and irreducible, this itself is philosophy.'

(1996 op. cit., p. 113). As a researcher concerned with using Foucault's concept of 'analysis as a multiplier of the forms and domains for the intervention of political action' I can move freely between the different philosophies and use their many tools.

Speculative knowledge and exploratory action

In these 'last words' to our book on research work in interesting times, I am arguing that the development of speculative knowledge is the means of generating this multiplier effect so that researchers can have much greater impact on the process of policy-formation and social change. Speculative knowledge creates best guesses for possible social futures on the basis of research into current social practices. It builds on powerful theories of innovation drawn from a number of disciplines. For example, that human activity is transformed by the development and use of new tools which may be either cognitive (such as language) or artefacts, physical or virtual (such as digital technologies), but that transformation depends not merely on having access to these tools, but on developing a vision of how they might be used. This process is clarified by Wartofsky's theory of human perception, which links (a) skilled use of tools (primary artefacts) with internal 'representations of modes of action' (secondary artefacts) based on awareness of possibilities built up by using these tools in exploratory ways, and (b) high-level skills in using them creatively to make radical changes in practice with the ability to play with these 'internal representations' by 'picturing in the mind' alternative forms of action (tertiary artefacts) (Wartofsky 1979, pp. 198–207). For Wartofsky 'perception is understood as a mode of human action (…) encumbered or endowed with all the qualities of human action or *praxis*' (ibid., p. 196). To have impact on policy formation researchers, therefore, need to develop scenarios of possibility and provide policy-makers with the means of seeing how these possibilities might play out in practice. Walker has already argued for forward-looking scenario-building of this kind and suggested that one way of doing this might be to develop digital ethnographies which allow readers/users to participate in the research study through exploring an extensive database of text, sounds and still and moving images (Walker 2002). The concept of speculative knowledge draws also on theories from complexity science, particularly that 'complex phenomena are *emergent*: they self-organize' (Davis and Sumara 2005). Complex systems are unpredictable, but they are also '*structure determined*; they are able to adapt themselves to maintain their coherence in the face of changing circumstances' (ibid., p. 455). Thus, although it is never possible to know in advance the outcome of any change in policy when it is implemented in practice (hence the endless possibilities for sociologists whose aim is to focus on unintended consequences with the benefit of hindsight), it is possible to modify structures and 'reconceptualise cognition as ongoing processes of adaptive activity' (ibid., p. 457). While it is never possible to manage change so that its outcomes are predictable, it is possible to 'improvise' transformative processes 'in the jazz music sense of engaging attentively and responsively with others in a collective project' (ibid., p. 461).

I argue that speculative knowledge capable of intervening effectively, so that analysis (research) multiplies the possibilities for political action, involves several key components. It needs to move imaginatively – using the theoretical sensitivity of Mills' sociological imagination – from analysis of the complexities of current and past activities to building scenarios of possibility, containing rich descriptions and possibly multi-modal representations capable of communicating a vision. By engaging with policy-makers in much more participatory ways it may be possible to improvise the co-construction of new visions. The process must be one of mutual engagement since perception, as Wartofsky tells us, is a form of action – new perceptions cannot be developed passively.

Speculative knowledge involves researchers in taking risks by going beyond what can be said with certainty on the basis of reliable and valid warrants. While our community already recognises that much of this paraphernalia of 'rigour' is a bogus technology, we are still locked into conventions of caution, routinely qualifying our knowledge claims so that we cannot be accused of assuming any final truth or reality – indeed perhaps resisting any responsibility to bring our research to a conclusion that claims any definite outcomes at all. This is not only infuriating for policy-makers who are tasked with taking 'purposive political action' – further, it makes it impossible for us, as a research community, to communicate our research knowledge persuasively in a world where power lies most with those who command the attention of the media. Castells suggests that in what he calls 'the network society' the whole process of politics and policy-making has shifted into the media spotlight: 'Outside the sphere of the media there is only political marginality' (Castells 2004, p. 370). In this world, as Wiles (2004, p. 33) puts it, it is 'difficult for specialist or nuanced voices to be heard'. Yet, when we work with public relations and media specialists – as I was required to do by a sponsor of one recent research project – the need to produce clear statements capable of translating into powerful soundbites creates considerable tension. Speculative knowledge must operate comfortably in this discourse frame and its generation requires courage in moving away from the 'regimes of truth' of our research community.

Speculative knowledge also involves policy-makers and politicians in moving away from an insistence on the myth that the aim of research is to produce knowledge that can be generalised across contexts, regardless of the complexities of socio-cultural variation. We need to employ our skills as teachers to find a discourse that is persuasive but insists on the exploratory, imaginative and visionary power of speculative knowledge. We almost certainly need to employ professionals to manage the larger process of effective communication in the media spotlight, but managing that aspect of our work is probably essential to building a change in relationships with policy people and allowing us, in Foucault's words, to 'develop new forms and domains for political action'.

References

Aristotle (1955) *Ethics*, translated by J.A.K. Thomson, London: Penguin Classics.

Bourdieu, P. (1980) *The Logic of Practice*, Cambridge: Polity Press.

Bourdieu, P. (1991) *Language and Symbolic Power*, Cambridge, MA: Harvard University Press.

Bourdieu, P. (1992) The purpose of reflexive sociology, *An Invitation to Reflexive Sociolology*, P. Bourdieu and L. Wacquant (eds), Chicago: University of Chicago Press.

Brewer, J. D. (2004) Imagining *The Sociological Imagination*: the biographical context of a sociological classic, *British Journal of Sociology* **55**(3): 317–33.

Brown, J. S. and P. Duguid (2000) *The Social Life of Information*, Boston, MA: Harvard Business School Press.

Castells, M. (2004) *The Information Age: Economy, Society and Culture. Volume II: The Power of Identity*, second edition, first published in 1997. Malden, MA and Oxford: Blackwell Publishing.

Cheville, J. (2005) Confronting the problem of embodiment, *International Journal of Qualitative Studies in Education* **18**(1): 85–107.

Davies, P. (2004) Sociology and policy science: just in time? *British Journal of Sociology* **55**(3): 447–50.

Davis, B. and D. Sumara (2005) Complexity science and educational action research: towards a pragmatics of transformation, *Educational Action Research* **13**(3): 453–64.

Deleuze, G. and F. Guattari (1983) *Anti-Oedipus: Capitalism and Schizophrenia*, Minneapolis, MN: University of Minnesota Press. Originally published as *L'Anti-Oedipe*, 1972, Les Editions de Minuit. First edition in English 1977.

Dewey, J. (1944) *Democracy and Education*, New York: Free Press.

Foucault, M. (1972) *Power/Knowledge: Selected Interviews and Other Writings 1972–77*, Bury St Edmunds: Harvester Press.

Foucault, M. (1983) Preface in *Anti-Oedipus*. G. Deleuze and F. Guattari. Minneapolis, MN: University of Minnesota Press. Originally published as *L'Anti-Oedipe*, 1972, Les Editions de Minuit. First edition in English 1977.

Haraway, D. (1991) *Simians, Cyborgs, and Women*, London: Free Association Books.

Hope, A. (2005) Panopticism, play and the resistance of surveillance: case studies of the observation of student Internet use in UK schools, *British Journal of Sociology of Education* **26**(3): 359–73.

Johnson, P. (2004) Making social science useful. *British Journal of Sociology* **55**(1): 23–30.

Kincheloe, J. L. (2005) On to the next level: continuing the conceptualization of the bricolage, *Qualitative Inquiry* **11**(3): 323–50.

Kuhn, T. S. (1970) *The Structure of Scientific Revolutions*, second edition, enlarged. Chicago, IL and London: University of Chicago Press.

Lather, P. (2003) Applied Derrida: (mis)reading the work of mourning in educational research, *Educational Philosophy and Theory* **35**(3): 257–69.

Lauder, H., P. Brown and A. H. Halsey (2004) Sociology and political arithmetic: some principles of a new policy science, *British Journal of Sociology* **55**(1): 3–22.

Levi-Strauss, C. (1964) *The Savage Mind*, Chicago, IL: Wiedenfeld and Nicolson.

Loveman, M. (2005) The modern state and the primitive accumulation of symbolic power, *American Journal of Sociology* **110**(6): 1651–83.

McLuhan, M. (1964) *Understanding Media*, London and New York: Routledge and Kegan Paul.

MacLure, M. (2005) 'Clarity bordering on stupidity': where's the quality in systematic review? *Journal of Education Policy* 20(4): 393–416. Reprinted as Chapter 4 of this book.

Mead, G. H. (1934) *Mind, Self and Society*, Chicago, IL: University of Chicago Press.

Mills, C. W. (1959) *The Sociological Imagination*, London and New York: Oxford University Press.

Mol, A. (2002) *The Body Multiple: Ontology in Medical Practice*, Durham, NC and London: Duke University Press.

Nancy, J.-L. (1996) The Deleuzian fold of thought, *Deleuze. A Critical Reader*. P. Patton (ed.) Oxford: Blackwell.

Pearson, M. and Somekh, B. (2006) Learning transformation with technology: a question of socio-cultural contexts? *Qualitative Studies in Education* **19**(4): 519–39.

Robertson, S., T. Shortis, N. Todman, P. John and R. Dale (2004) ICT in the classroom: the pedagogical challenge of respatialisation and reregulation, *Culture and Learning: Access and Opportunity in the Curriculum*, M. Olssen (ed.) Westport, CT: Greenwood Press.

Shilling, C. (2004) Physical capital and situated action: a new direction for corporeal sociology, *British Journal of Sociology* **25**(4): 473–87.

Somekh, B. (2006) *Action Research: A Methodology for Change and Development*, Buckingham and Philadelphia, PA: Open University Press.

Somekh, B. and Saunders, L. (2007) Developing knowledge through intervention: meaning and definition of 'quality' in research into change, *Research Papers in Education* **22**(2): 183–98.

Stronach, I. and M. MacLure (1997) *Educational Research Undone: The Postmodern Embrace*, Buckingham: Open University Press.

Stronach, I., D. Garratt, C. Pearce and H. Piper (2007) Reflexivity, the picturing of selves, the forging of method, *Qualitative Inquiry* **13**(2): 179–203.

Walker, M. (2005) Race is nowhere and race is everywhere: narratives from black and white South African university students in post-apartheid South Africa, *British Journal of Sociology of Education* **26**(1): 41–54.

Walker, R. (2002) Case study, case records and multimedia, *Cambridge Journal of Education* **32**(1): 109–27.

Wartofsky, M. (1979) *Models: Representation and Scientific Understanding*. Dordrecht: Reidel.

Wenger, E. (1998) *Communities of Practice: Learning, Meaning and Identity*, Cambridge, New York and Melbourne: Cambridge University Press.

Wildavsky, A. (1993) *Speaking Truth to Power: The Art and Craft of Policy Analysis*, New Brunswick, NJ and London: Transaction Publishers.

Wiles, P. (2004) Policy and sociology, *British Journal of Sociology* **55**(1): 31–4.

Index